IMAGES
of America

AROUND CURWENSVILLE

On the cover: A crew works on constructing a concrete road on what is now Route 879 in Arnoldtown, right outside Curwensville in 1891. The road ran parallel to the railroad tracks at this point in time. Note the steam-powered concrete mixer. (Courtesy J. Duane Test.)

IMAGES
of America

AROUND CURWENSVILLE

Julie Rae Rickard

ARCADIA
PUBLISHING

ISBN 978-0-7385-5506-5

Published by Arcadia Publishing
Charleston SC, Chicago IL, Portsmouth NH, San Francisco CA

Printed in the United States of America

Library of Congress Catalog Card Number: 2007928792

For all general information contact Arcadia Publishing at:
Telephone 843-853-2070
Fax 843-853-0044
E-mail sales@arcadiapublishing.com
For customer service and orders:
Toll-Free 1-888-313-2665

Visit us on the Internet at www.arcadiapublishing.com

For R. K. Way, who sold local postcards at his stationery store. His attempt to document history by having postcards made from local photographs is represented in this book. Also for all those who go out of their way to document the present for history's sake.

Contents

ACKNOWLEDGMENTS

I am lucky to live in an area where history is preserved by several different historical societies and their hardworking volunteers. Royalties from this book will benefit the Curwensville-Pike Township Historical Society, as my previous books have supported the Clearfield County Historical Society. Both societies contributed to the contents of this book, which also includes submissions from local collectors J. Duane Test, Dan McDonald, Mark Coudriet (who supplied photographs from the E. S. Shuck Estate), Jim Bennett, Jeff Gates, and Aletta Singley. Several people were extremely helpful in putting together this new collection of photographs and postcards. My sincere gratitude goes out to Carolyn Rowles, Hildred Rowles, Warren Fox, Pat Murphy, Joy Rickard, Deuwain Rickard, Terry Rickard, Twila Briskar, Cathy Howe, Douglas Beard, Lenore McDonald, Lori Norris, Charlie McGarry, David McNaul, Cathie Hughes, Jim Curry, Gary Jewart, Dr. A. G. Williams, Helen Way, Larry Kelly, Jerry Learn, and Doe Augustine, as well as the collectors listed above. Special thanks to the late William "Smokey" Osborn, who, in 1987, put together a wonderful program called "Smalltown USA," which featured a slide show with audio commentary. This program, now the property of the Curwensville-Pike Township Historical Society, also provided images for this book. Resources used for the information contained in the book include *Curwensville: In Celebration of 200 Years*; *150th Anniversary: Curwensville, PA*; *History of Clearfield County* by Lewis Cass Aldrich; *The Progress Presents A View From*; *Clearfield County, Present and Past* by Thomas Lincoln Wall; *Clearfield Today and Tomorrow: Railroads of the Area*, by George A. Scott; *Around DuBois* by the DuBois Area Historical Society; *DuBois Where and When* by Janice Flood Nichols; and the newsletters of the Clearfield County Historical Society; as well as my previous books and my play, *Hidden Treasures: A History of Clearfield County*. Special thanks to Robert M. Kurtz Jr. for starting me on this local history writing path.

INTRODUCTION

Although I did not technically grow up in Curwensville, I did spend plenty of time there in my childhood because both my grandparents lived on Irvin Hill. My first library books came from the Curwensville Library. When I started working as a newspaper reporter, I was assigned to cover Curwensville Borough. One way or another, I have always come back to Curwensville.

When Carolyn Rowles of the Strawberry Tree gift shop told me people were asking when I was going to do another local history book, Curwensville was a natural choice. While working on *Clearfield* from the Postcard History Series and *Clearfield County* from the Images of America series, I was surprised to find so many interesting and fun postcards and photographs of Curwensville in the early 20th century. Research revealed that many of these had the same source, R. K. Way, who owned Way's Stationery Store, which was located on State Street in downtown Curwensville.

During the early 1900s, it was common for photographers from Germany to travel to the area where they took many scenic photographs, which were turned into postcards for local merchants. Way also supplied many local photographs to these companies, which printed them as postcards featuring everything from vanishing forests to children in an unofficial parade across the main street. Also Way's family photographs have found their way into the archives of the Curwensville-Pike Township Historical Society. This is why I decided it was appropriate to dedicate this book to him.

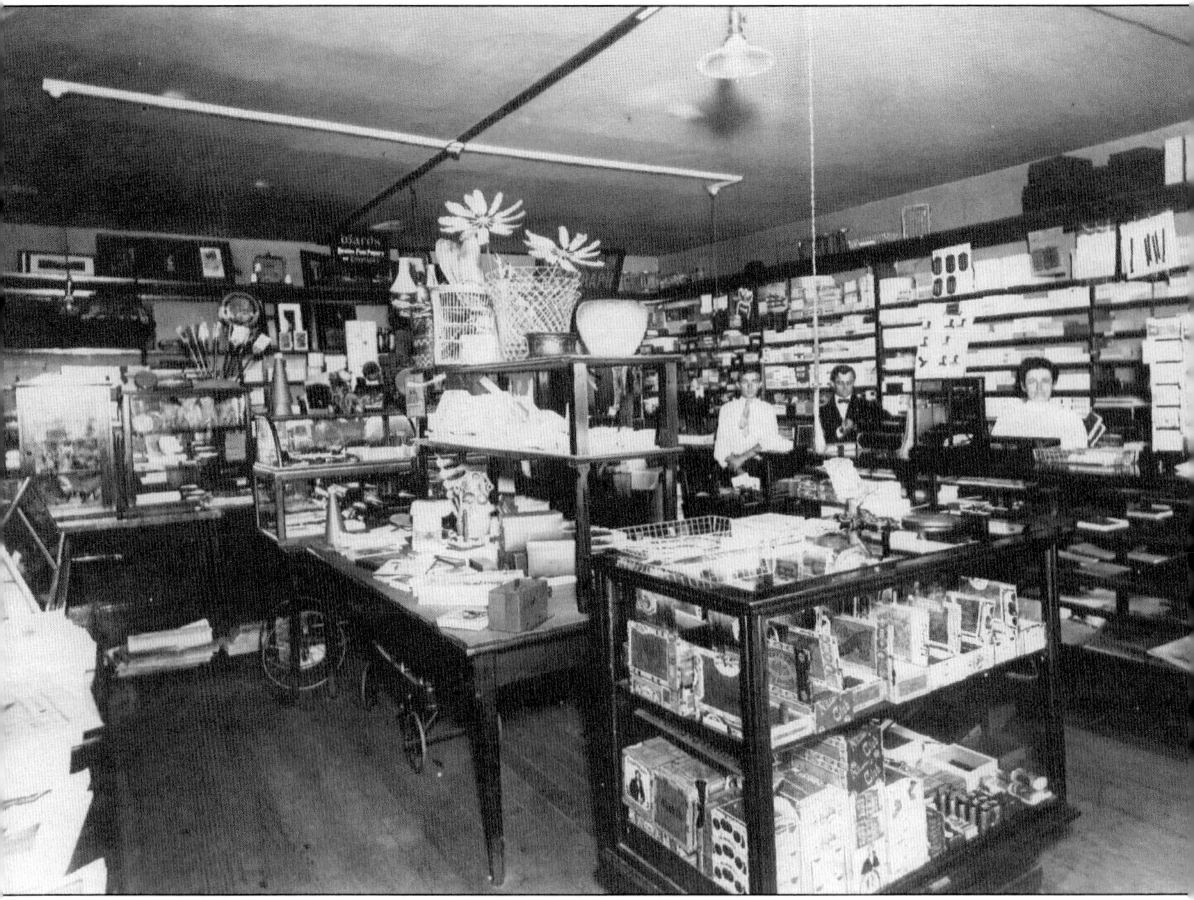

Way's Stationery Store was established in 1896 by R. K. Way. This photograph shows the merchandise available around 1910. The store was later owned by Alex Kantar and operated in the 1970s as Buzzard's Stationery Store. (Courtesy Curwensville-Pike Township Historical Society.)

One

Businesses

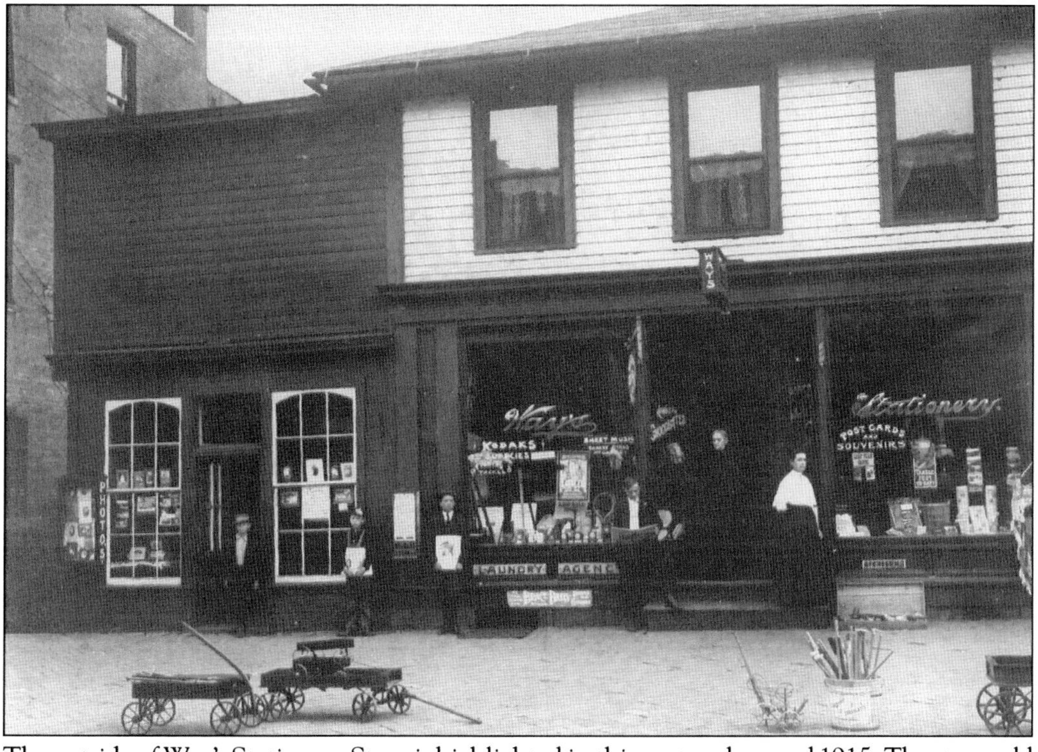

The outside of Way's Stationery Store is highlighted in this postcard around 1915. The store sold photograph supplies, sheet music, postcards, souvenirs, candy, and newspapers and also served as the Western Union telegraph station for the area. Clara Way, R. K.'s mother, is standing inside the doorway, and next to her on the right is Tensie Way. (Courtesy Curwensville-Pike Township Historical Society.)

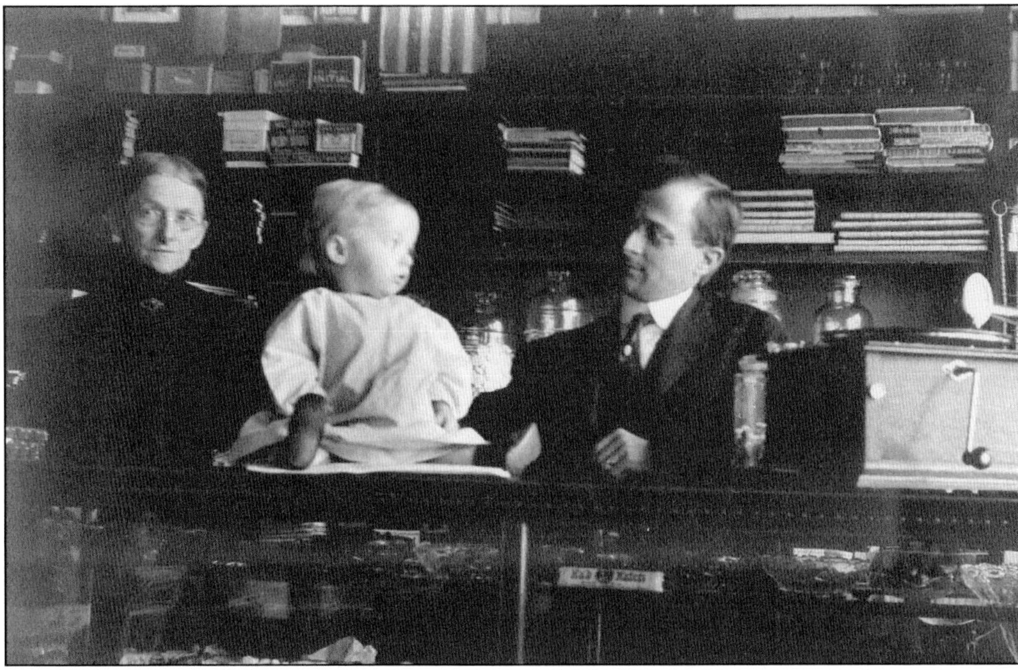

R. K. Way poses with his son, Reeder, aged 17 and a half months, sitting on the counter and his mother, Clara Way, in this photograph from March 3, 1915. R. K. was responsible for many of the photographs on the postcards sold in his store. (Courtesy Curwensville-Pike Township Historical Society.)

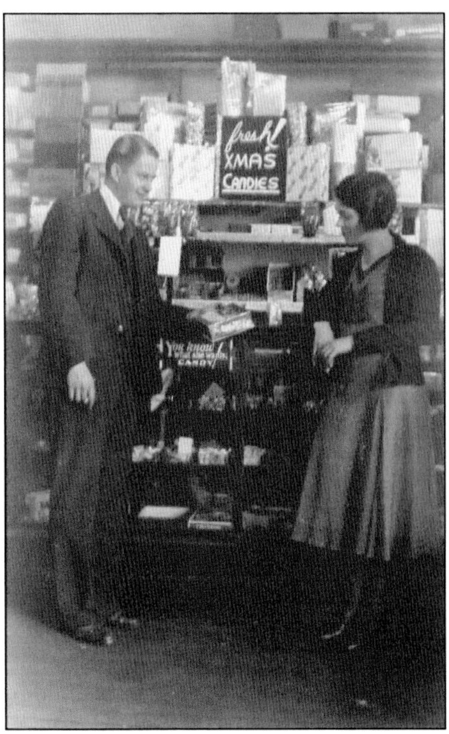

In the 1930s, a now-grown Reeder Way works in the store. He assists a customer, Miss Doughman, in choosing the right Christmas candy. Reeder was a talented magician who eventually left the area to perform elsewhere. Unfortunately, he died while only in his late 20s. (Courtesy Curwensville-Pike Township Historical Society.)

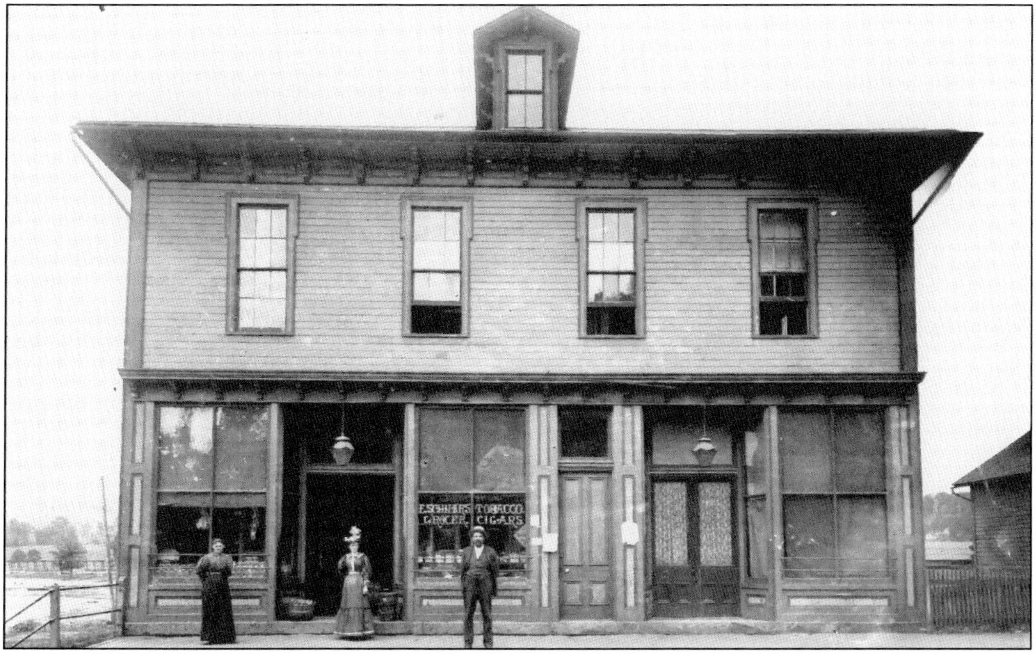

The E. Schnarrs store was a grocery store, which also sold tobacco in the early 1900s. This building, located near the river (on the left), was once called the corner store. It has been many things over the years, including a video store, but the name on the building now is Berndt's Tobacco Outlet. (Courtesy Curwensville-Pike Township Historical Society.)

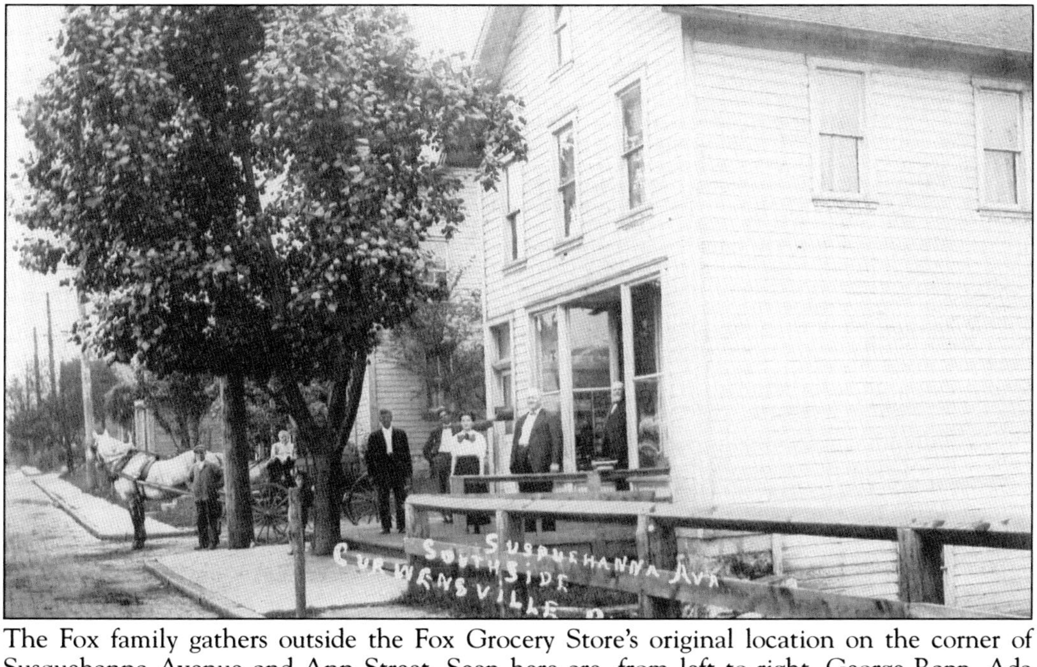

The Fox family gathers outside the Fox Grocery Store's original location on the corner of Susquehanna Avenue and Ann Street. Seen here are, from left to right, George Rapp, Ada Bell (in wagon), John Fox, Vern Fox, Pearl Fox, and W. B. Fox. The man in the doorway is unidentified. The store began in 1898 and later moved two doors down the street. This building was then used as a warehouse. (Courtesy Curwensville-Pike Township Historical Society.)

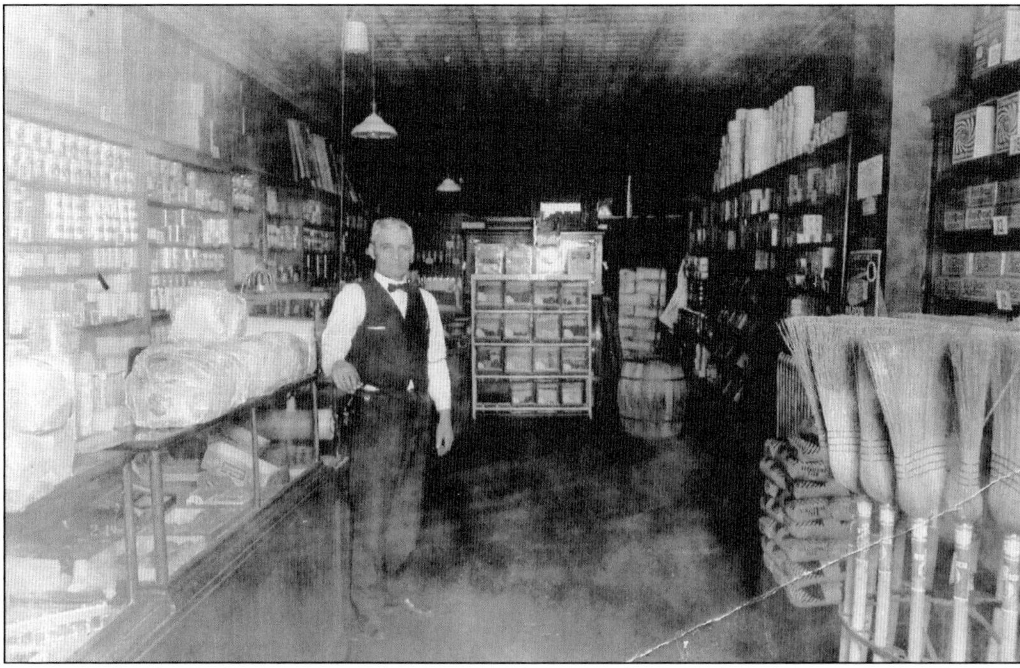

In 1919, the Acme Store was run by Harry Robison. Robison is listed as an employee of the tannery in the 1912 city directory. He lived on Bloomington Avenue with his wife, Jennie, and three children. In 1949, the store was located in the Patton Block. (Courtesy Clearfield County Historical Society.)

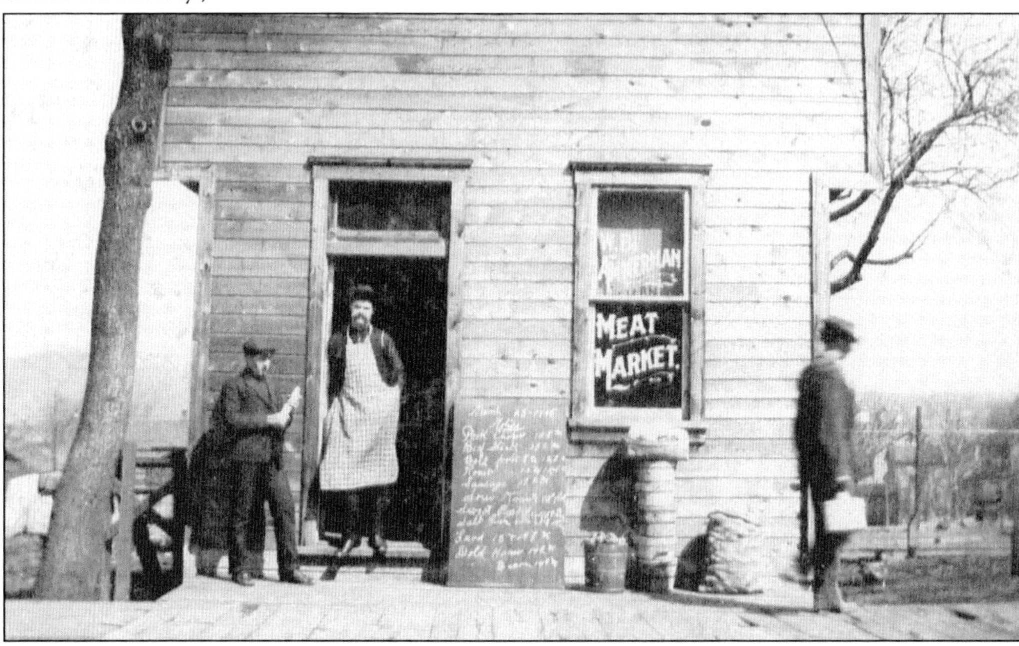

W. B. Ammerman, proprietor, stands in the doorway of his meat market, which was located on Susquehanna Avenue in Curwensville in the early 1900s. The sign outside appears to have the date as March 15, 1905. The day's offerings included pork chops, beefsteak, roast, sausage, and sauerkraut. By 1912, the store was gone. (Courtesy Clearfield County Historical Society.)

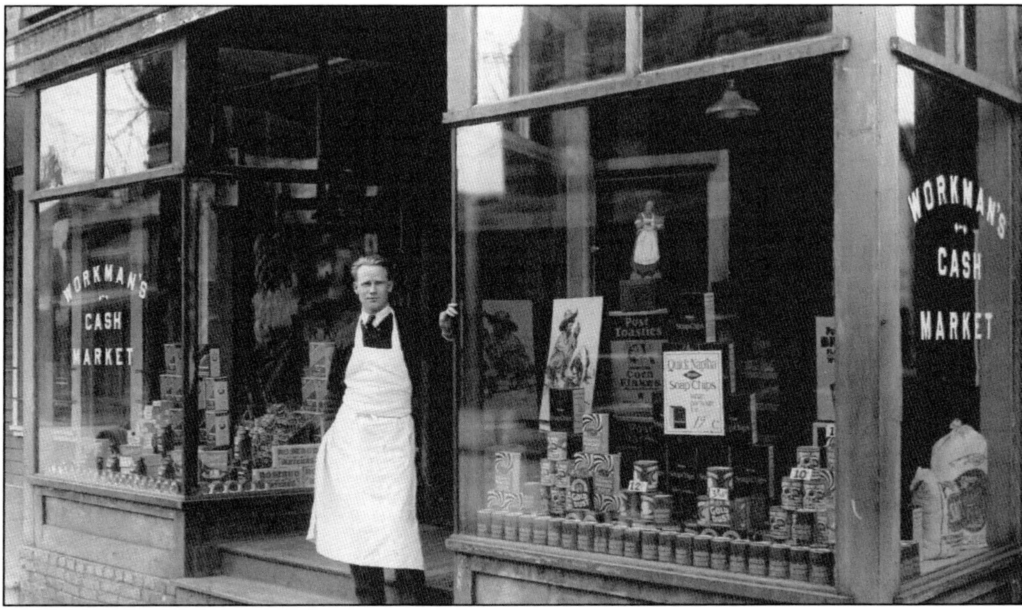

Clifford Kelly poses in front of Workman's Cash Market on Filbert Street. Kelly worked here from 1924 to about 1927. In the 1940s, Kelly ran his own business, a shoe store that was located near where Dollar General is now. The shoe store closed in 1966. (Courtesy Curwensville-Pike Township Historical Society.)

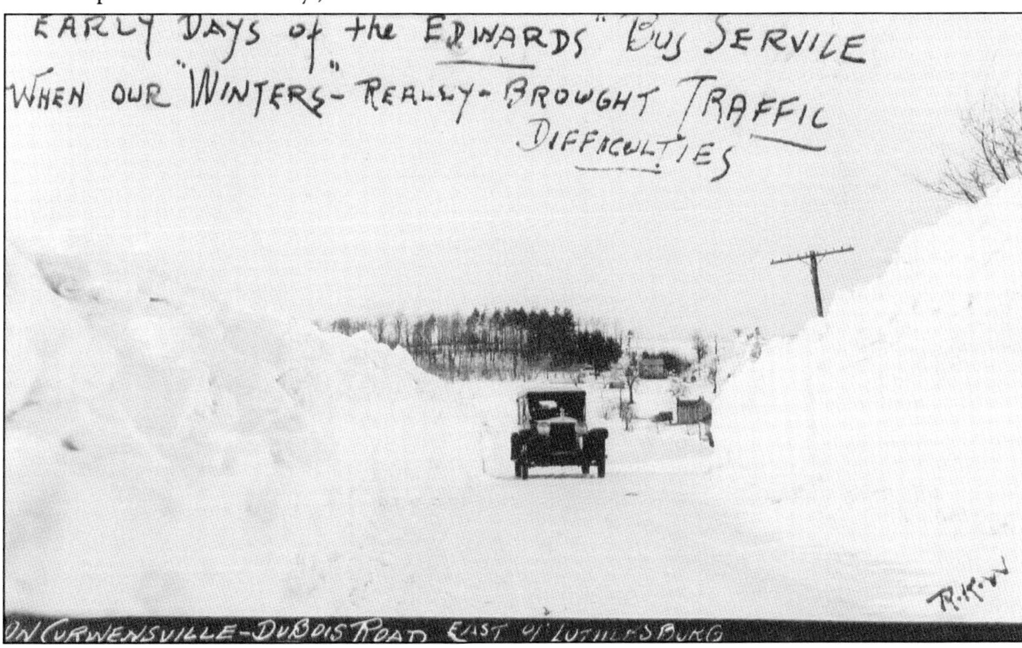

Shown here are the early days of the Edwards Bus Service. "When our winters really brought traffic difficulties," reads this postcard from R. K. Way (his initials are in the bottom, right-hand corner). The "Edwards' Lakes to Sea System" was started in 1918 and originally only had a route between Clearfield and Curwensville. Later it branched out as illustrated by this photograph, which was taken on the Curwensville-DuBois Road east of Luthersburg. (Courtesy Curwensville-Pike Township Historical Society.)

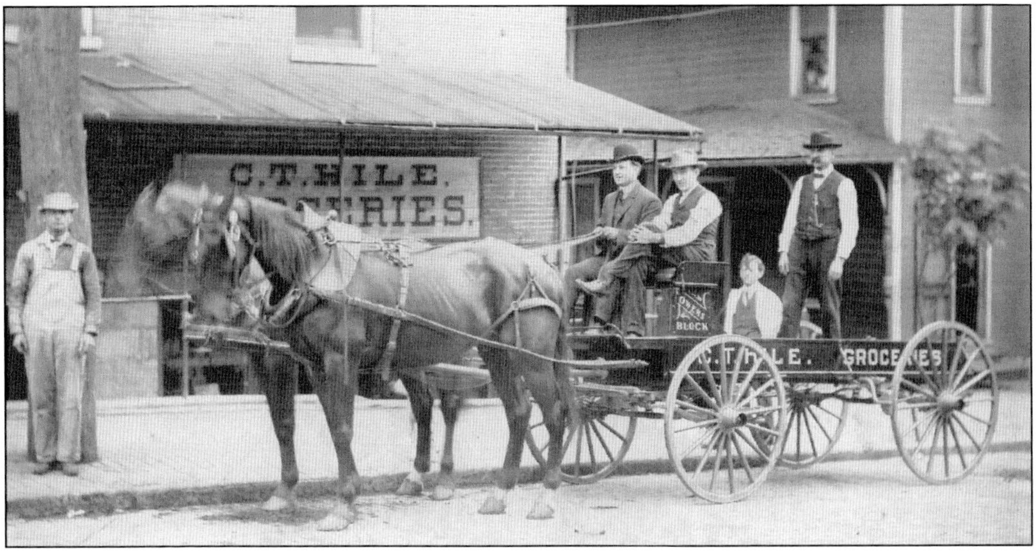

The delivery team for the Hile Grocery Store in Curwensville in 1912 is ready to roll. They are, from left to right, Frank Hile in front of telephone pole; Furman F. Tate, driver; C. T. Hile; Sam Norris (on street behind the wagon); and standing in the wagon is William B. Hile. The horse on the inside was not patient with the photographer and moved, causing a blurry image. (Courtesy Clearfield County Historical Society.)

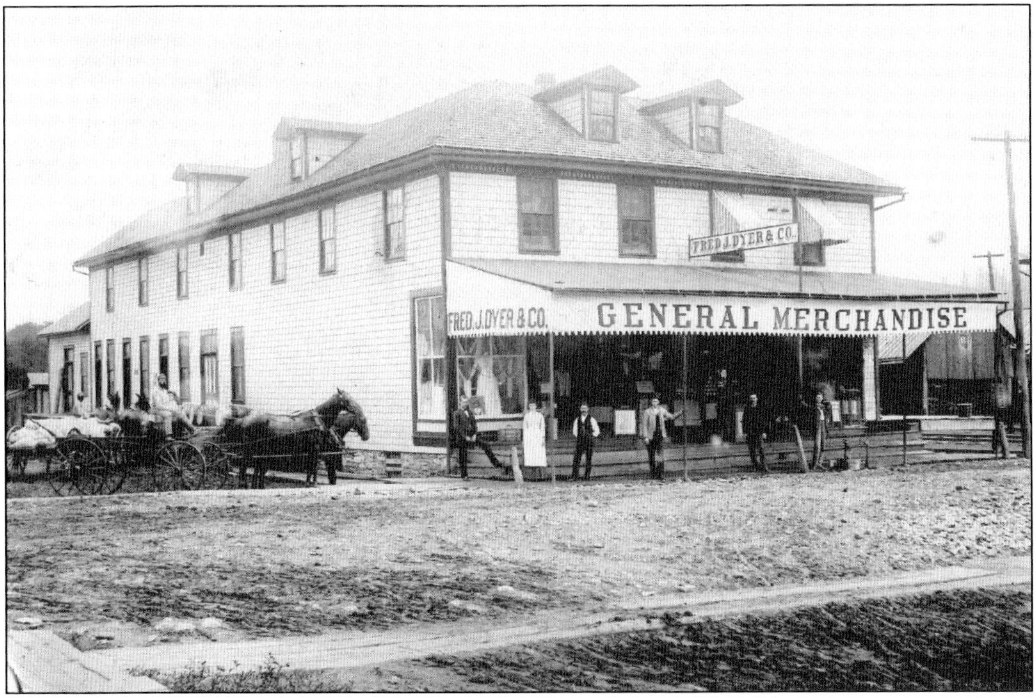

The Fred J. Dyer and Company store in Curwensville later became Bloom's Grocery and was known as McNeal and Smith until 1960. The building is now the location of Harner's Mobile Home Supplies and Service on Meadow Street. Standing in front of the store are Lou Addelman, Will Greer, Jack Draucker, Fred Bard, and Richard Wright. (Courtesy Curwensville-Pike Township Historical Society.)

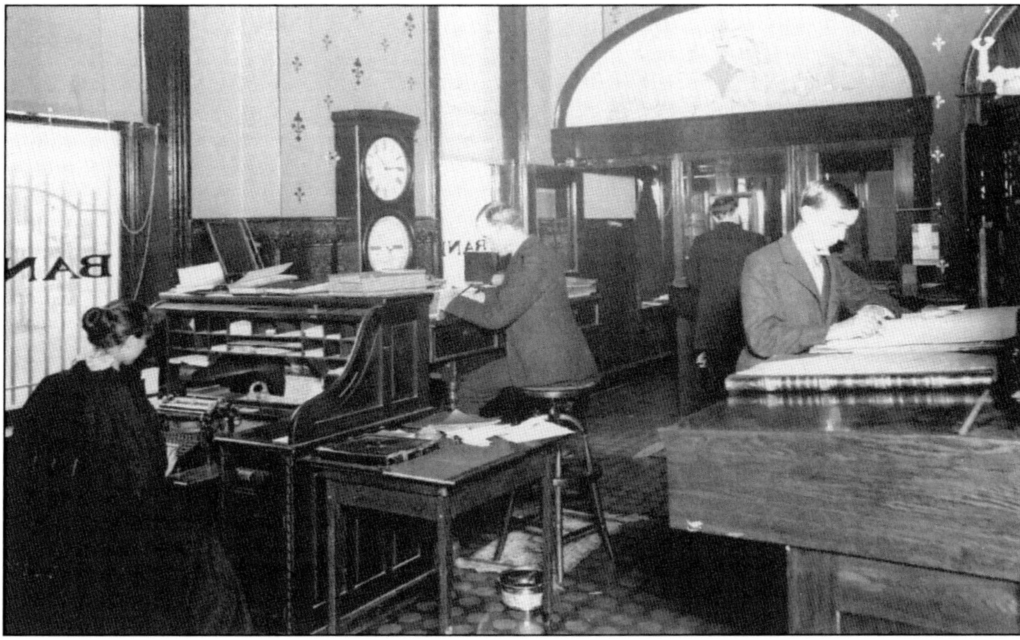

Since 1864 when the First National Bank of Curwensville was organized, Curwensville has always had a home-based bank. The Curwensville Bank, pictured here around 1895, existed until 1904 when it became the Curwensville National Bank. In 1945, it merged with Curwensville State Bank, which later was known as CSB. CSB was recently sold to Northwest Savings Bank, ending the tradition of a hometown bank. Seen here are, from left to right, Minnie Bilger (married to Walter Welch), Anthony Hile, C. S. Russell, and Joel McKeehan. (Courtesy Clearfield County Historical Society.)

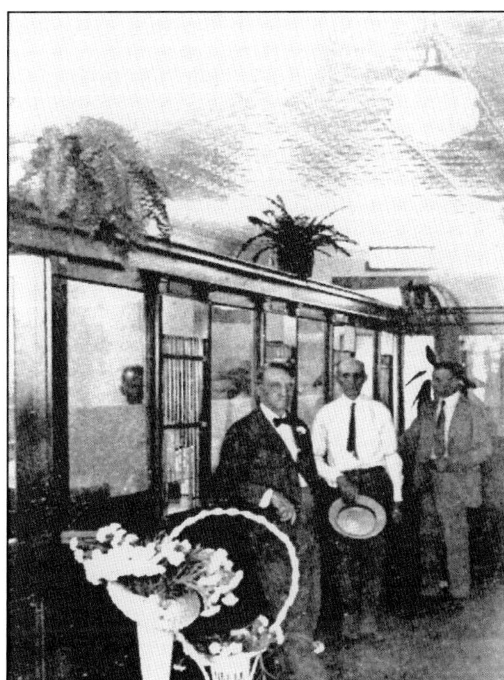

In 1924, the Curwensville State Bank opened its new banking room on State Street. Its initial cash deposits totaled over $100,000. At its open house, between 3,000 and 4,000 visitors stopped in to see the new room. In 1949, a new bank building was constructed at the corner of State and Filbert Streets and was used by Curwensville State Bank until 2007. (Courtesy Curwensville-Pike Township Historical Society.)

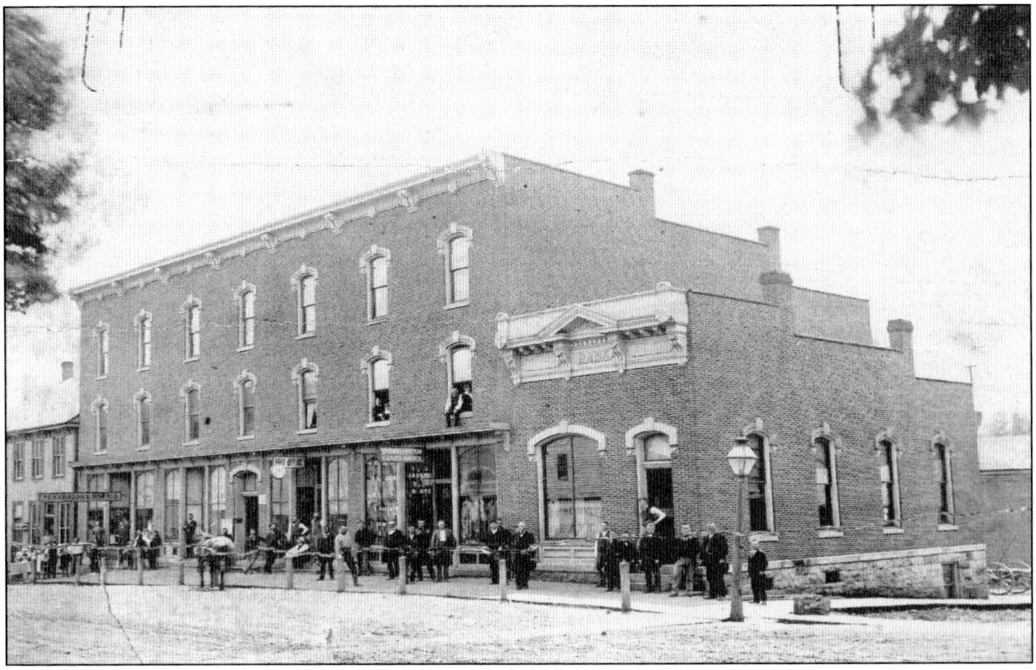

The Patton Block of Curwensville on State Street around 1878 housed, from left to right, the offices of Rorabaugh and Norris, Arnold Lumber Company, the post office, Sprenkel and Patton Ladies Shoes, Dry Goods and Carpets, and Curwensville Bank. Today it houses a variety store, the *Progress* newspaper office, a beauty salon, Kathy's School of Dance, and Mabel's Pizza. (Courtesy Clearfield County Historical Society.)

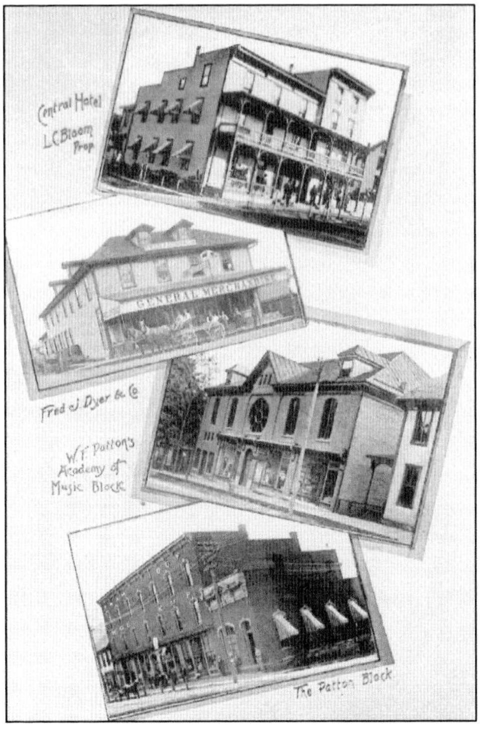

This *c.* 1895 postcard shows several Curwensville businesses. Included here are the Central Hotel, which is still in business today; Fred J. Dyer and Company; the W. F. Patton Academy of Music, which is the current site of Northwest Savings Bank; and the Patton block, which was the home of the original Curwensville Bank. (Courtesy Clearfield County Historical Society.)

A jeweler or watchmakers shop was located in the opera house building near the Academy of Music. It was torn down in 1946. This is the current location of the former CSB Bank at the corner of Filbert and State Streets. The building also housed Wrigley's Drug store. (Courtesy Curwensville-Pike Township Historical Society.)

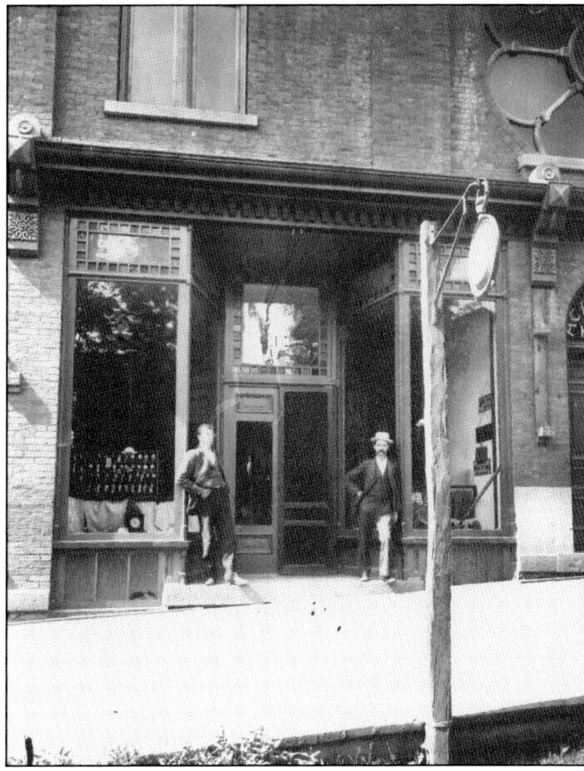

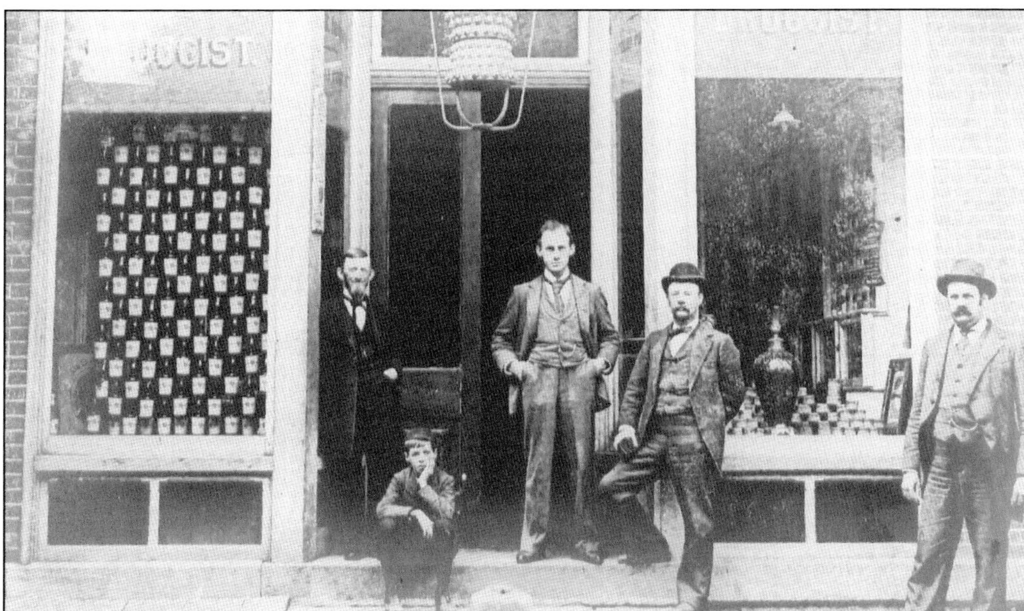

In 1865, Joseph Irwin started the first drugstore in Curwensville, and in the early 1900s, he sold it to William K. Wrigley, who moved it to the old opera house building. In 1919, it was sold to J. W. Murphy, who operated it until the 1950s, when it was bought by Cosmo "Gus" Guglielmi. He ran it until 1985, when it became Curwensville Pharmacy. (Courtesy Curwensville-Pike Township Historical Society.)

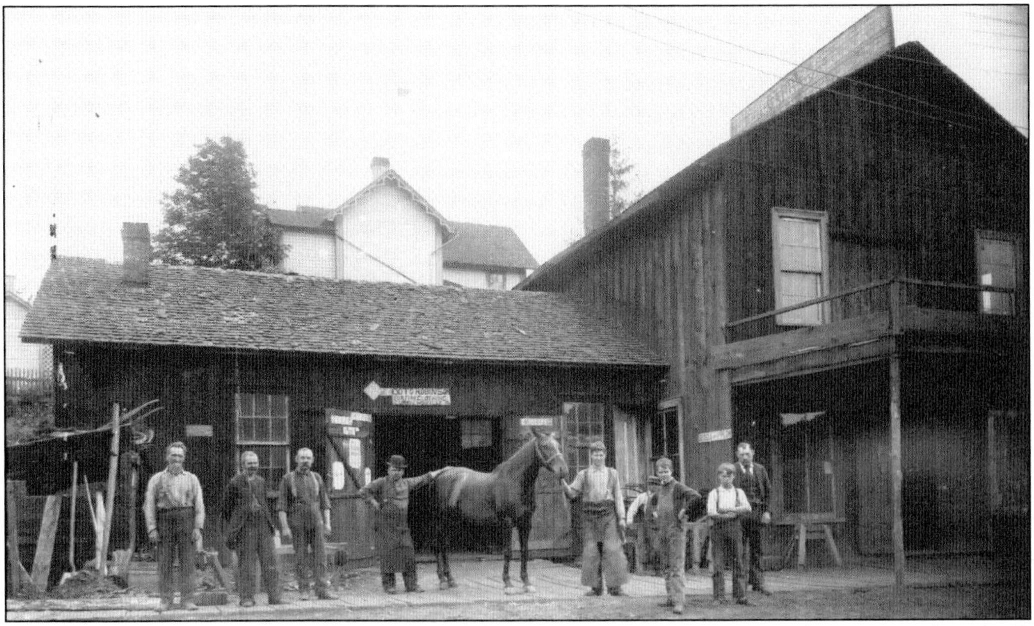

Samuel J. McKenrick, third from left, stands in front of Garrison and McKenrick, which manufactured the "Curwensville Wagon." The business, which was located at Meadow and Thompson Streets, also repaired wagons. According to an advertisement from 1912, he also was a dealer in "stock food, poultry supplies" and was an agent for "Queen washing machines and wringers." (Courtesy Curwensville-Pike Township Historical Society.)

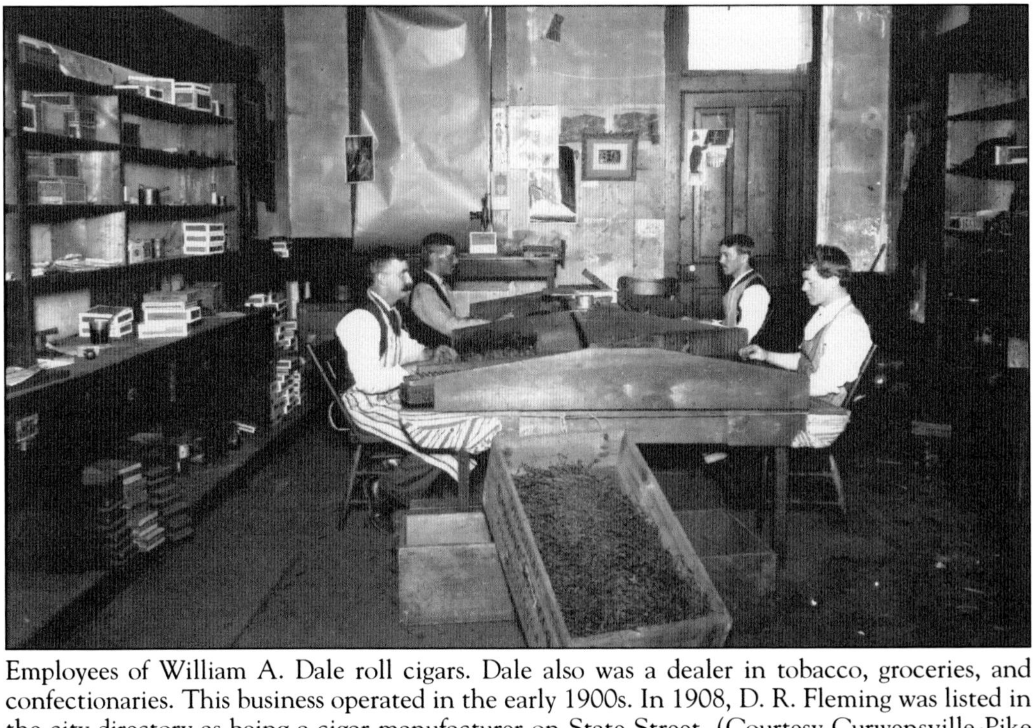

Employees of William A. Dale roll cigars. Dale also was a dealer in tobacco, groceries, and confectionaries. This business operated in the early 1900s. In 1908, D. R. Fleming was listed in the city directory as being a cigar manufacturer on State Street. (Courtesy Curwensville-Pike Township Historical Society.)

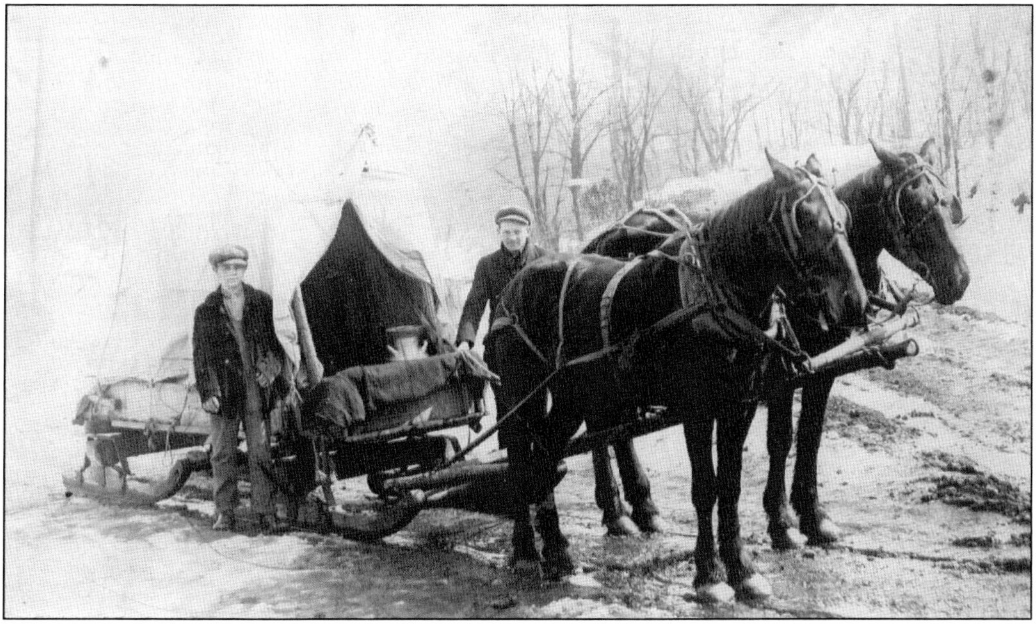

The Neeper Dairy delivered no matter what the weather, using this sled in the winter. The dairy, started by Leonard Neeper, was located on Chestnut Ridge. His sons are also seen; Arthur Neeper is on the left, and Oscar Neeper is on the right. After Leonard's death in 1938, another son, Dorsey, ran the business until 1946. (Courtesy Dan McDonald.)

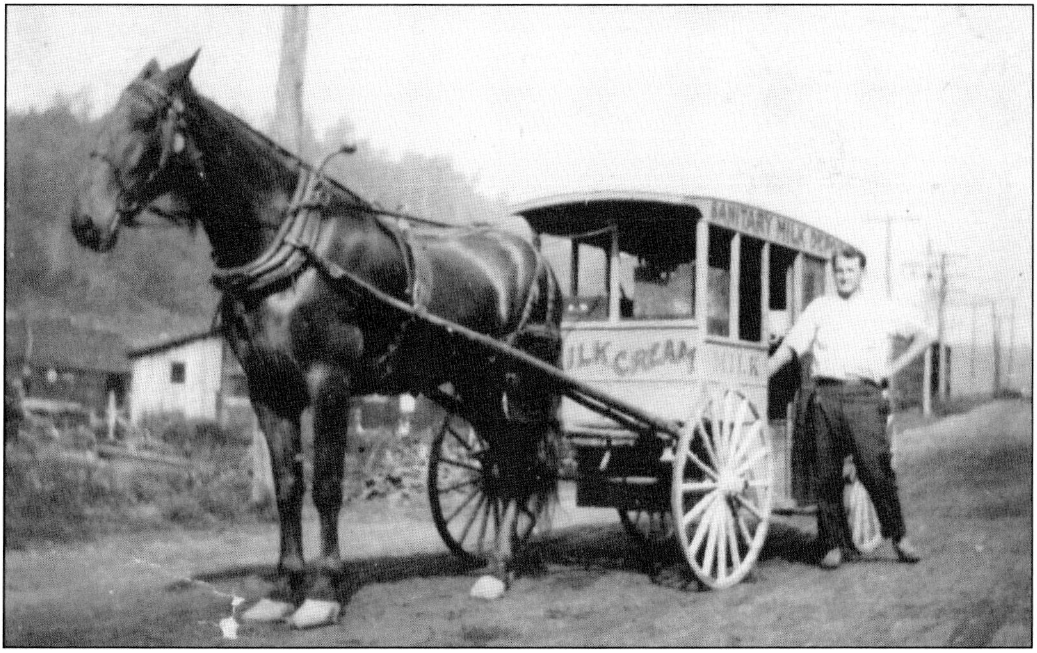

In the 1920s, Sanitary Dairy delivered milk, buttermilk, cottage cheese, condensed milk, and ice-cream mix to homes within a 100-mile radius of Curwensville using a horse and buggy. With the wagon is Hugh Way. The company, started by Scott Ammerman in 1919, continued until 1977, when it was sold to Sani-Dairy of Johnstown. (Courtesy Curwensville-Pike Township Historical Society.)

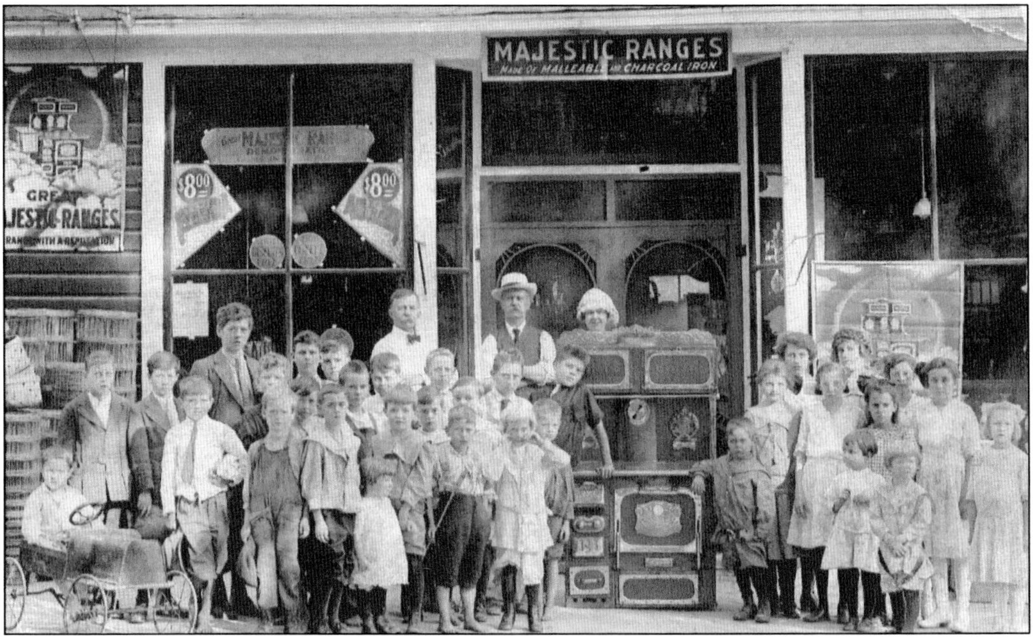

Gates Hardware has been operating in Curwensville since 1877. Posing outside the original store, which was located next door to the current location on Filbert Street, are some of the neighborhood children. The store began as a blacksmith shop and later added farm machinery. (Courtesy Jeff Gates.)

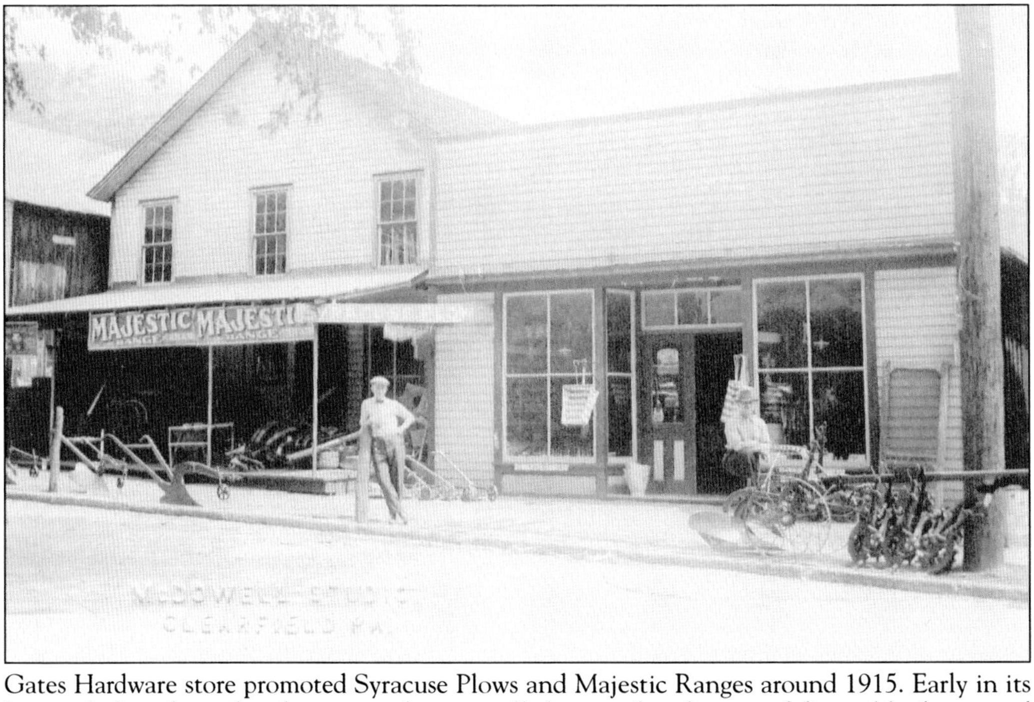

Gates Hardware store promoted Syracuse Plows and Majestic Ranges around 1915. Early in its history before the railroad came to the area, all the merchandise was delivered by horse and wagon from Philipsburg or Tyrone. Wagons also delivered merchandise from the store to the nearby quarries that were regular customers. (Courtesy Jeff Gates.)

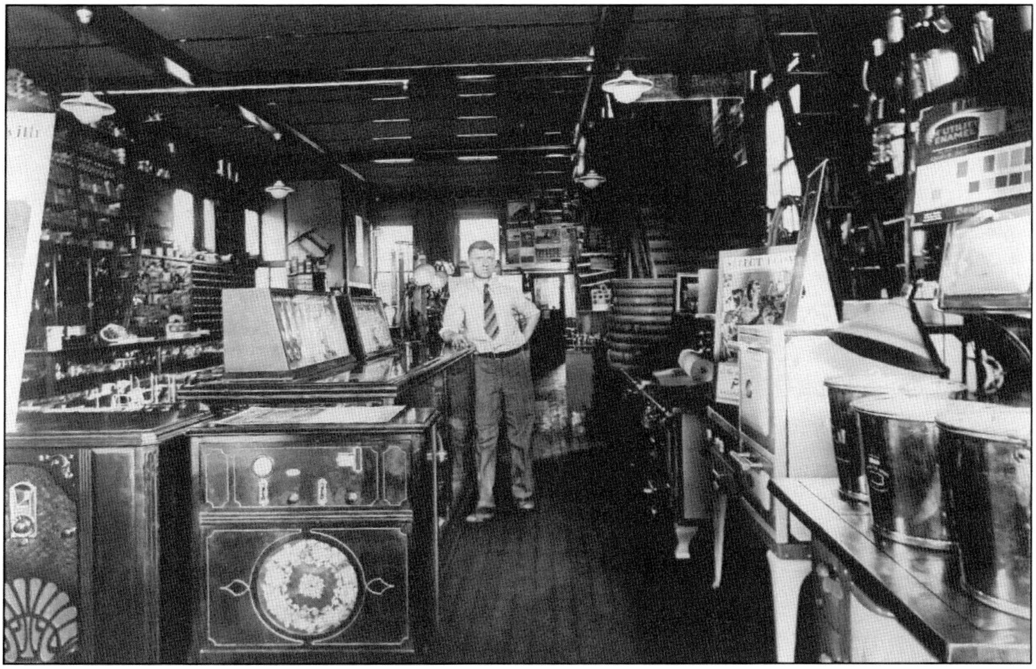

Harry G. Gates poses in the current Gates Hardware store around 1920. In front can be seen Philco radios, and stacked on the counter are Model-T tires. Five generations of the Gates family have served the hardware needs of the people of Curwensville, beginning with Solomon Gates and his son William in 1877. (Courtesy Jeff Gates.)

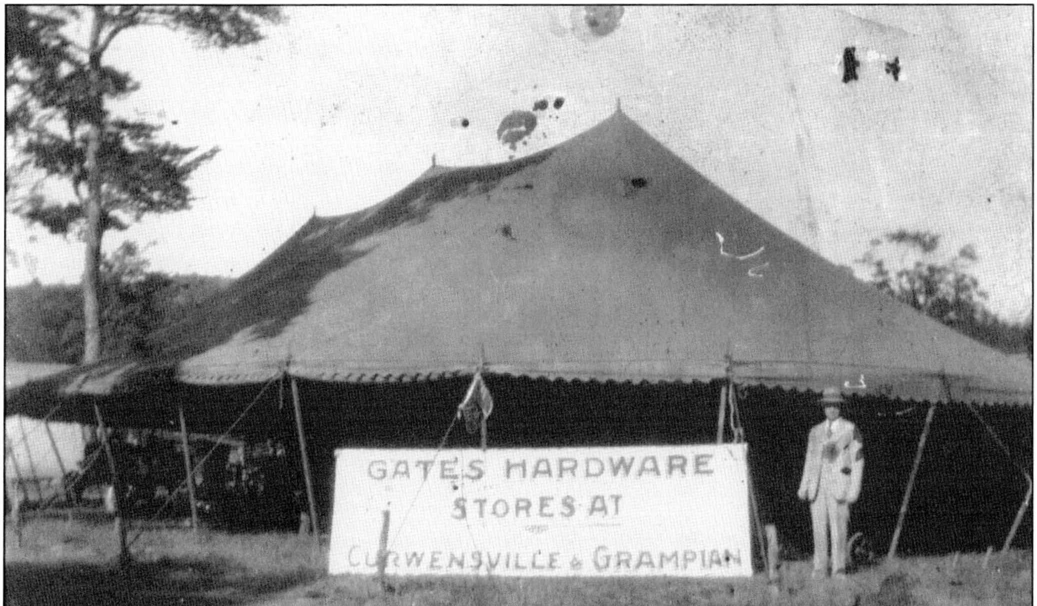

During the 1940s, Gates Hardware had a tent set up at the Clearfield County Fair to advertise the business, which at that time had a store in Grampian as well. At one point, there were Gates Hardware stores in Curwensville, Grampian, Westover, Osceola Mills, and Clearfield. They also operated two Clover Farm Stores. (Courtesy Jeff Gates.)

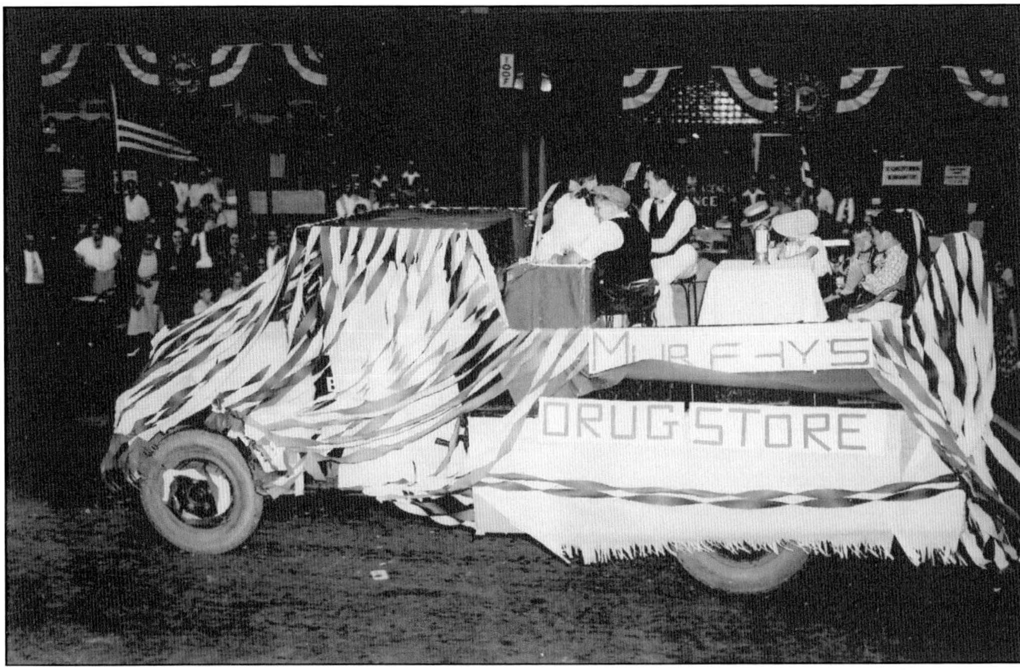

During the sesquicentennial, Murphy's Drug Store created a mobile soda shop float. Jay W. Murphy bought the store in 1919 from William K. Wrigley, who started the business in 1865. It was favorite hangout for teenagers, who enjoyed sundaes made with special homemade toppings. In 1954, the store was sold to Cosmo "Gus" Guglielmi, who ran it until the mid-1980s, when it became Curwensville Pharmacy. (Courtesy Pat Murphy.)

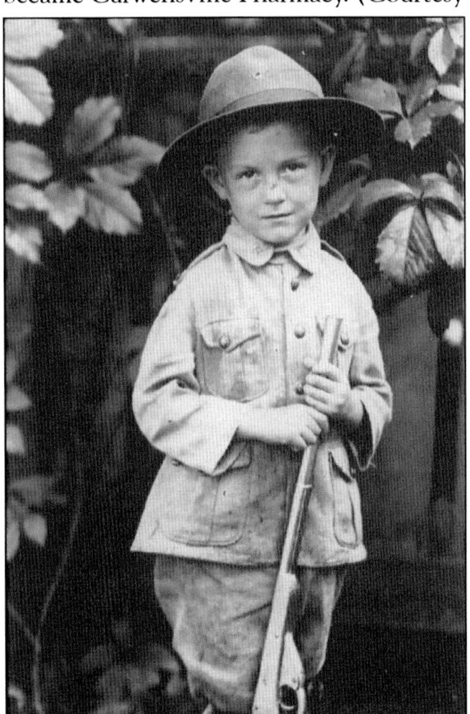

This youngster grew up be a doctor who delivered about 8,000 babies, "not with a smack on the bottom, but mostly with a gentle tickle on the foot." Born in Curwensville in 1914, Dr. James H. Murphy, the son of Jay Murphy, was in the army from 1942 to 1946, during which he participated in the Normandy Invasion. He began his practice in Curwensville in 1947 and retired in 1983. Dr. Murphy died in 1987. (Courtesy Pat Murphy.)

Two

Lifestyle and Celebrations

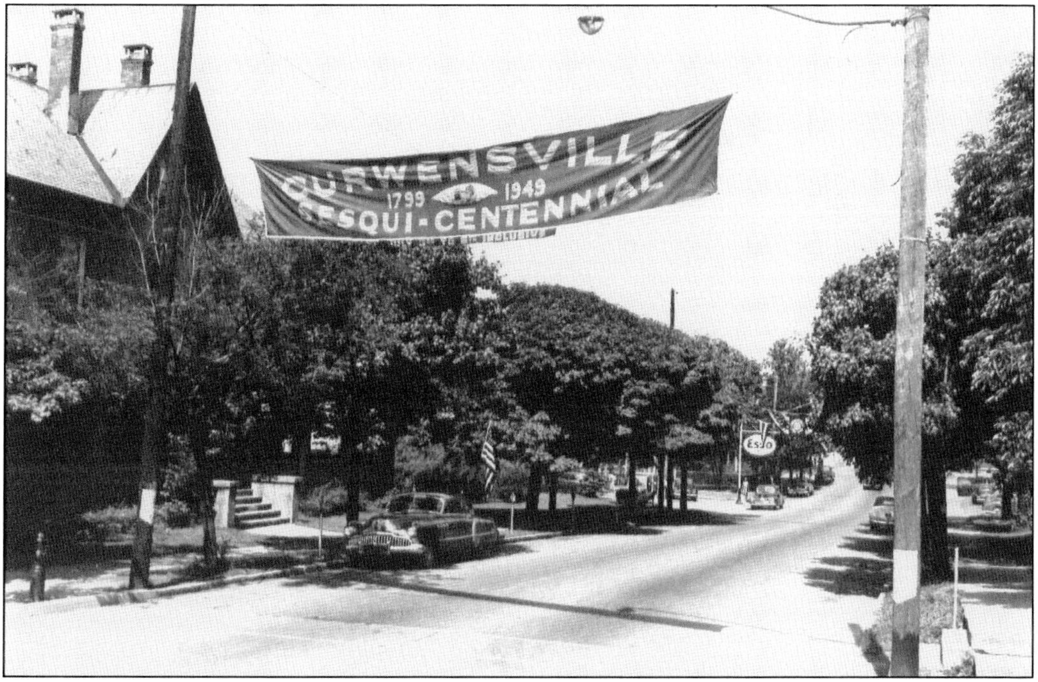

In July 1949, Curwensville marked its sesquicentennial with a six-day celebration. Each day had its own theme honoring churches, veterans, manufacturers and industrial workers, founders and merchants, firemen, and the schools. There were parades and "outstanding attractions at the stadium in the evening." Here a street-wide banner decorates State Street to mark the occasion. (Courtesy Curwensville-Pike Township Historical Society.)

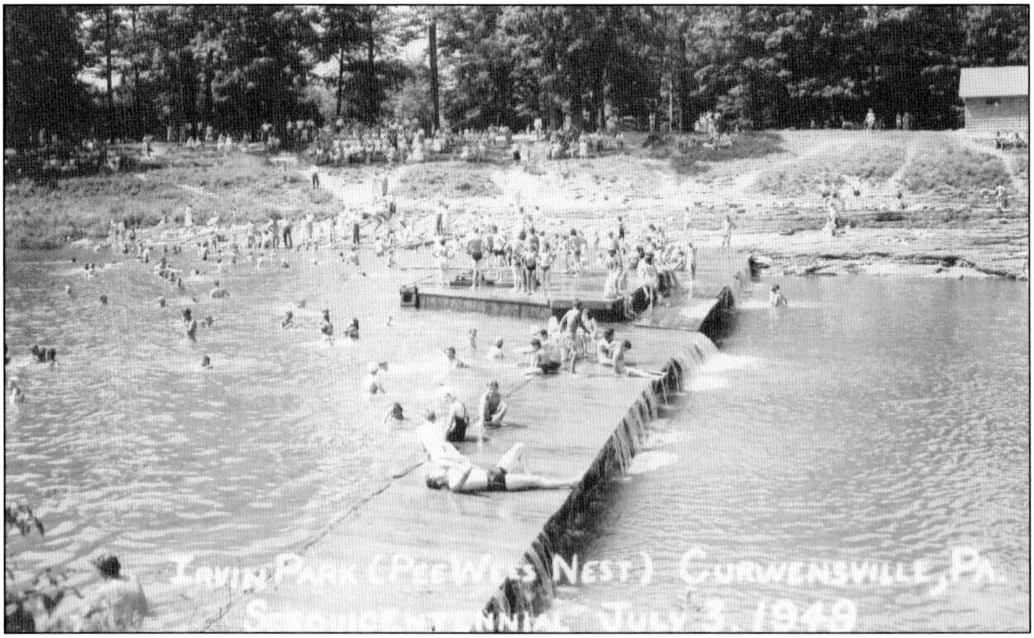

"Pee Wee's Nest," or Irvin Park, was a hot spot for a cool swim in 1949 during the sesquicentennial. The park has been a gathering place for families since 1921, when the land on the West Branch of the Susquehanna River was donated to the community by Elizabeth and Hugh M. Irvin. The nickname Pee Wee's Nest came from the small birds that nested there. (Courtesy Curwensville-Pike Township Historical Society.)

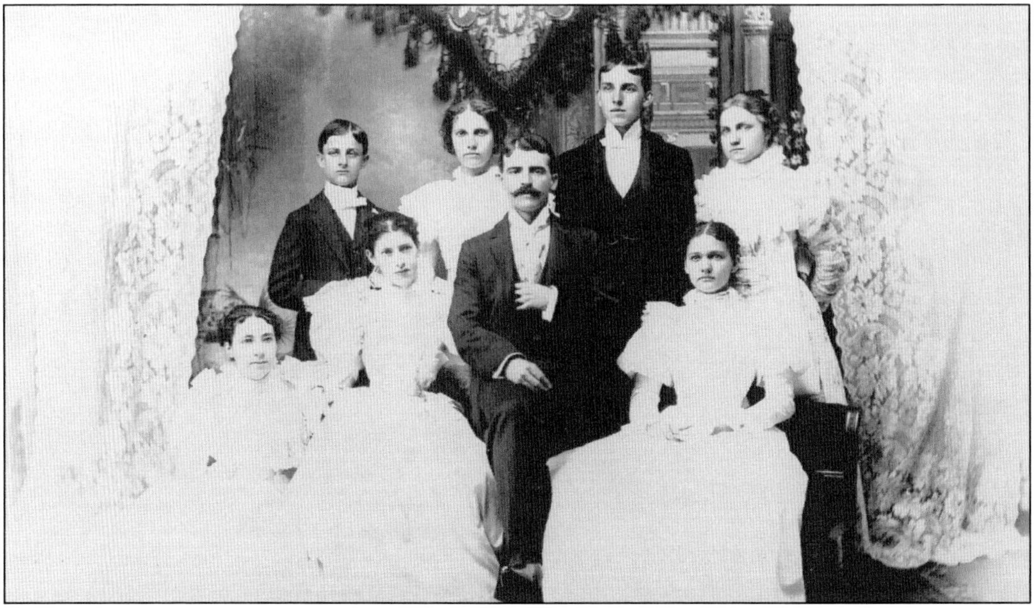

The graduating class of the Patton High School in May 20, 1897, included, from left to right, (first row) Mary Scott (Albert), Mary Garretson, Principal Harry M. Weigle, and Margaret Bloom (Burtnette); (second row) Reeder King Way, Alice Maude Leech (Crocker), Harry Joseph Kittelberger, and Alamand K. Kerns (Gaylor). (Courtesy Curwensville-Pike Township Historical Society.)

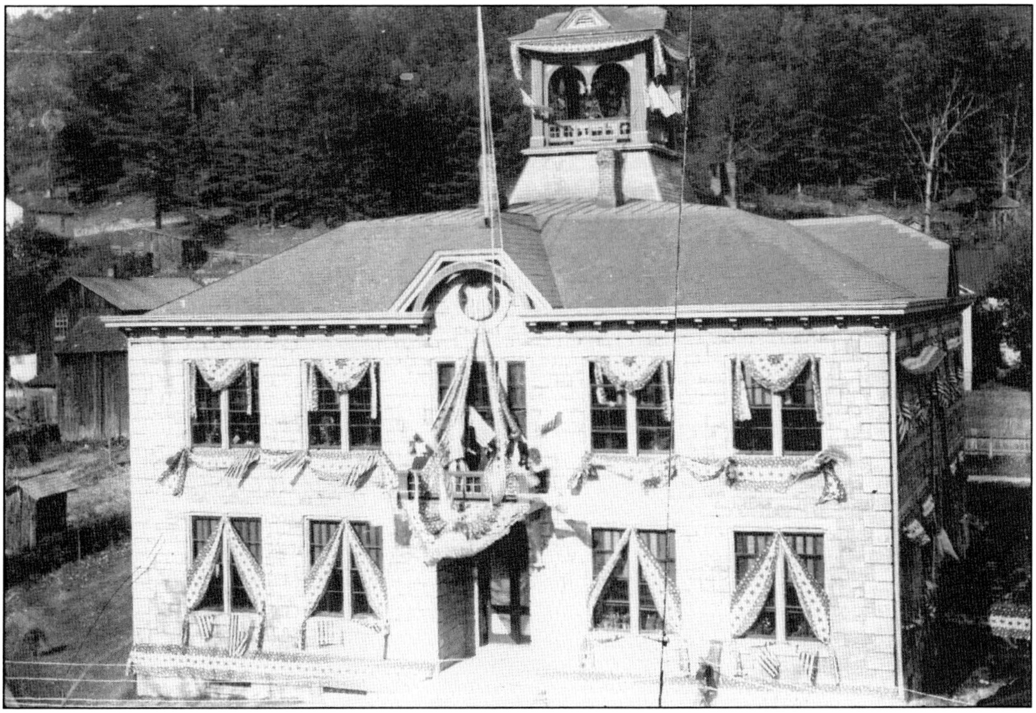

The Patton School is decorated for a Columbus Day celebration in this photograph from the 1890s. The building, which was located at the corner of Walnut and State Streets, was built in 1885 with funds provided by John Patton. It was torn down in 1968. (Courtesy Curwensville-Pike Township Historical Society.)

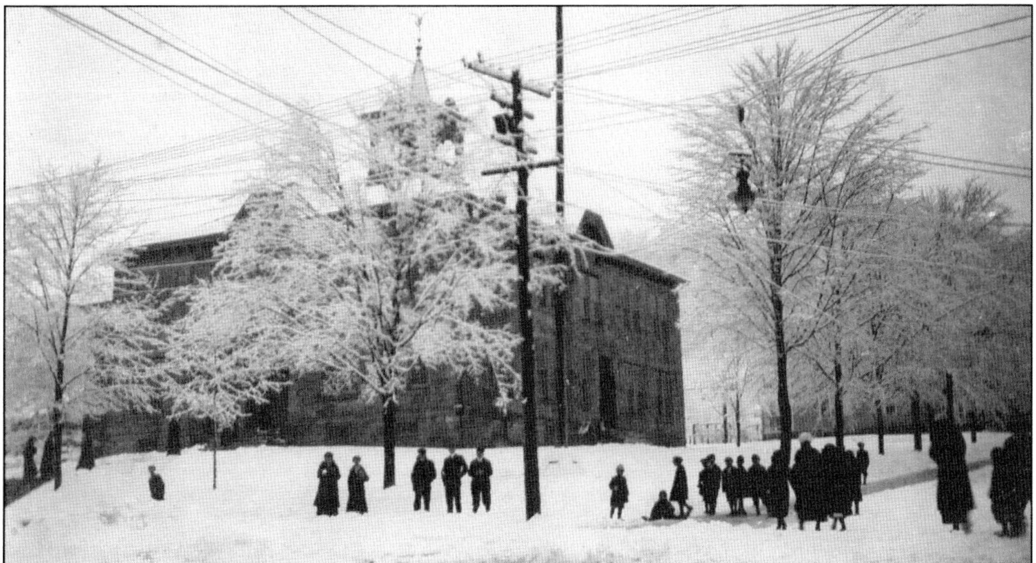

This lovely view of the Patton School, "to school on a winter's morning," was featured on a c. 1910 postcard. The school was constructed of native sandstone and housed eight classrooms, four on each of its two floors. Around 1900, a two-room annex was added, and later the basement was also used for classes. (Courtesy Curwensville-Pike Township Historical Society.)

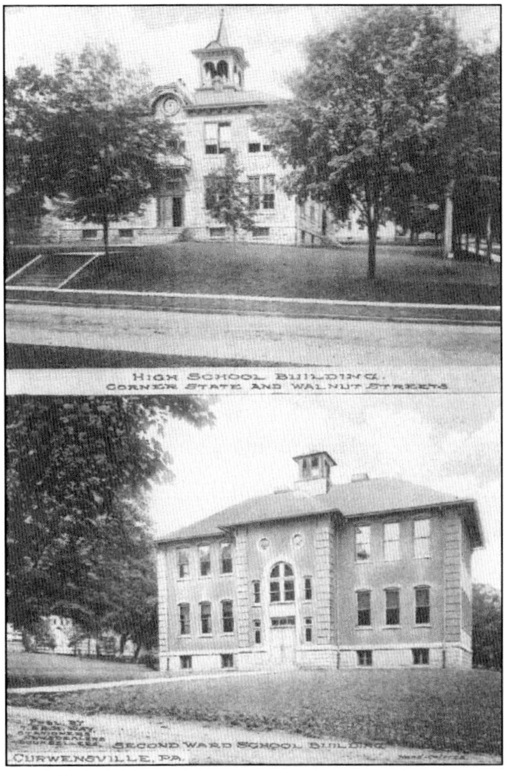

This postcard from 1913 features both the Patton School and the Locust Street School, which was built in 1908. In 1955, 794 students from these schools packed their books and walked to the new junior-senior high school on Beech Street. (Courtesy Clearfield County Historical Society.)

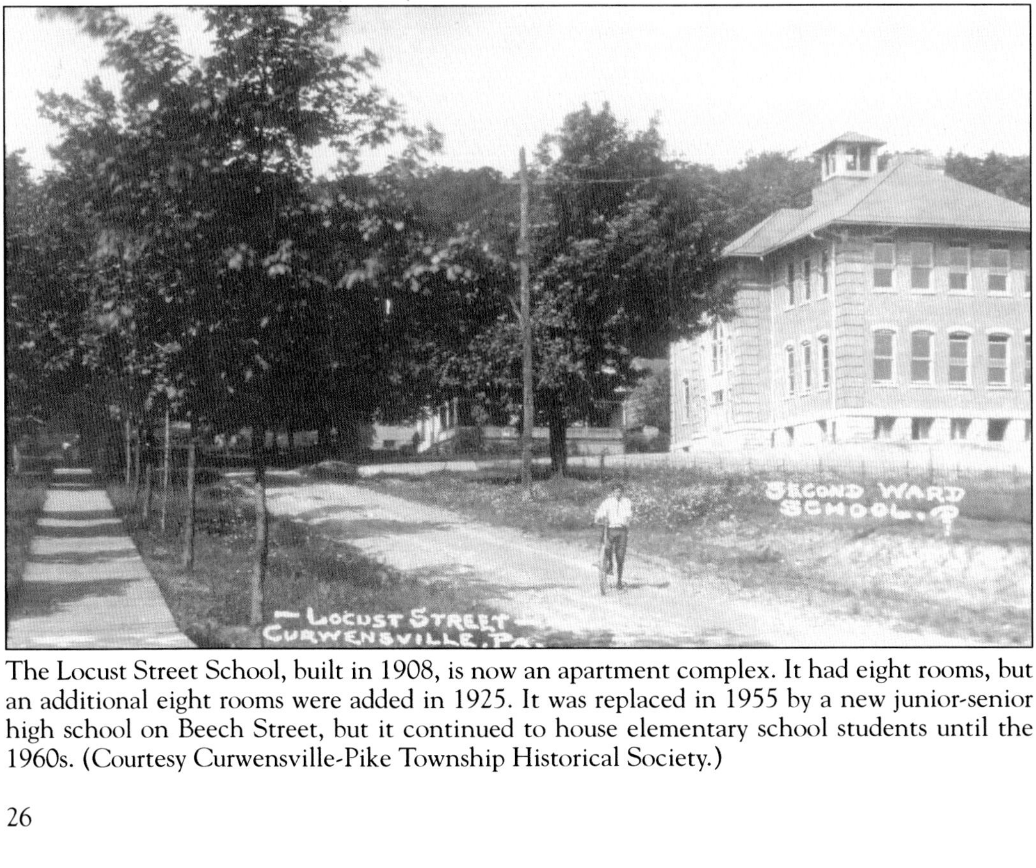

The Locust Street School, built in 1908, is now an apartment complex. It had eight rooms, but an additional eight rooms were added in 1925. It was replaced in 1955 by a new junior-senior high school on Beech Street, but it continued to house elementary school students until the 1960s. (Courtesy Curwensville-Pike Township Historical Society.)

Born in 1794, William McNaul moved to Curwensville in 1819, where he and his wife, Hannah Way, lived for the rest of their lives. When Curwensville was made a United States post office in 1821, McNaul was named its first postmaster. He also started one of Curwensville's first tanneries, which was located on State Street, also in 1819. (Courtesy David McNaul.)

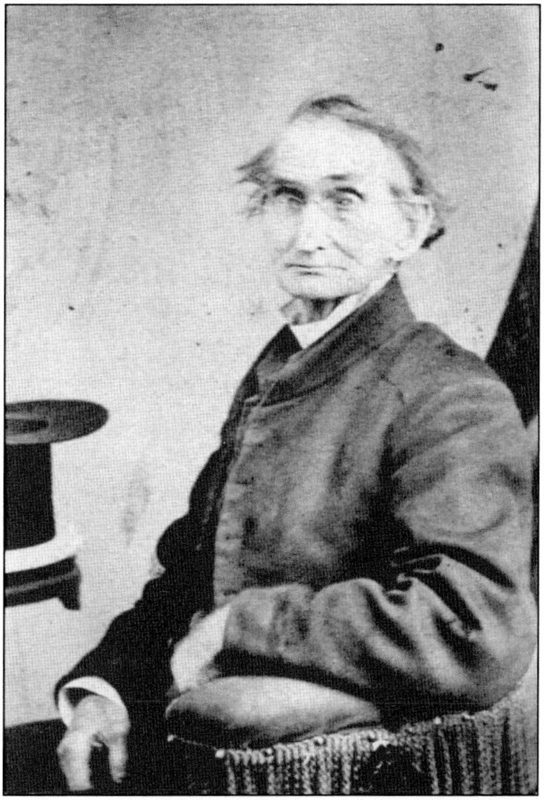

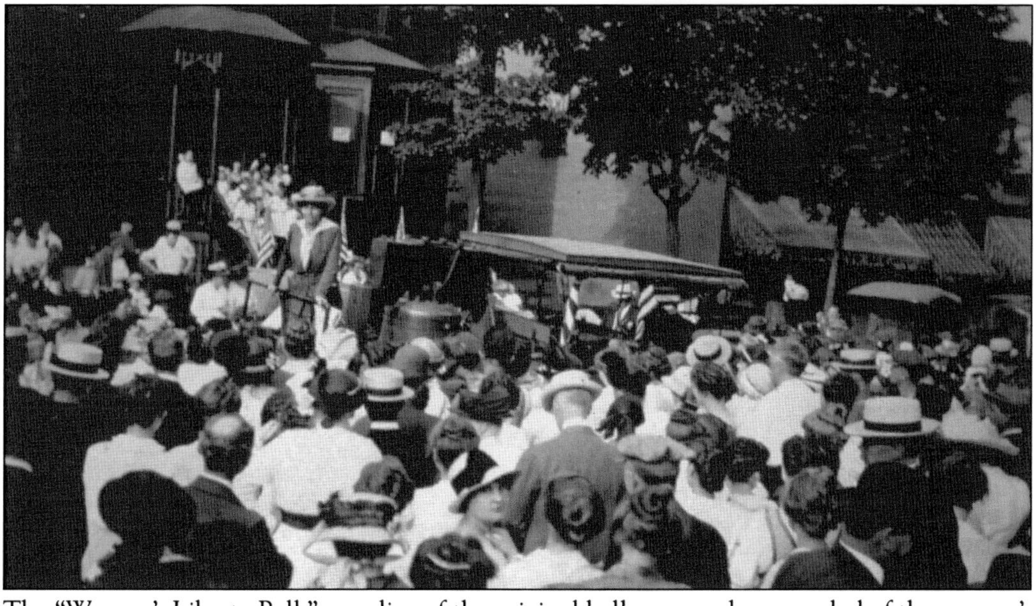

The "Woman's Liberty Bell," a replica of the original bell, was used as a symbol of the woman's suffrage movement in 1915. The bell accompanied speakers who traveled to every county asking men to "help break the chains that hold the bronze clapper silent. Vote yes on the suffrage amendment on election day." The bell and its speaker visited Curwensville on July 27, 1915. (Courtesy Curwensville-Pike Township Historical Society.)

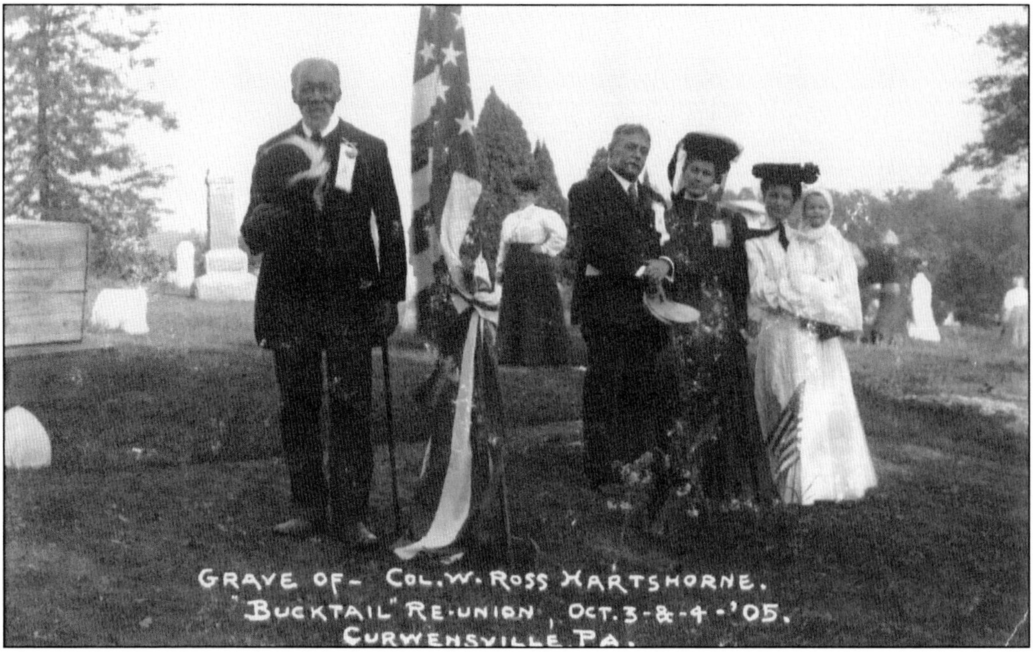

A small crowd gathers at the grave of Brig. Gen. W. Ross Hartshorne as part of the Bucktail Reunion in October 1905. Hartshorne, who was the highest-ranking officer in Clearfield County, helped plan the reunions, which began in 1887. This was the 19th reunion of the Civil War's Pennsylvania Bucktail regiment, which was known for its fine marksmanship and courage. The man on the left is Elijah Only, who served as Col. E. A. Irvin's personal aide during the war. (Courtesy Dan McDonald.)

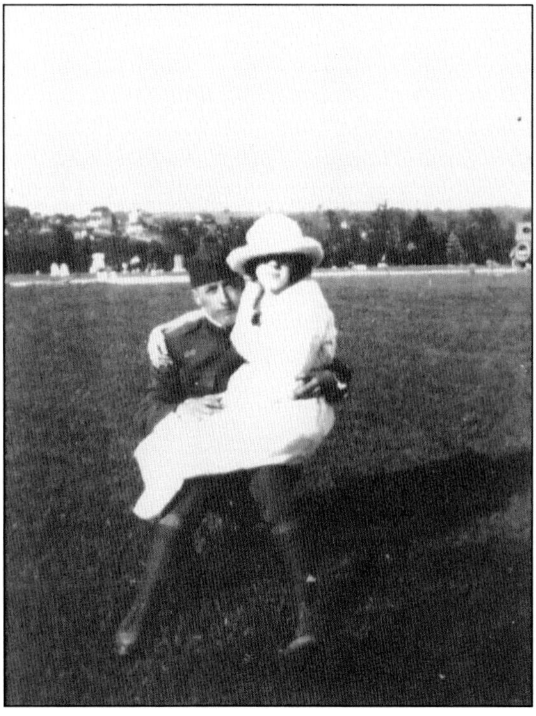

Violet Craddock and Arthur Winters visit while at a Memorial Day celebration 1921 at Oak Hill Cemetery. Winters joined the cavalry at an early age and was with the group that chased Pancho Villa around Mexico. After that, he was sent to Europe in World War I, where he spent years in a London hospital after being gassed. Winters and Craddock were married in August 1922. (Courtesy Joy Rickard.)

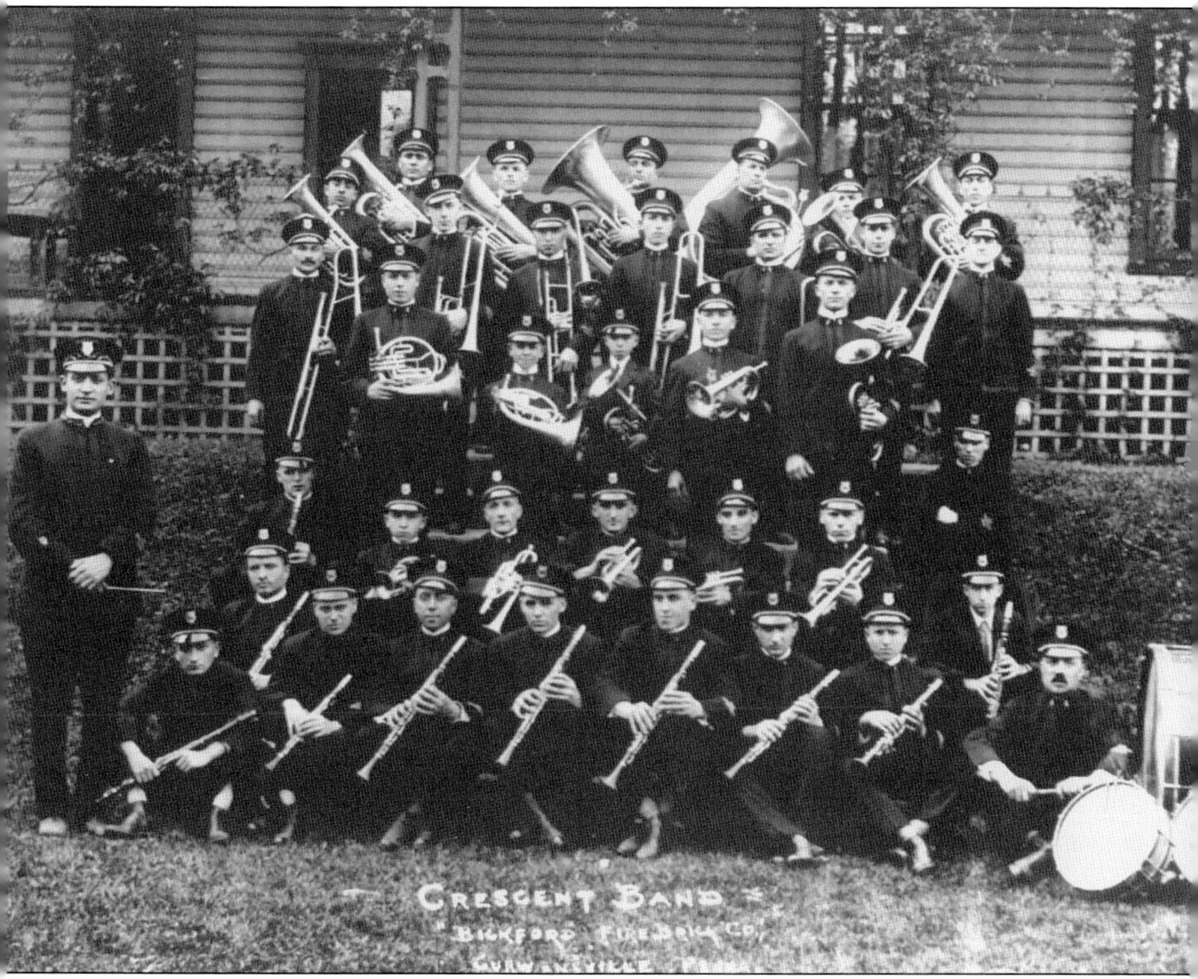

The Crescent Band was named for the local factory where several of the members worked. They are, from left to right, (first row) director Orazio Circolo, Armando Passarelli, Boyd Smith, Tom Brunetti, Dean Doughman, Jim Volpe, Jim Lombardo, Pete Grande, and Joe Pedro; (second row at opposite ends between first and third rows), Amilcare Cavaterra and Reuben Moose; (third row) Guy Woodel, Guy Yacabucci, Teddy Ricci, John Bellone, Frank Maurey, and Lawrence Girardi; (fourth row) Tucci Errigo, Guerry Brunetti, Rudy Yacabucci, Frank Feola, Tony Zwolski, and Percy Maurey; (fifth row) Amerigo Abrino, Harvey Smith, Guy Lozardo, Premo Yacabucci, Charles Maurey, Raymond Volpe, and Danny Sullivan; (sixth row) John P. Errigo, Anthony P. Errigo, Frank Stricek, Themjstocle Cavaterra, Jess Richards, Anthony S. Errigo, and Foreste Brunetti. (Courtesy Curwensville-Pike Township Historical Society.)

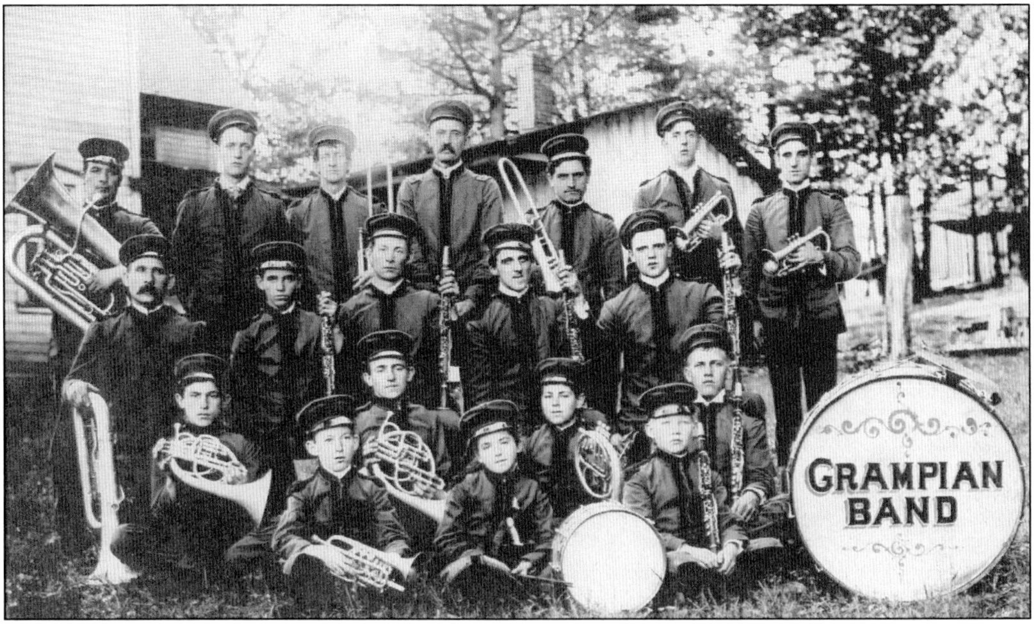

The Grampian Band was a favorite of composer George Rosenkrans, who wrote the *Grampian March*. Seen here are, from left to right, (first row) Fred Thompson, Esther Doughman, and Edgar Chelgren; (second row) two unidentified, Dudley Doughman, and Warner Chelgren; (third row) Gus Chelgren Sr., Deon Doughman, Cobe Thompson, Chas Mowrey, and Guy Woodel; (fourth row) Jess Richards, unidentified, Wilmet Wall, W. G. Doughman, Albert Bartacci, unidentified, and Frank Mowrey. (Courtesy J. Duane Test.)

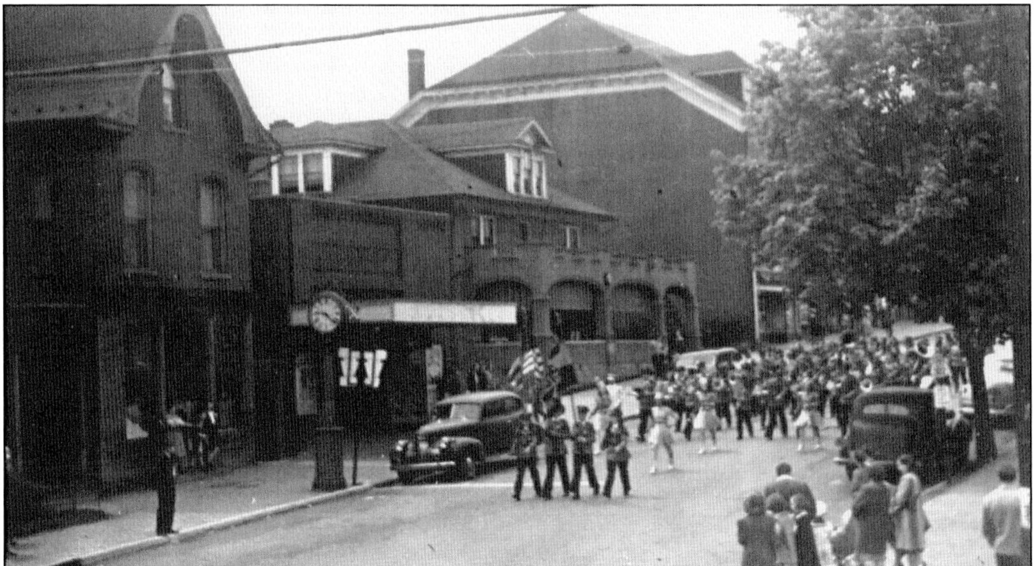

A parade on State Street around 1950 passes by the Rex Theater (on the left). The theater was built in 1920 and originally called the Strand. It was sold to H. J. Thompson in 1935. After remodeling it, he changed the name to the Rex Theater. It was torn down around 1979 to make way for a new parking area for the Curwensville State Bank. (Courtesy Clearfield County Historical Society.)

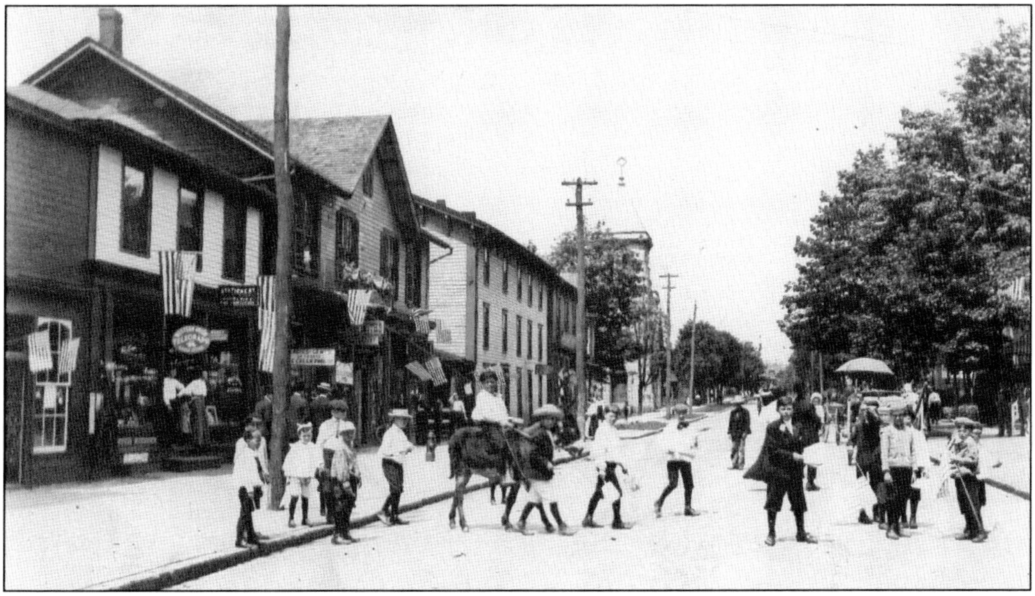

A group of children decides to make their own parade to mark a patriotic occasion as they cross State Street in this *c.* 1910 postcard. On the left is Way's Stationery Store, the white building is the Draucker House, and farther down the street, the Curwensville United Methodist Church can be seen. (Courtesy Curwensville-Pike Township Historical Society.)

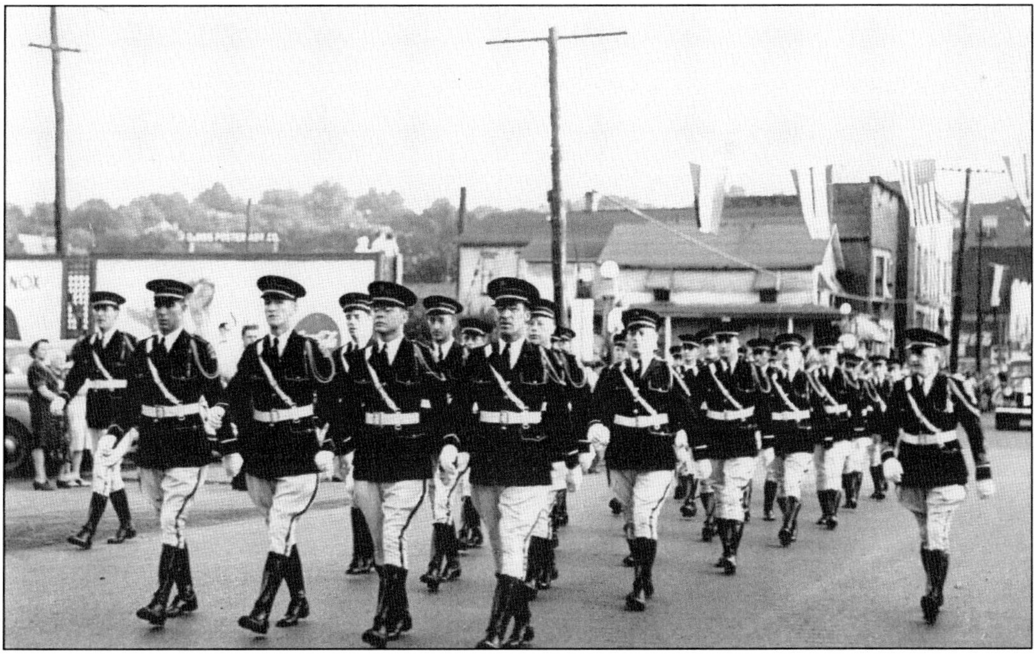

The Rescue Hose and Ladder Drill Team is on the march in 1930. A news article from that time described them as having put on a "splendid exhibition" at a district firemen's convention where they earned top honors. The exhibition was reenacted later on State Street. "There were 39 men in line and each and every one acted as though they had studied Upton's tactics for a lifetime. The liberal applause they received was well merited," the article read. (Courtesy Curwensville-Pike Township Historical Society.)

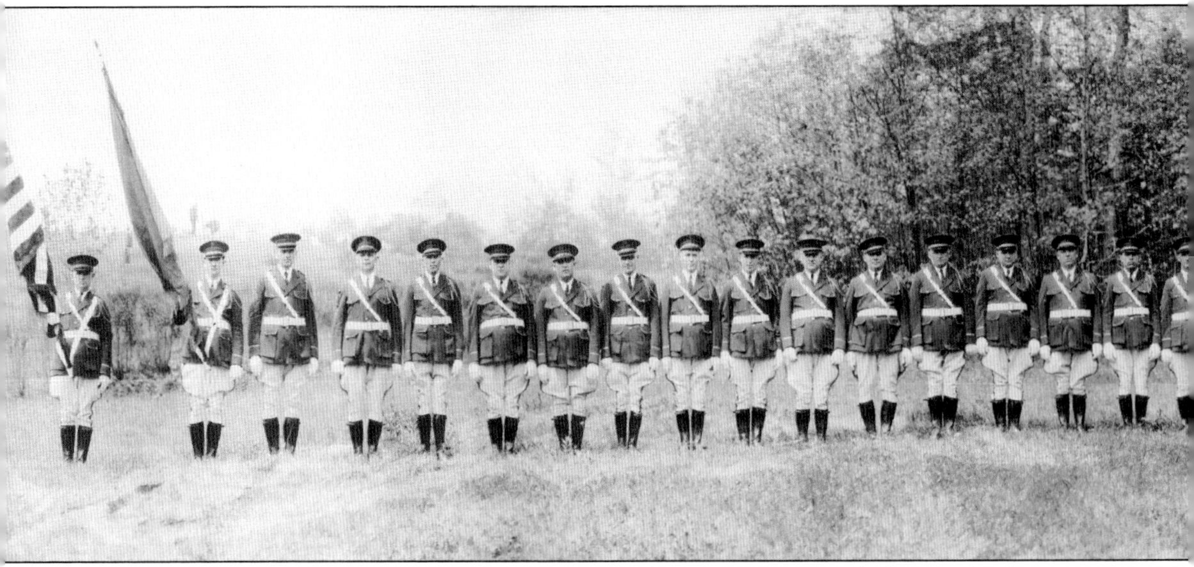

The Rescue Hose and Ladder Drill Team poses in this team photograph from 1930. During its history, the team became acclaimed for its skill and won many awards. In 1942, the group was named the best in the state. They are, from left to right, Charles Norris, William Cowdrick, Wilbur Wall, Alex Gabrielson, Earl McFadden, Jay Murphy, Joseph Vesco, Furman Smith, Allen Passmore, Edward Frankhouser, Walter Olson, Vern Palmgren, George Ardary, Isaac Whitaker, Dewey Hummell, Burton Bloom, Ralph Cruikshank, Steven Sovinsky, Joseph Hipps, Droze

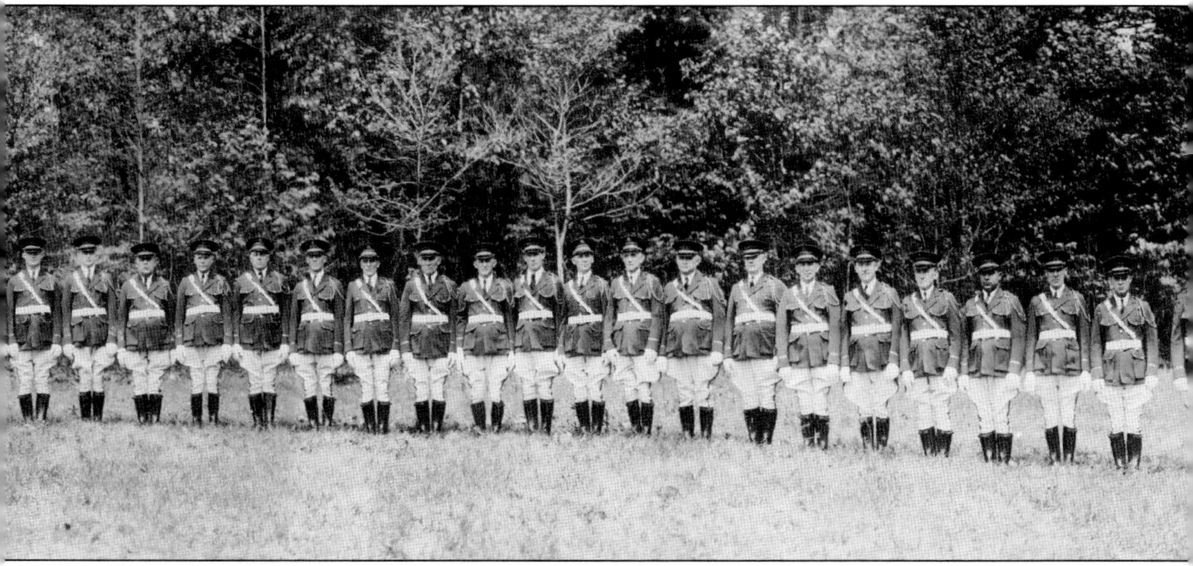

Dotts, George Benner, George Whitaker, Howard Thompson, Forest Bornhoft, Clair Williams, Hugh Mallon, Alex Frankhouser, Clifford Kelly, Arthur Swanson, Charles Smith, Ralph Johnston, Edward McLaughlin, James Edmiston, Peter O'Laughlin, Jared McNaul, Anthony Errigo, Peter Ross, Chester Smith, and Edward Norris. (Courtesy Curwensville-Pike Township Historical Society.)

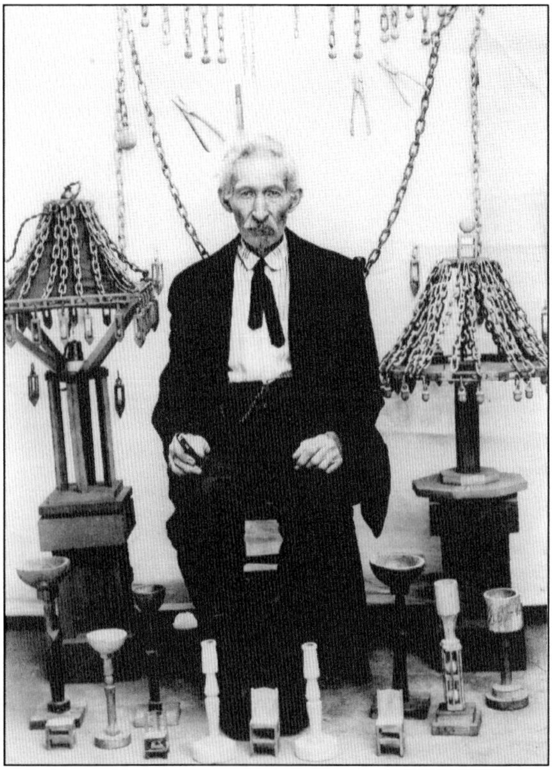

Jacob Hawk poses with some of his handiwork. Hawk's hobby was carving wood. Born in 1845, he was the first of 14 children. He died in 1939 and is buried in Oak Hill Cemetery. In his long life, he had many different jobs, including steering a raft to market, for which he received $45; owning both a sawmill and gristmill; and making cement blocks. (Courtesy Dan McDonald.)

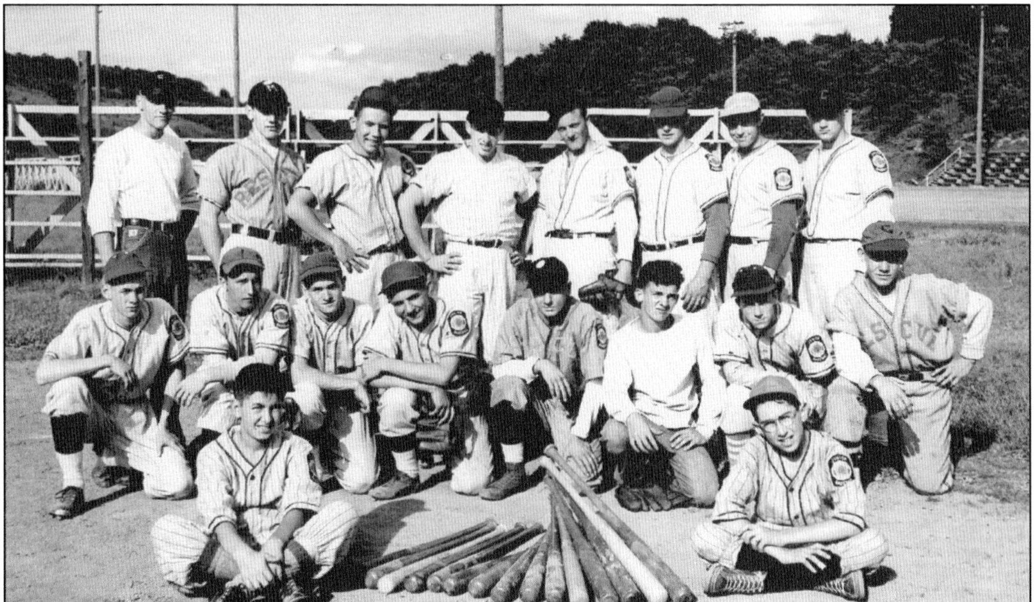

A Curwensville baseball team poses in this c. 1945 photograph. Seen here are, from left to right, (first row, sitting) Jack Errigo and Morty Kanter; (second row) Russ Clark, Don Shuberts, Chris Cullen, Zeke Fye, "Pucky" Rybbee, Donnie Thurston, Eddie Flick, and Lance Duttry; (third row) Sonny Cramer, Don Sponterelli, only identified as "8 Ball," Jack Riddle, Muzzy Miles, Bud Sunderland, Ken Spencer, and Harry Bunnell. (Courtesy J. Duane Test.)

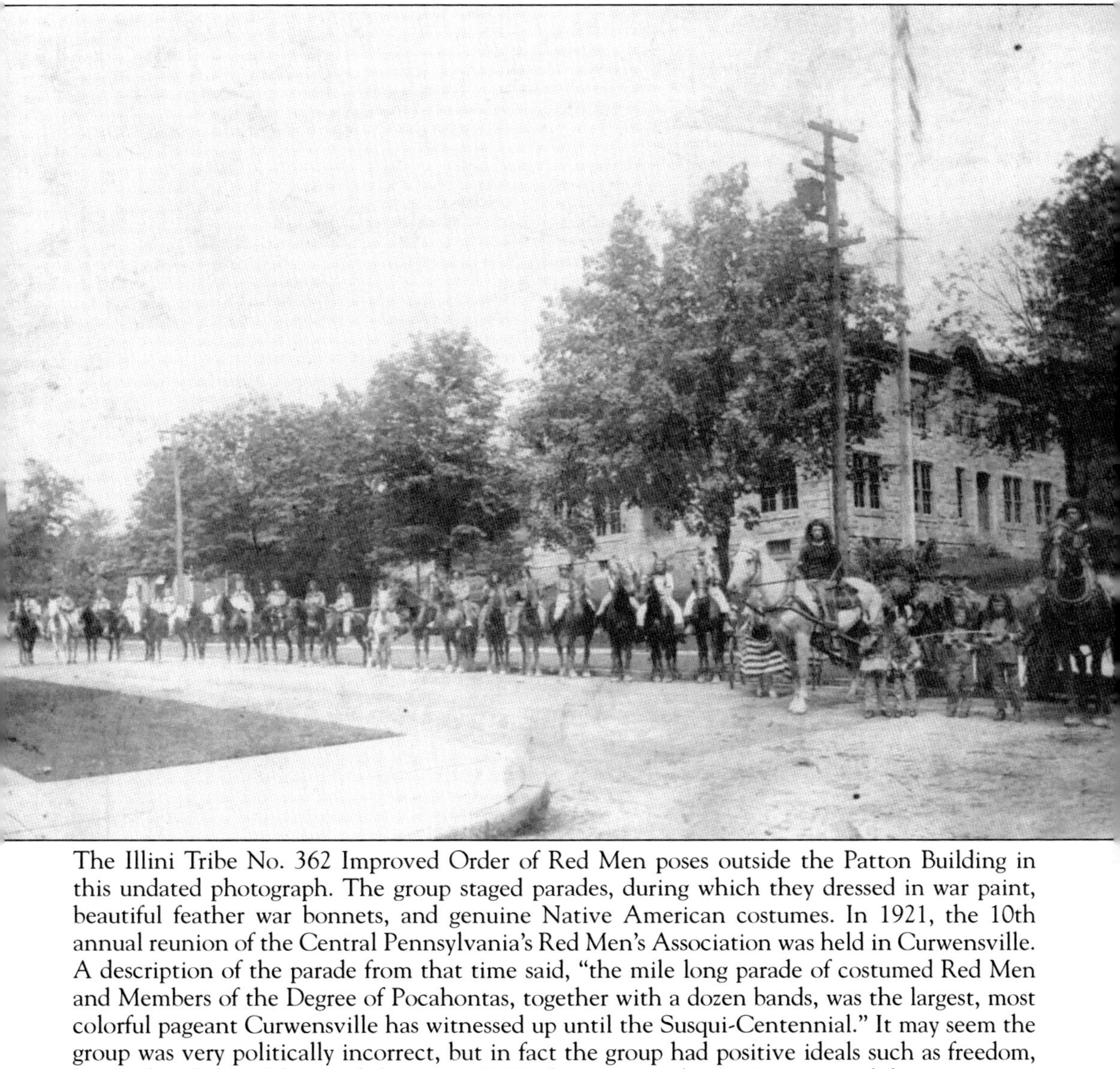

The Illini Tribe No. 362 Improved Order of Red Men poses outside the Patton Building in this undated photograph. The group staged parades, during which they dressed in war paint, beautiful feather war bonnets, and genuine Native American costumes. In 1921, the 10th annual reunion of the Central Pennsylvania's Red Men's Association was held in Curwensville. A description of the parade from that time said, "the mile long parade of costumed Red Men and Members of the Degree of Pocahontas, together with a dozen bands, was the largest, most colorful pageant Curwensville has witnessed up until the Susqui-Centennial." It may seem the group was very politically incorrect, but in fact the group had positive ideals such as freedom, brotherhood, friendship, and charity. In 1920, there were orders in 46 states and there were over half a million members. The organization, which started after the War of 1812, still exists today with a national office in Waco, Texas. (Courtesy Test collection.)

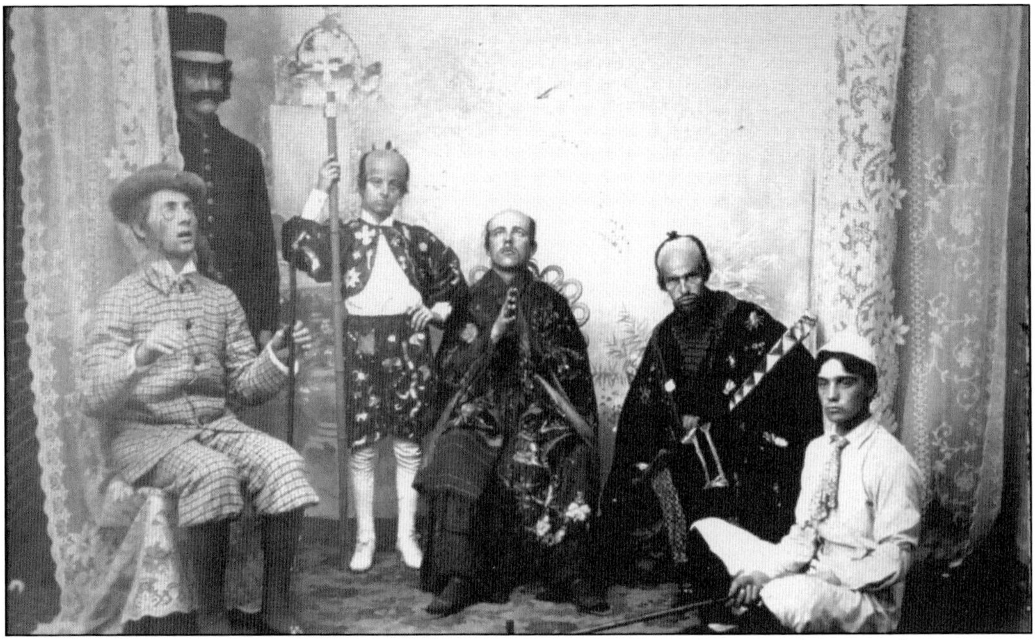

The opera house, which was located on State Street, had a second floor auditorium that was used for many things, including graduation ceremonies and plays. The musical *Tycoon* was performed there in 1891 with a cast that included R. K. Way, third from left. The building was torn down in 1946. (Courtesy Curwensville-Pike Township Historical Society.)

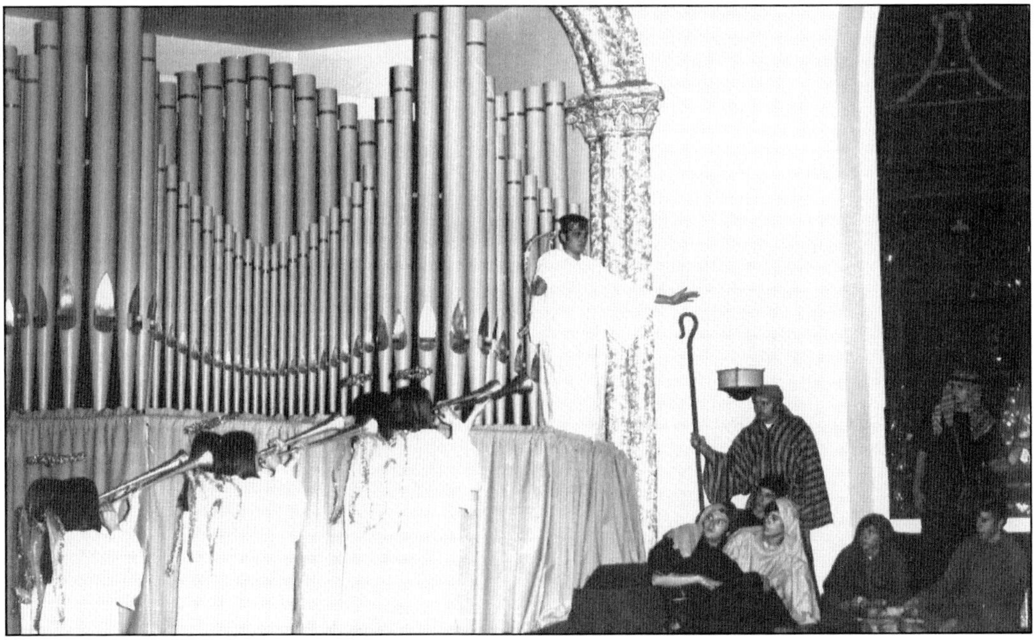

When Laura Wright, unsatisfied with other Christmas pageants, decided to write her own, no one suspected it would become a beloved annual event. *The Search for Peace* has been performed at the Curwensville United Methodist Church for 46 years. Many of the actors have played the same roles year after year. In this *c.* 1968 photograph, the angel Gabriel, played by Hildred Rowles, speaks to the shepherds. (Courtesy Curwensville United Methodist Church.)

The original brick Methodist church was built in 1862. Then John Patton suggested building a new structure with stone from the Roaring Run Quarry. He agreed to supply the funds, which were estimated at $18,000. This building was demolished in 1893 to make way for the new and current stone structure. (Courtesy Curwensville-Pike Township Historical Society.)

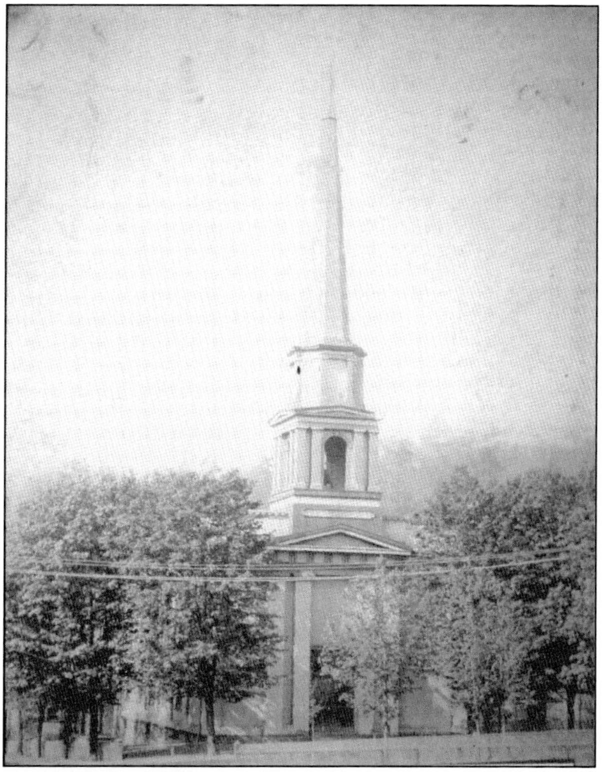

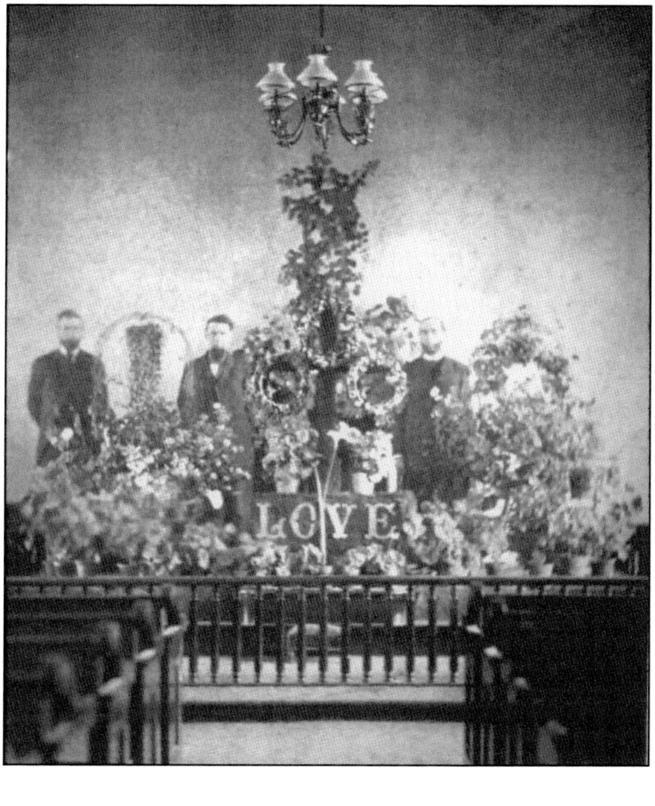

An altar at the old brick Methodist church is decorated in this photograph around 1884. Following the Civil War, the church thrived and in 1872, was "improved" for $3,600. Prior to constructing this church, the congregation met at a building across the street, which is the current site of Clearfield Bank and Trust Company. They began meeting in a log school in 1812. (Courtesy Curwensville-Pike Township Historical Society.)

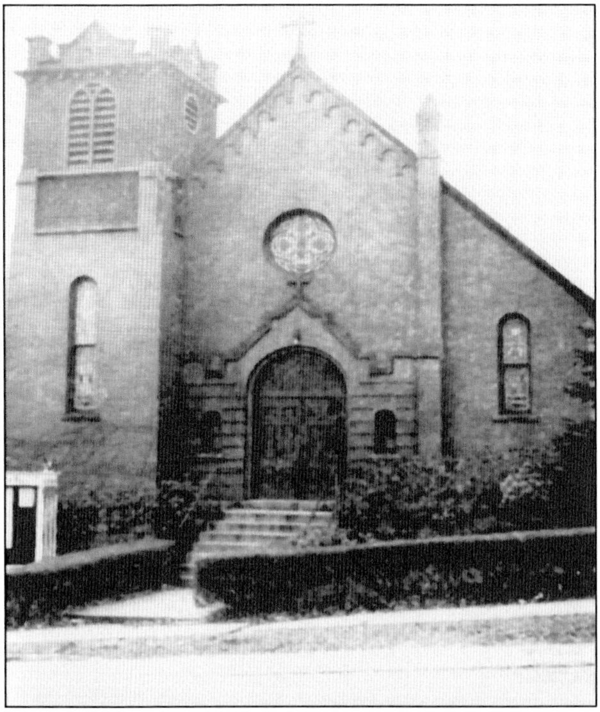

The cornerstone of St. Timothy's Church was laid in 1815. Fr. Peter J. Sheridan, who was the pastor of the St. Francis Church in Clearfield, also served as pastor at St. Timothy's Church at this time. He was instrumental in building both churches. Some of the funds came from collections made by Timothy Cavan of workers building the Pennsylvania Railroad between Curwensville and Grampian. (Courtesy Curwensville-Pike Township Historical Society.)

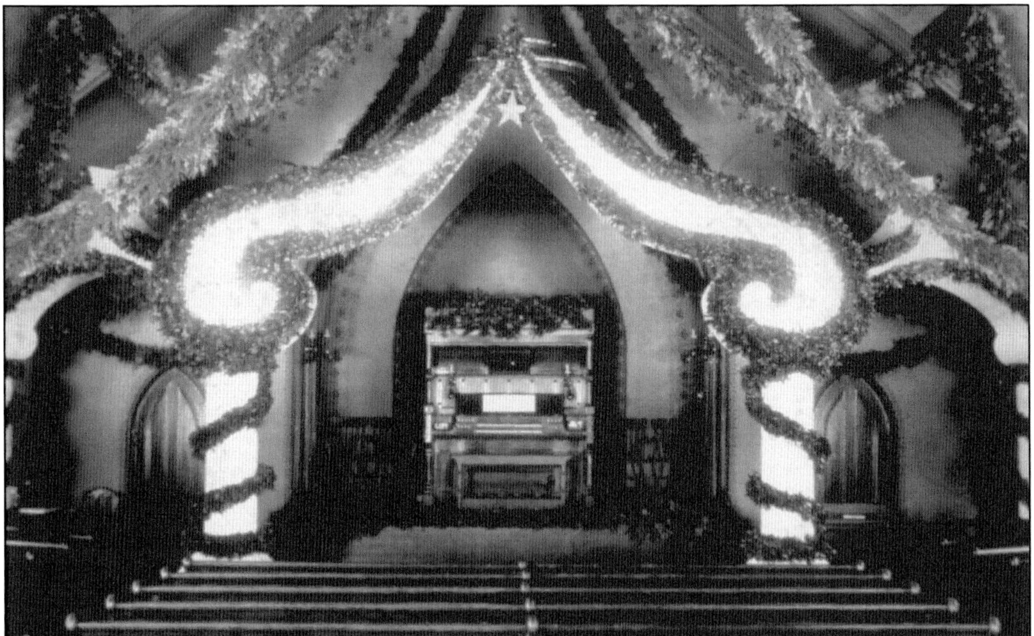

The inside of the Curwensville Presbyterian Church is decorated in this c. 1905 photograph. The church had its beginnings in McClure Cemetery in the 1820s, making it the oldest church in Clearfield County. In 1843, it moved to Curwensville. Originally the Pike Presbyterian Congregation, the name was changed in 1848 to the Curwensville Presbyterian Church. The current church was built in 1869 for $16,000. (Courtesy Curwensville-Pike Township Historical Society.)

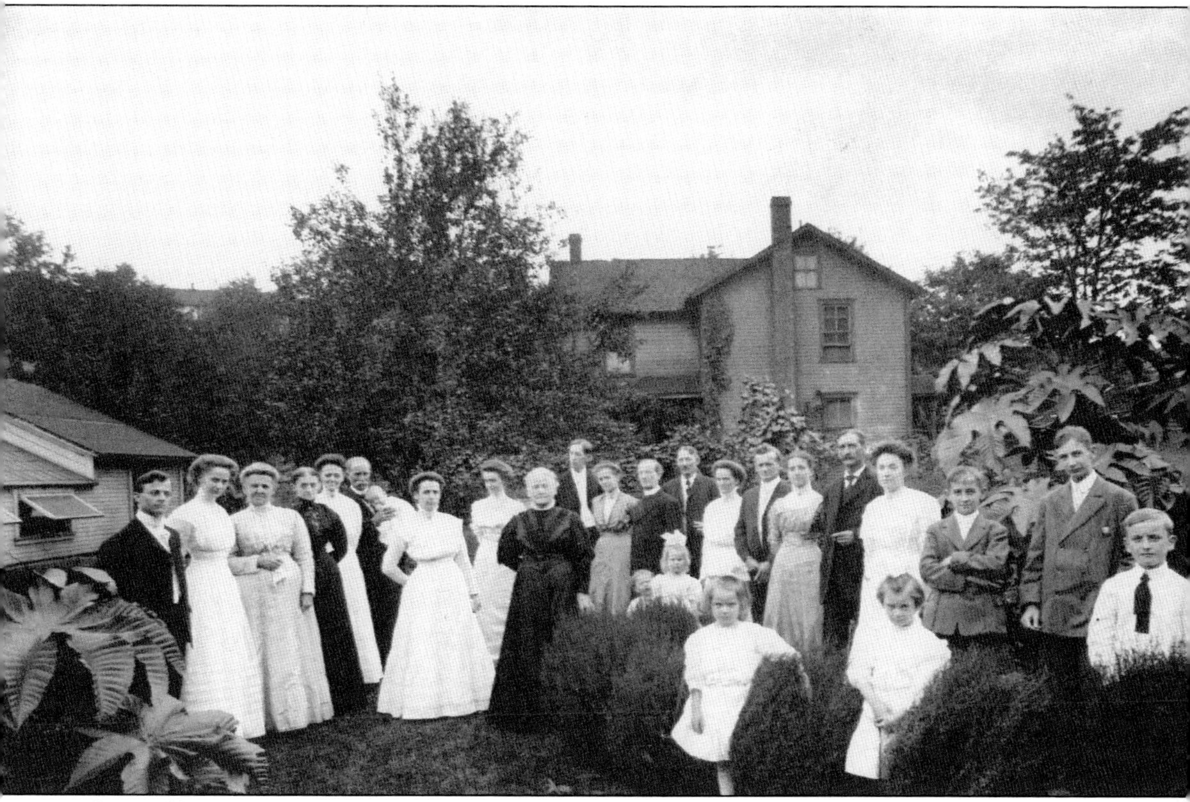

The wedding of R. K. Way and Edna Owens, on September 22, 1909, was a big event. It took place at her home on Anderson Avenue. Seen here are, from left to right, (first row, children) Margaret Brownlee, Julia Powell, and Way Powell; (second row) R. K. Way, Edna Owens Way, Sue Owens (aunt), Clara Way (groom's mother), Mrs. Owens (mother of the bride), Alfred Owens (father of bride) holding William Brownlee (son of Alice Owens Brownlee), Tensie Way (sister of groom), Mrs. T. J. Norris, grandmother Catherine Thompson (sister Clara's mother-in-law), Truman Norris, Ella Norris (sister of groom), Reverend Ganoe, Ord Norris, Alice Owens Brownlee (sister of bride), Lee Powell, Gertrude Powell (sister of groom), William Watson (husband of Olive Watson, sister of groom who was ill and did not attend), Clara Thompson, Clarence Watson, and Paul Watson. The two small children in front of Reverend Ganoe are Kenneth and Irene Brownlee. (Courtesy Curwensville-Pike Township Historical Society.)

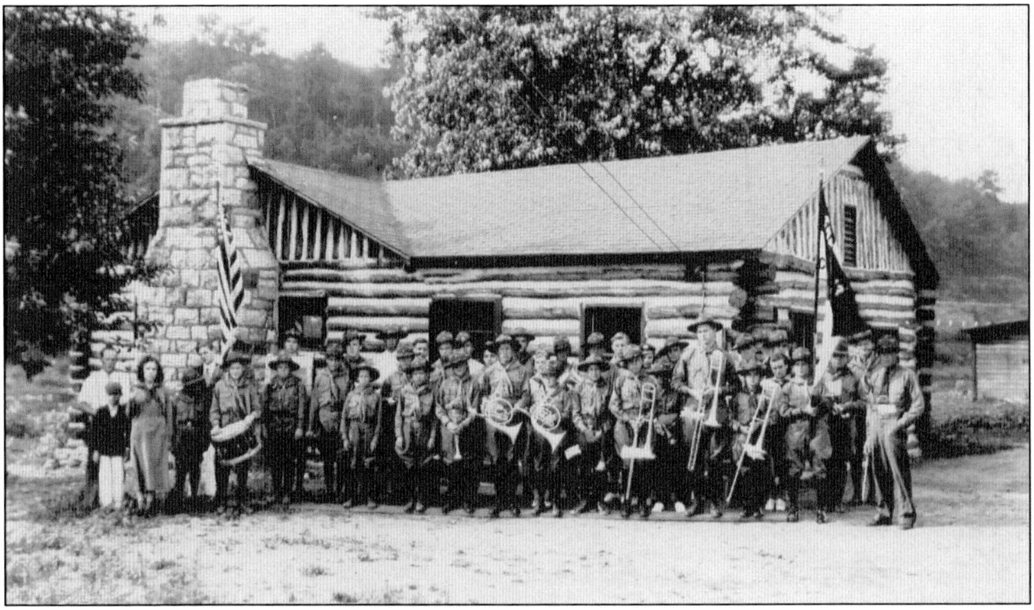

This Boy Scout cabin was built in the 1930s, shortly after Curwensville Troop 13 of the Bucktail Council was organized. It was later owned by the school district and used by players of the sports teams to change clothes before and after games. The cabin, which was located near where the civic center is now, was torn down in 1967. (Courtesy Aletta Singley.)

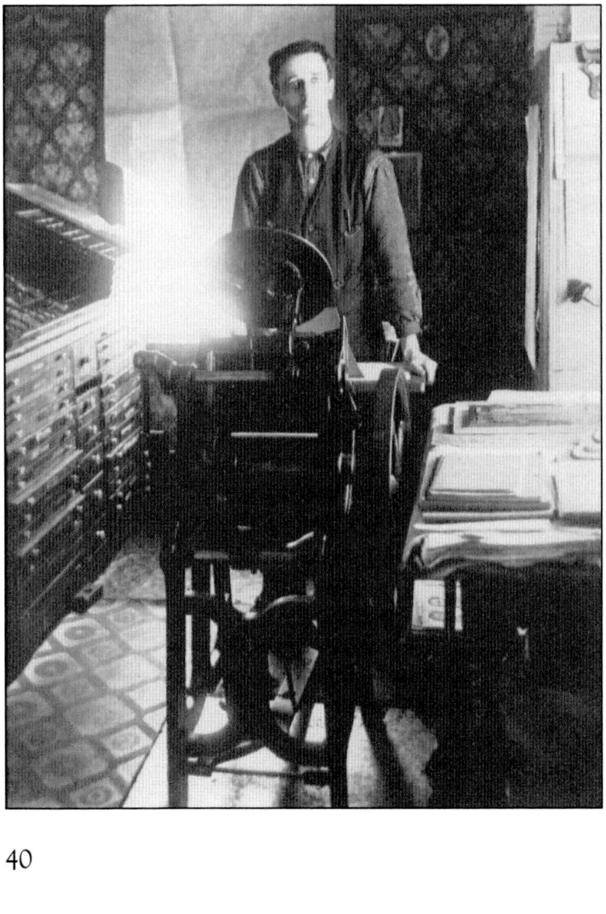

Dallas Kirk of Rockton poses with his printing press. He printed and published the *Home Review*, a monthly community newspaper that was sold throughout the area in the 1930s. It featured local news, gossip, special events, opinions, and helpful household hints, as well as various recipes. (Courtesy Aletta Singley.)

Three

Industry

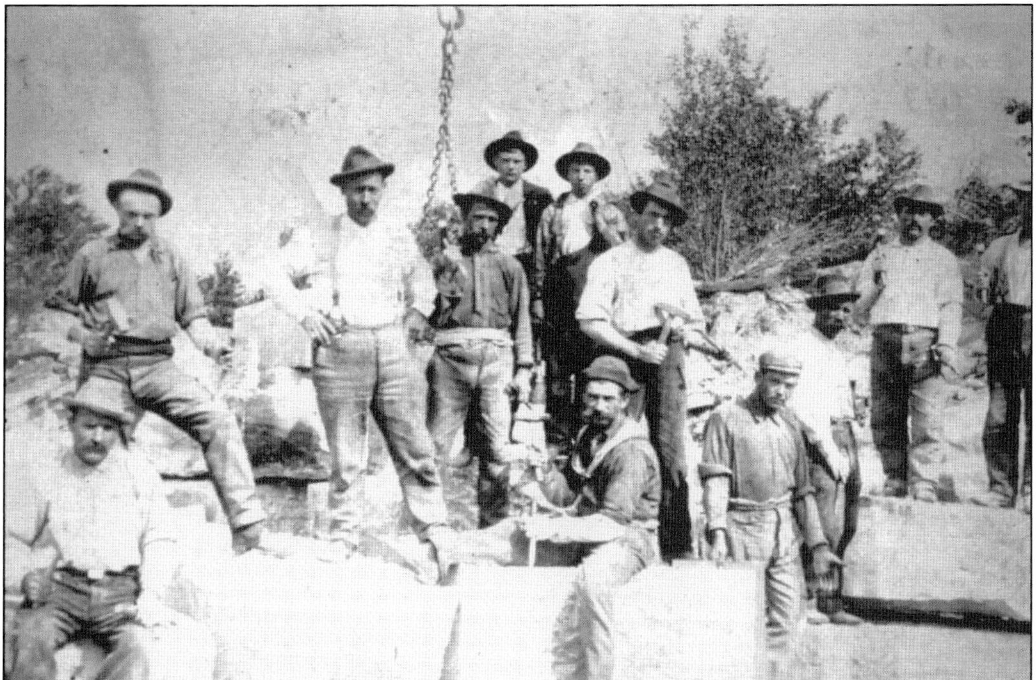

In the latter part of the 19th century, the quarries outside Curwensville were a vital part of the economy. Stone from the Bailey Quarry, shown above, was used to build a railroad bridge at Rockville that crosses the Susquehanna River and goes to Harrisburg. The Bailey Quarry was eventually used as a source of sand taken from the stone. (Courtesy Curwensville-Pike Township Historical Society.)

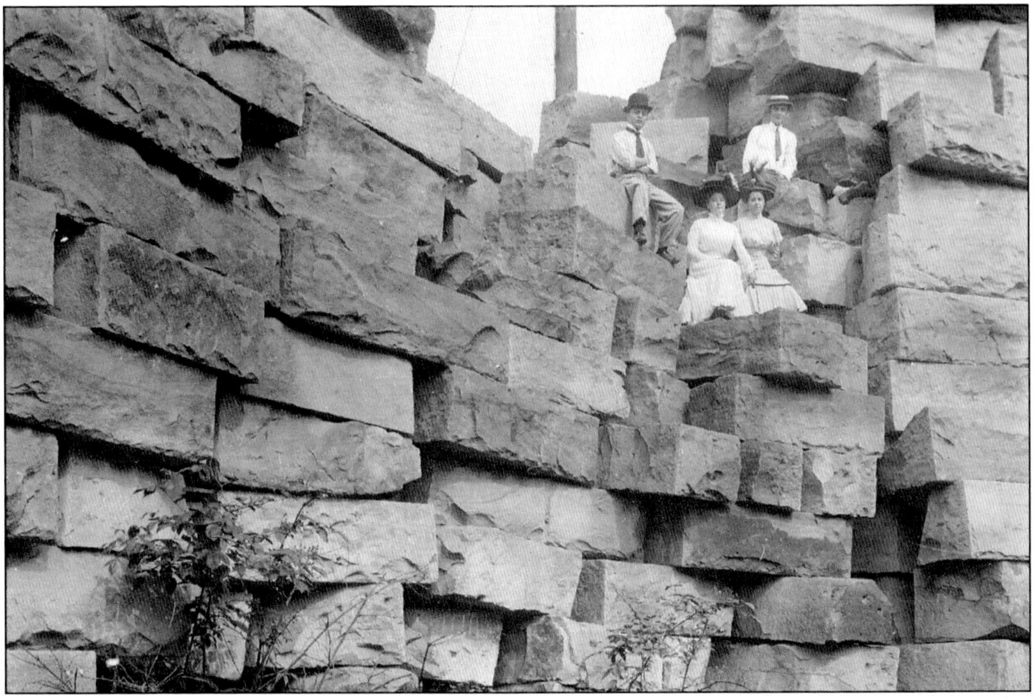

The Snyder Quarry was owned by Fredrick Snyder and later by Sen. A. E. Patton. In 1888, Snyder spent $25,000 to add a railroad line to the quarry, which was two miles north of Curwensville. The quarry was later owned by the Roaring Run Stone Company. (Courtesy J. Duane Test.)

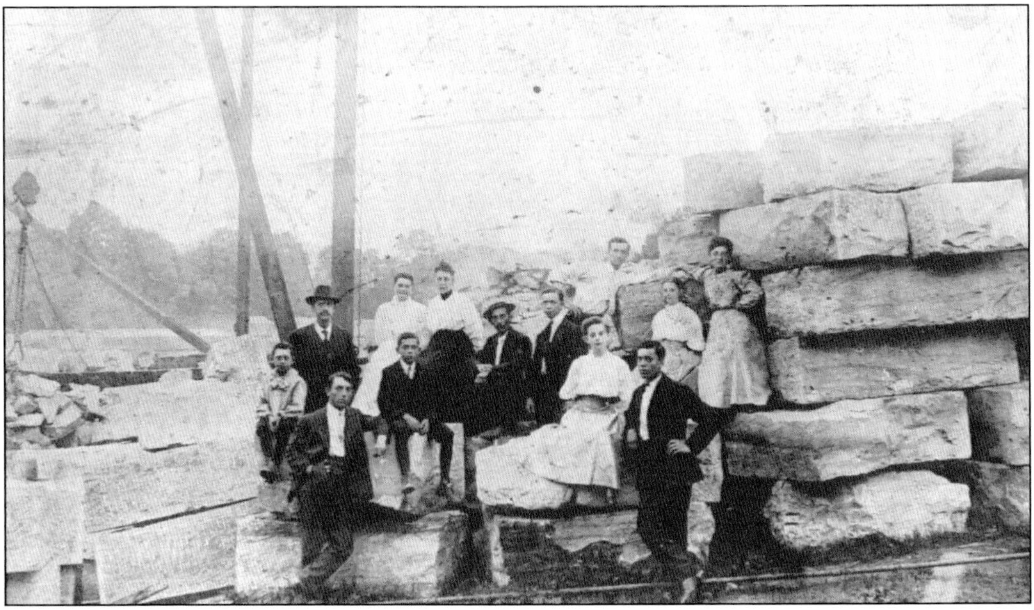

The Roaring Run Quarry, which was opened in 1888, was still being used as a source of ground stone to make bricks in the 1940s. Stone from this quarry was used to build the chapel at Princeton University and locally the Methodist church, the chapel at Oak Hill Cemetery, and the Curwensville Post Office, which was one of the last built from local stone. (Courtesy Dan McDonald.)

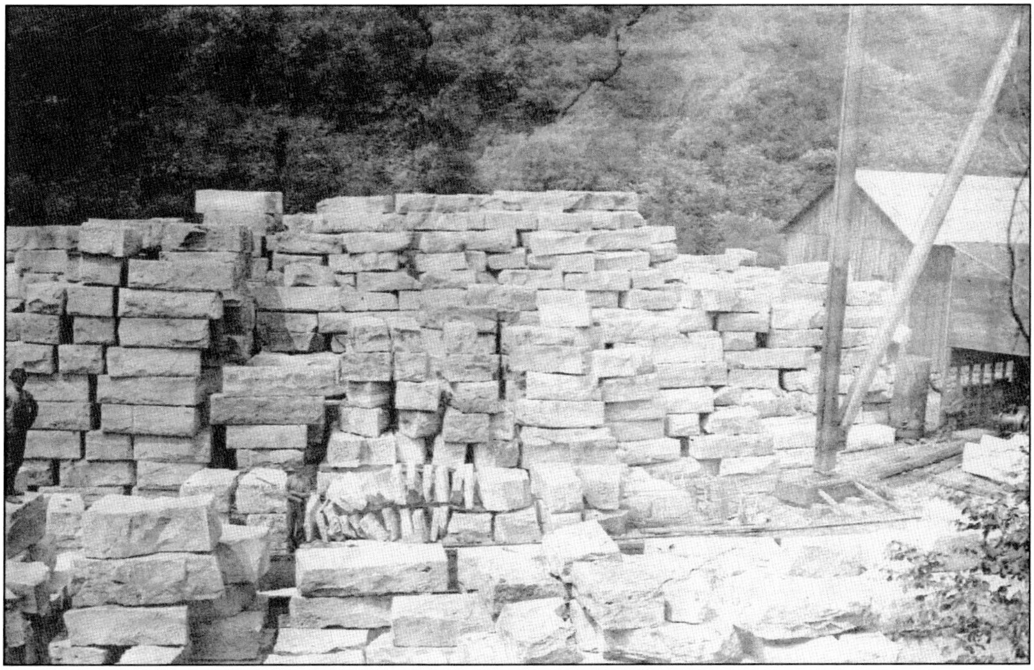

Blocks are stacked and ready to go in this photograph of the Roaring Run Quarry. The high-grade sandstone was used for heavy construction work. Its texture also allowed it to be used for fine stonework for ornamental purposes. After the Johnstown Flood in 1889, the stone was in high demand for the rebuilding of bridges. (Courtesy Dan McDonald.)

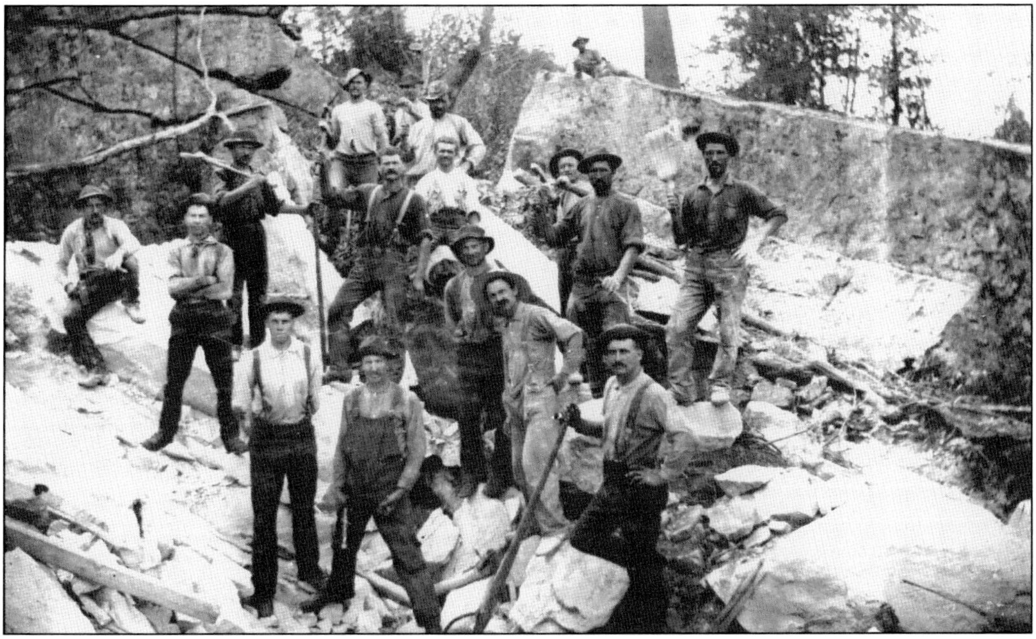

Workers quarrying sandstone pause to pose for a photographer in this picture around 1905. Men came from Italy and Ireland to work in the quarries, with many staying to raise their families in Curwensville even after the quarries closed. (Courtesy Curwensville-Pike Township Historical Society.)

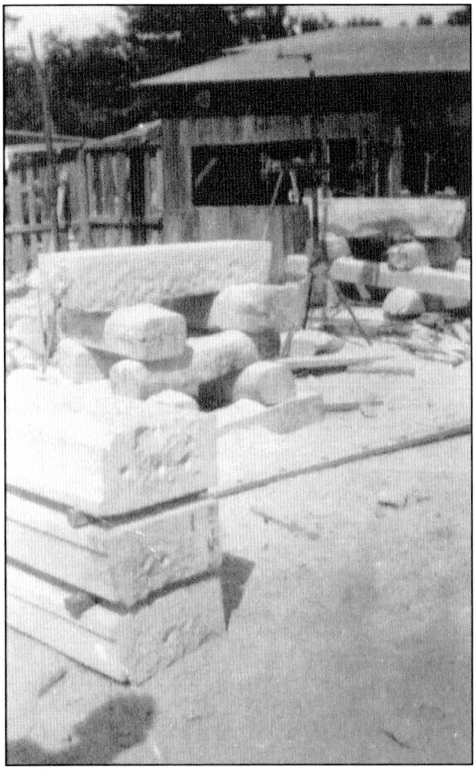

Three quarries, the Bailey, Roaring Run, and Bloom Run, were located around Curwensville. They each employed over 600 people on average during their peak periods. Once concrete became more popular, blocks like the ones at left were less in demand. The quarries suffered and eventually shut down. (Courtesy Dan McDonald.)

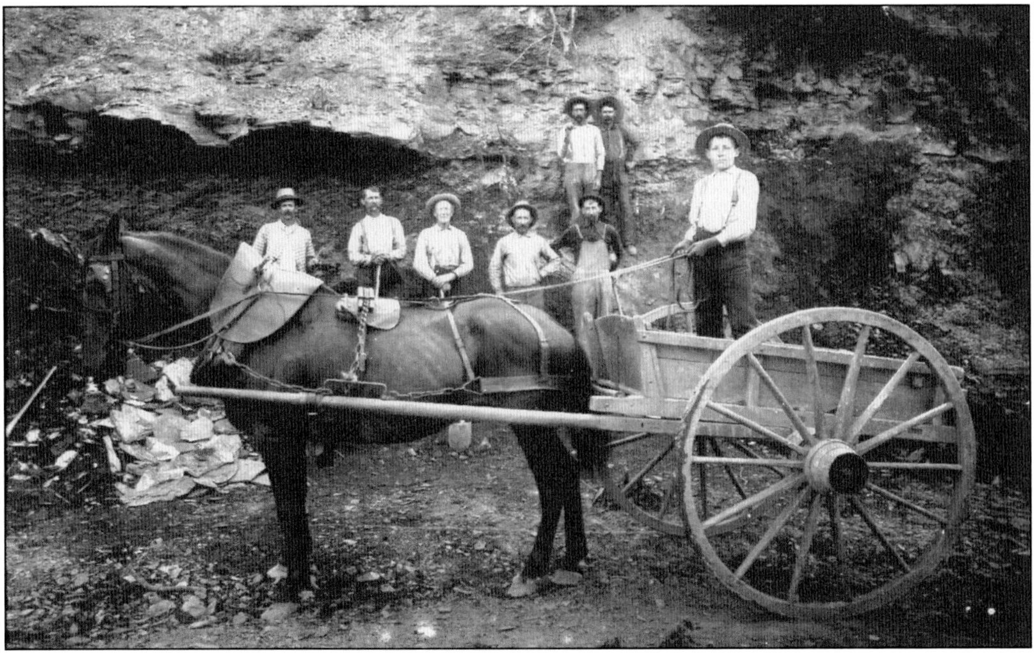

One of the most important industries early in the 20th century was coal mining. This early coal mine around 1885 used a wagon to haul its product. Information with the photograph identified it as the Country Bank Mine. Horses and mules were both vital tools in early coal mining. (Courtesy Curwensville-Pike Township Historical Society.)

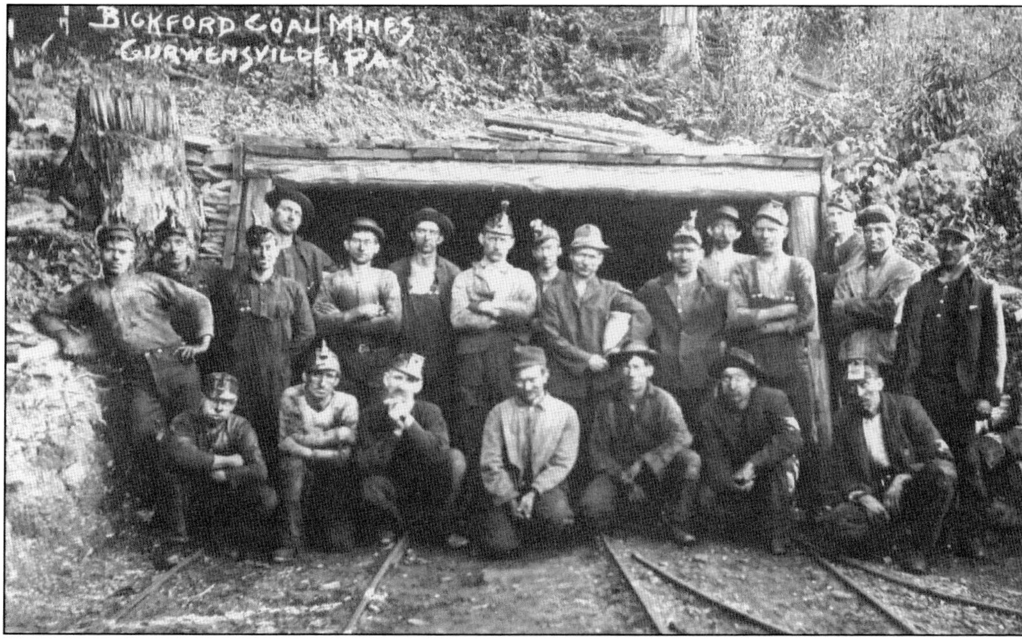

The Bickford Coal Mine was located just outside Curwensville. In 1911, these miners took a break to pose for this postcard. During World War I, miners were paid 98¢ per ton for loading coal. (Courtesy Curwensville-Pike Township Historical Society.)

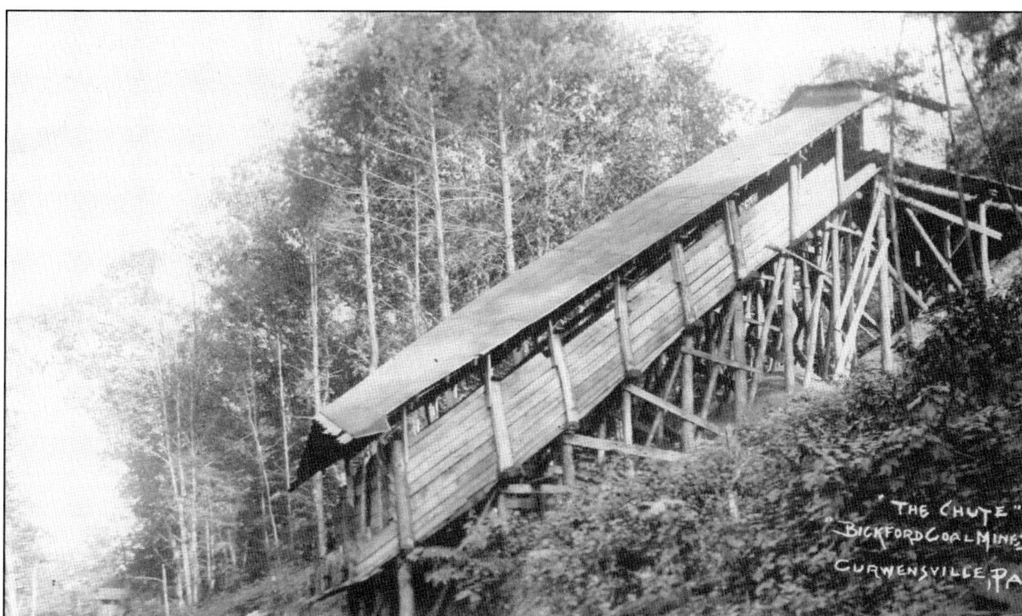

The chute at the Bickford Coal Mine was located near the Curwensville Dam on Bloomington Hill. The chute was used to send coal from the mines down to waiting wagons or train cars. Coal was a major employer in the area with many little "coal towns" springing up wherever it was found. (Courtesy Curwensville-Pike Township Historical Society.)

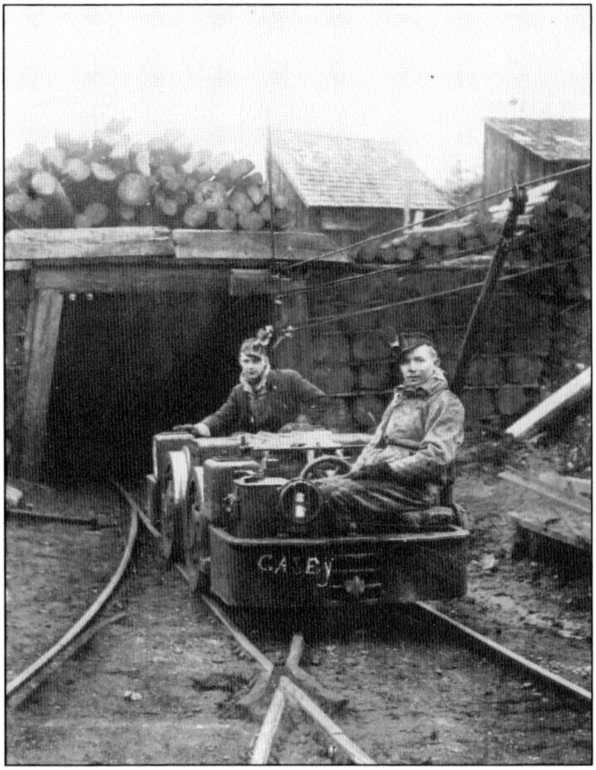

Two miners are ready to head off to work in this undated photograph. One of the miners is Alvin Johnson, but information with the photograph was unclear as to which was Johnson. In the 1950s, deep mining began to be replaced with strip mining. (Courtesy J. Duane Test.)

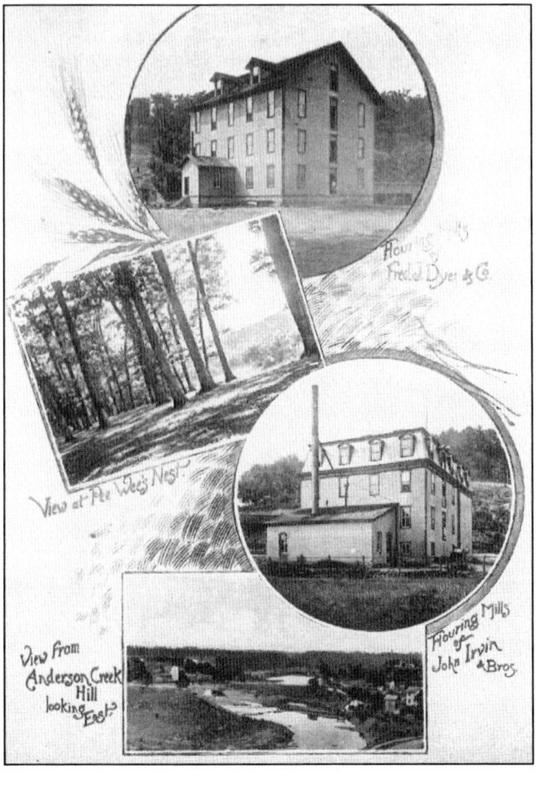

This group postcard from the 1895 *Souvenir of Curwensville* booklet portrays the "flouring" mills of Fred Dyer and John Irvin as well as two scenic shots. The mills, usually powered by water, ground grain into flour. Both of these mills were located on the West Branch of the Susquehanna River, which was also the location of Pee Wee's Nest. (Courtesy Clearfield County Historical Society.)

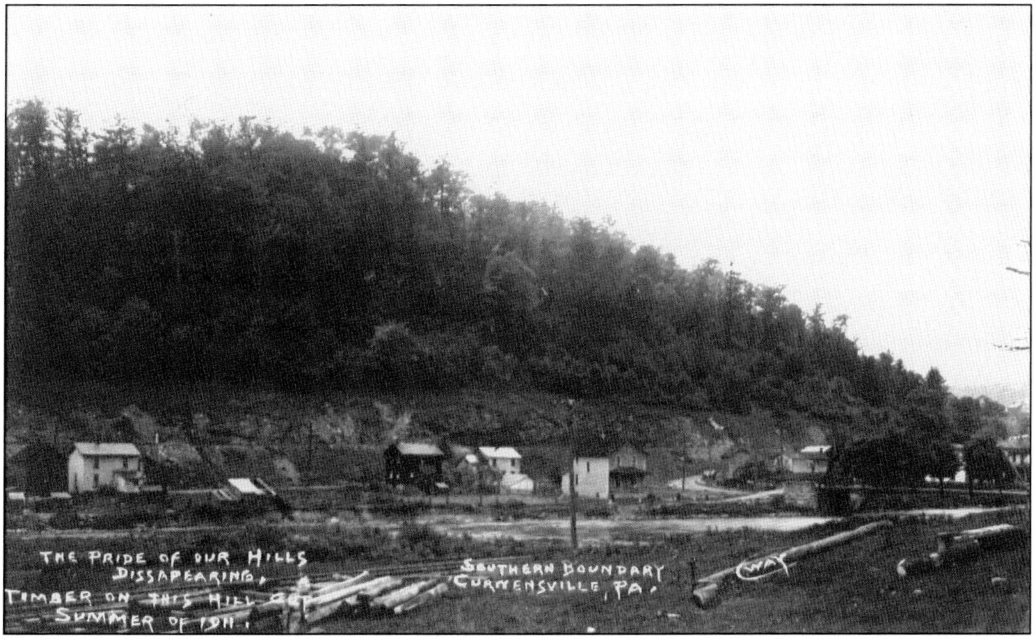

"The Pride of our hills disappearing" reads this postcard from 1911. It also notes that the "timber on this hill cut summer of 1911." This was one of Way's Stationery Store's cards as the Way name can be seen on a log on the right. (Courtesy Curwensville-Pike Township Historical Society.)

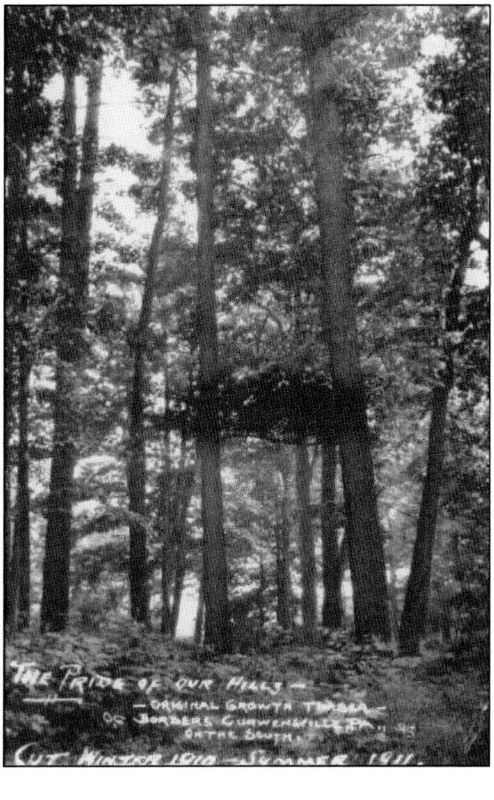

R. K. Way also documented this wood with a second postcard. "The Pride of our hills, original growth timber, borders Curwensville PA on the south. Cut winter 1910-summer 1911," it reads. The lumber industry was instrumental in the early growth of Curwensville. (Courtesy Curwensville-Pike Township Historical Society.)

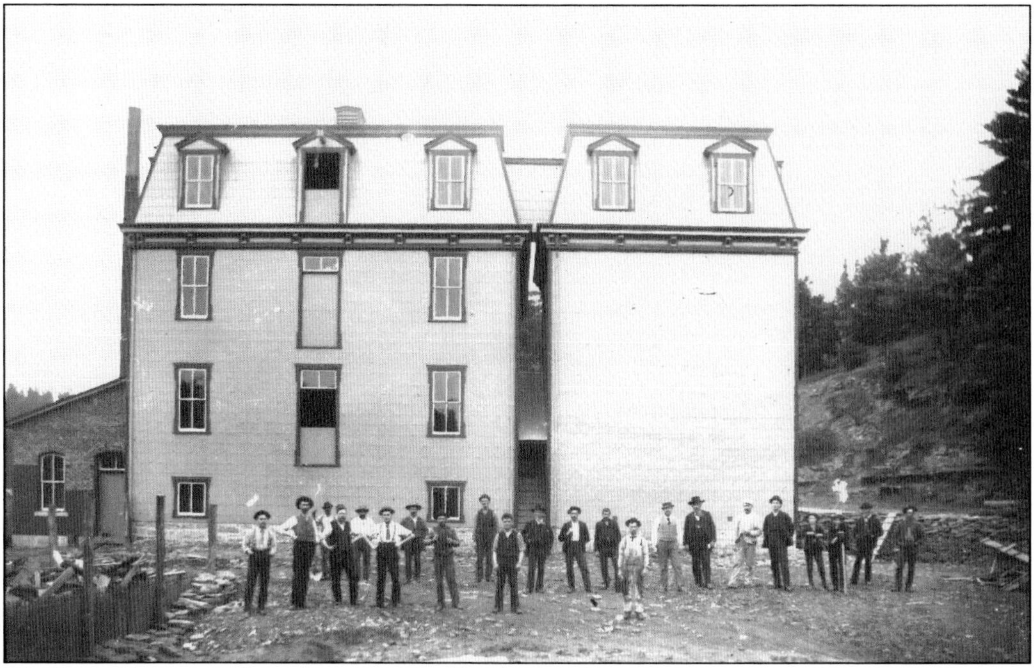

The Irvin Planing Mill produced surfaced lumber in the mid-1880s. It was located on the river near Irvin Hill. It was owned by Col. John Irvin, who served in the Pennsylvania Bucktails during the Civil War, and his brothers, Jared and James. (Courtesy Curwensville-Pike Township Historical Society.)

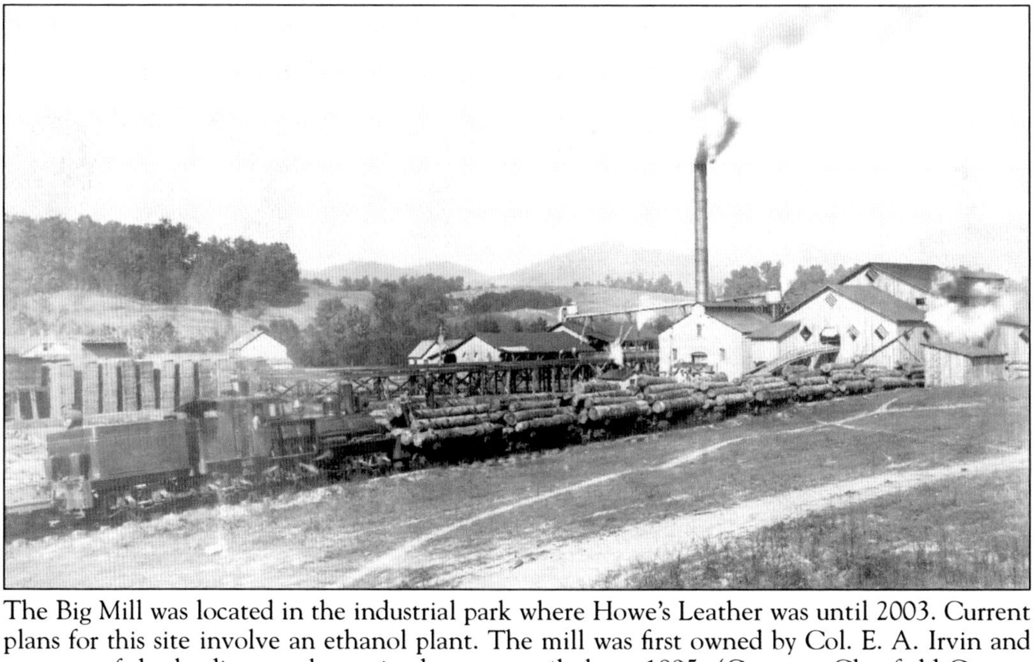

The Big Mill was located in the industrial park where Howe's Leather was until 2003. Current plans for this site involve an ethanol plant. The mill was first owned by Col. E. A. Irvin and was one of the leading employers in the area until about 1895. (Courtesy Clearfield County Historical Society.)

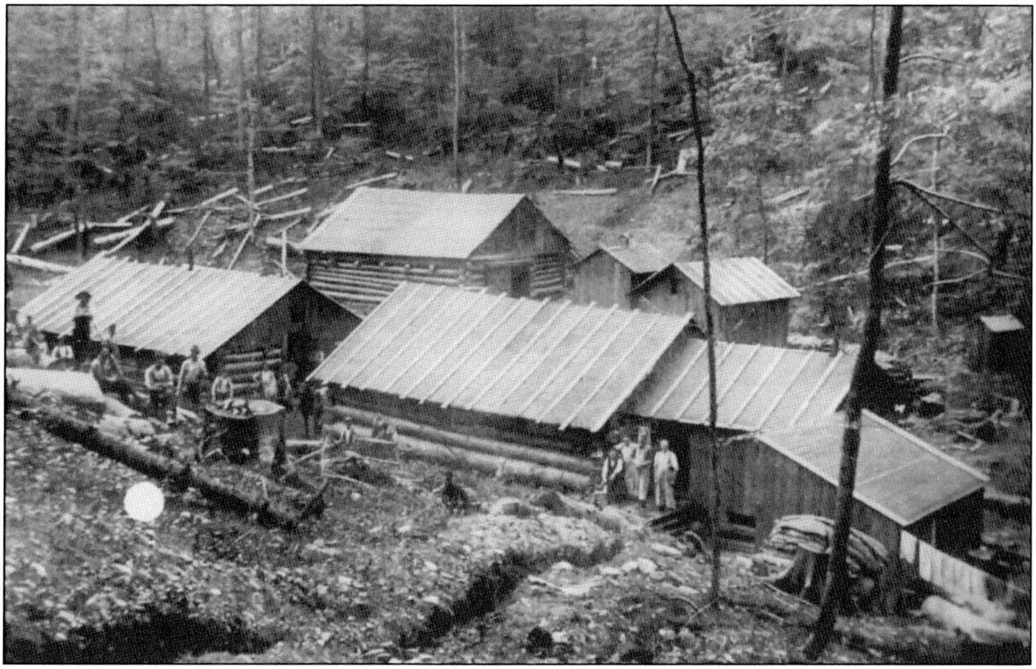

This Curry Run logging camp seen around 1880 was owned by Cy Richards. The group of men on the right includes Richards, with the bow tie, and Ed Flynn, the cook who is wearing an apron. Col. E. A. Irvin and James Mitchell also owned some of the timber in this area. (Courtesy Jim Bennett.)

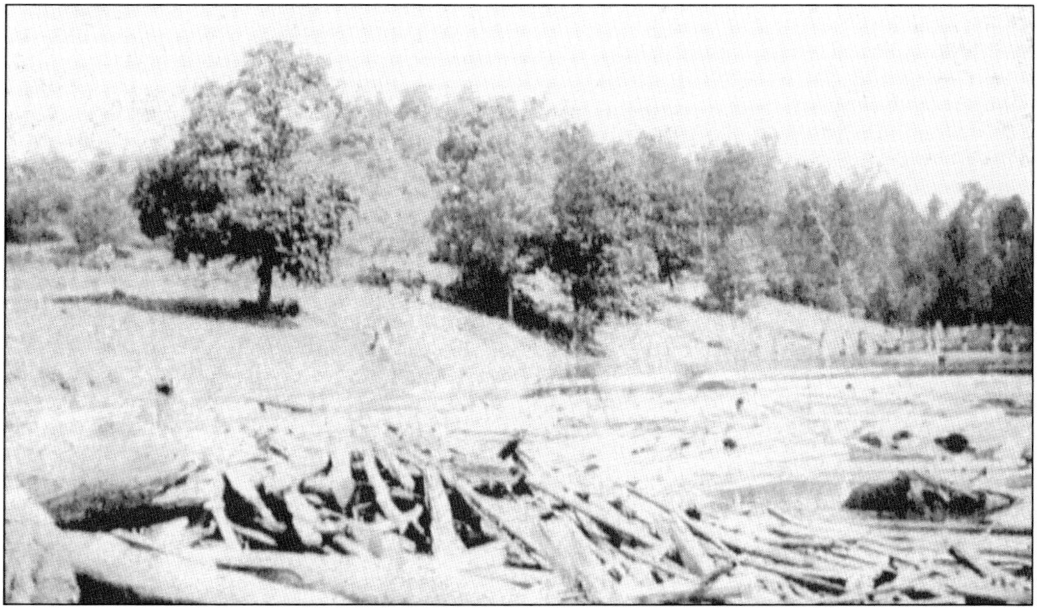

Pioneers came to Walltown because of the large amount of timber available. One of the first mills was operated by the Wall family and may have been the reason the original name for the town was Walls Mill. Lumber was a longtime industry here, making it difficult to date this photograph. Logs from here were often peeled, and the bark was taken to the tannery in Curwensville. (Courtesy Dan McDonald.)

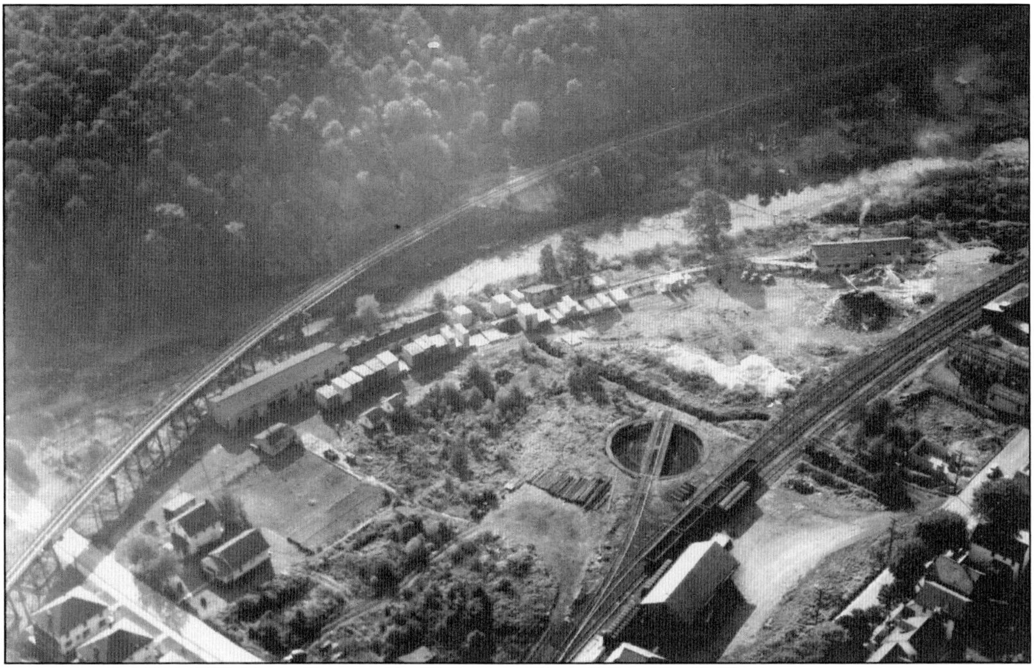

Haley's Lumberyard was still going strong in 1949. This aerial view shows the yard with Filbert Street on the left. The company started with John Haley of Maine who came to Pennsylvania in 1865. He worked in several parts of the state, including the Grier Bell tract at Lumber City. His son William P. Haley moved to Curwensville after Haley's death in 1931. (Courtesy Test collection.)

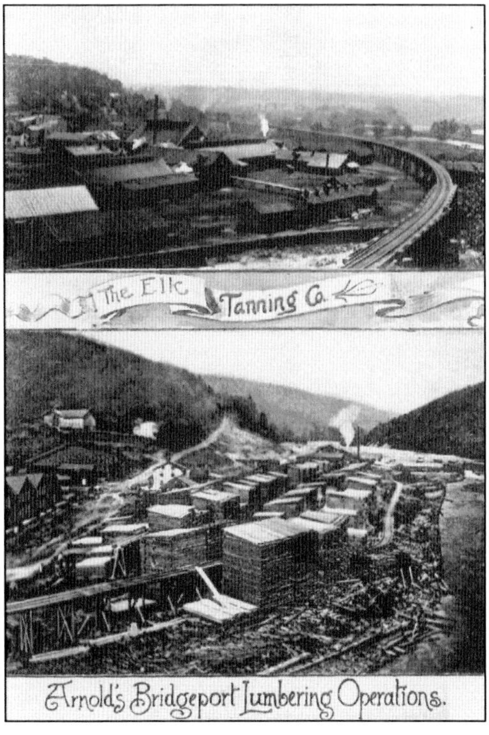

This postcard from 1895's *Souvenir of Curwensville* booklet portrays the Elk Tanning Company and Arnold's Bridgeport Lumbering Operations. The Elk Tanning Company was a subsidiary of the United States Leather Company. The Arnold Mill, built in 1881, was one of the largest sawmills in the area. Its capacity was 30,000 feet per day. (Courtesy Clearfield County Historical Society.)

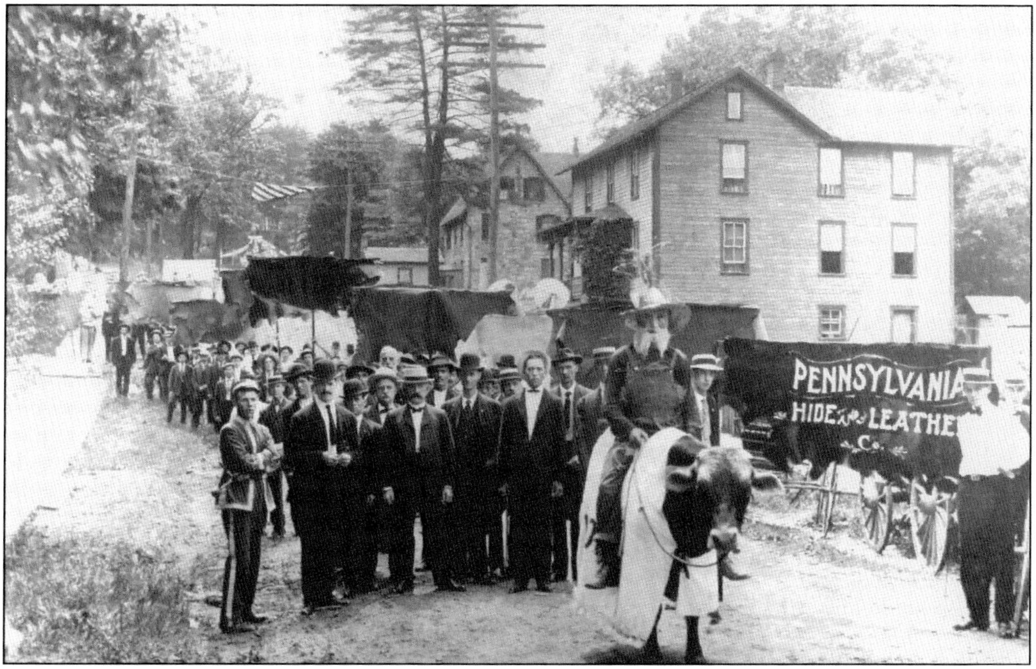

The Pennsylvania Hide Leather Company was built around 1900, on the site of the former Big Mill. It partially burned in 1928 and then was sold to Franklin Tanning Company. Later it became Howes Leather Company, which closed in 2003. This parade, led by a cow, features men holding poles topped by several types of hides. (Courtesy Curwensville-Pike Township Historical Society.)

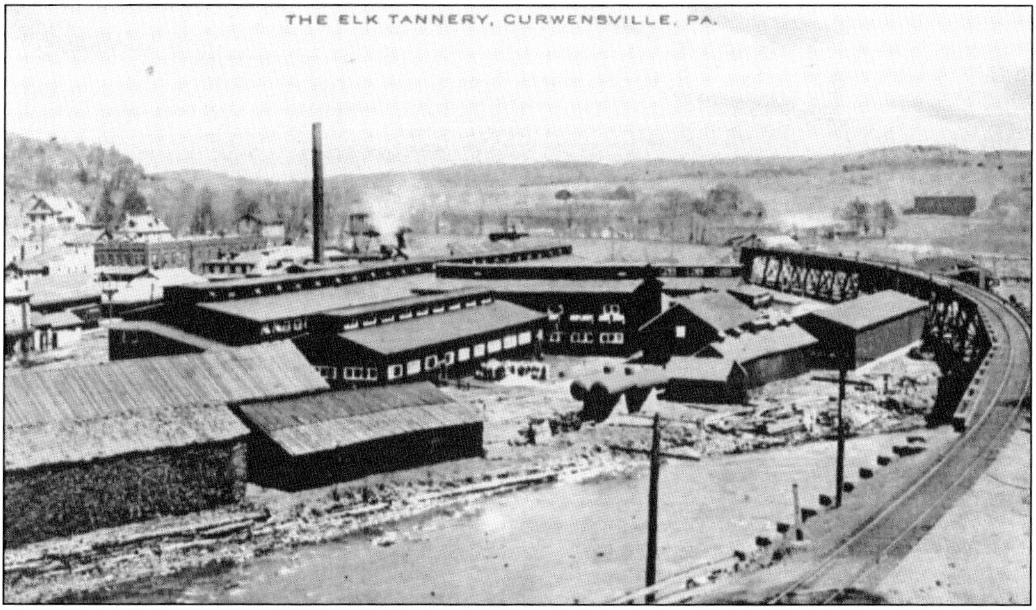

This tannery, started in 1877, was the first steam tannery in Curwensville. Later it was sold several times, becoming the Elk Tanning Company in 1893. In 1897, it was damaged by a huge fire and was rebuilt later that year with lumber from Arnold's Mill. It was eventually destroyed by a second fire a few years later. (Courtesy Clearfield County Historical Society.)

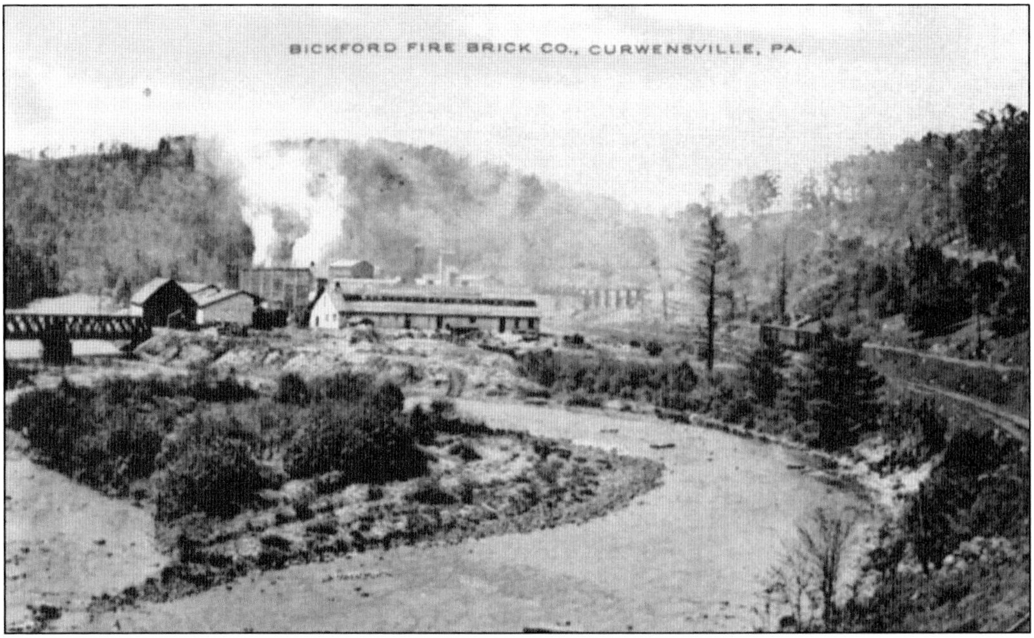

Originally the brick plant was built in 1899 and was known as the Curwensville Fire Brick Company. It became the Bickford Fire Brick Company in 1906 and was billed as "the largest fire brick plant in the world under one roof." In the 1940s, it employed about 300 people in the plant as well as in the mines the company owned. (Courtesy Clearfield County Historical Society.)

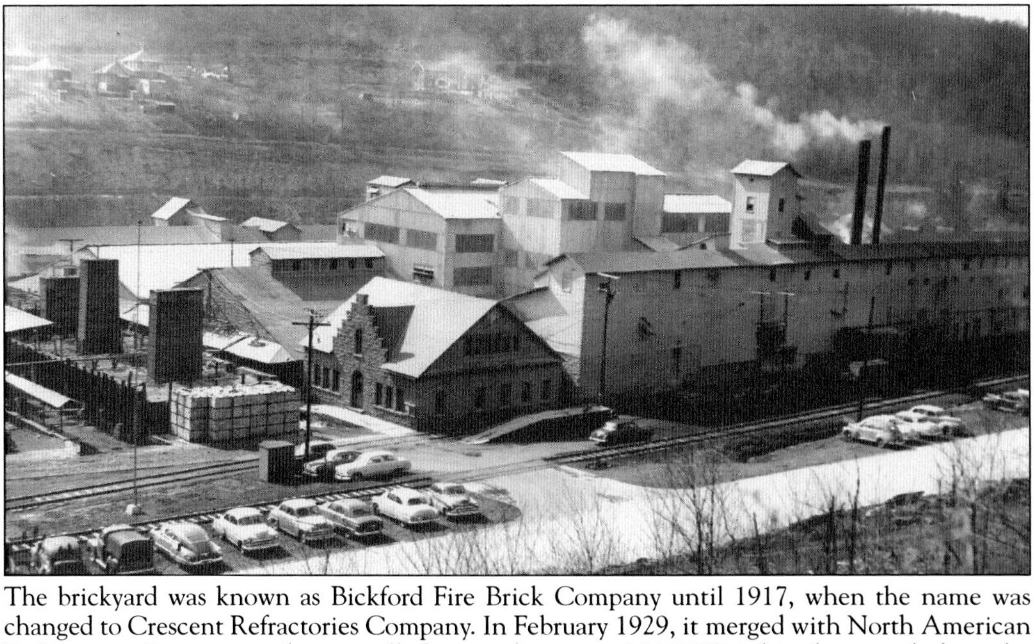

The brickyard was known as Bickford Fire Brick Company until 1917, when the name was changed to Crescent Refractories Company. In February 1929, it merged with North American Refractories Company and eventually became known as NARCO. This photograph from the 1950s shows how the factory appeared in that decade, complete with employee parking. Today the complex is owned by Mount Savage Specialty Refractories. (Courtesy Curwensville-Pike Township Historical Society.)

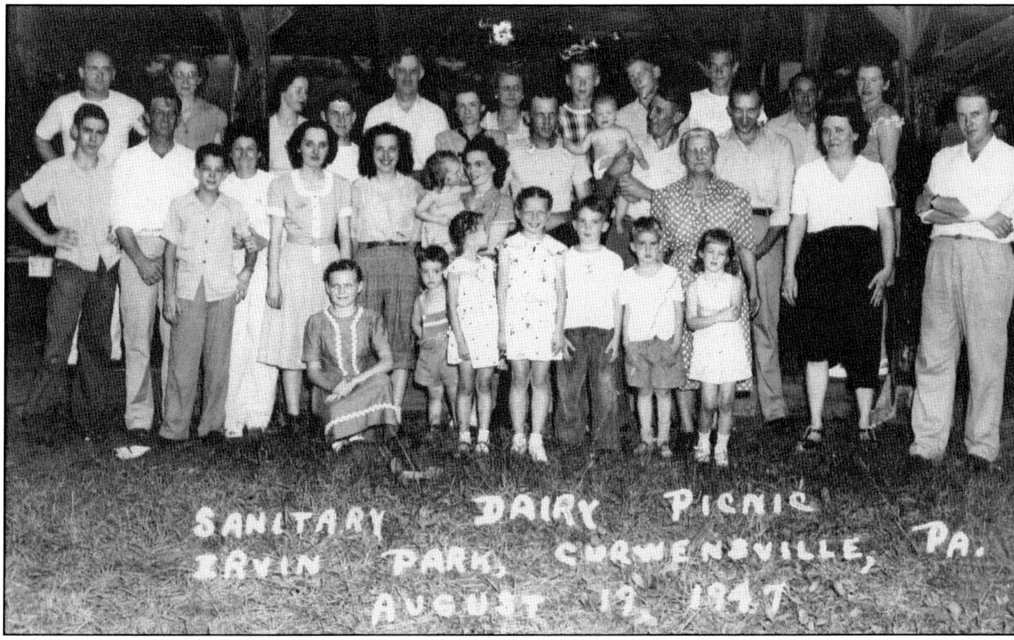

Employees of the Sanitary Dairy and their families pose for this photograph taken at a company picnic at Irvin Park on August 19, 1947. The company, started in 1919 by Scott Ammerman, operated until 1977, when it was purchased by Sani-Dairy of Johnstown. (Courtesy Curwensville-Pike Township Historical Society.)

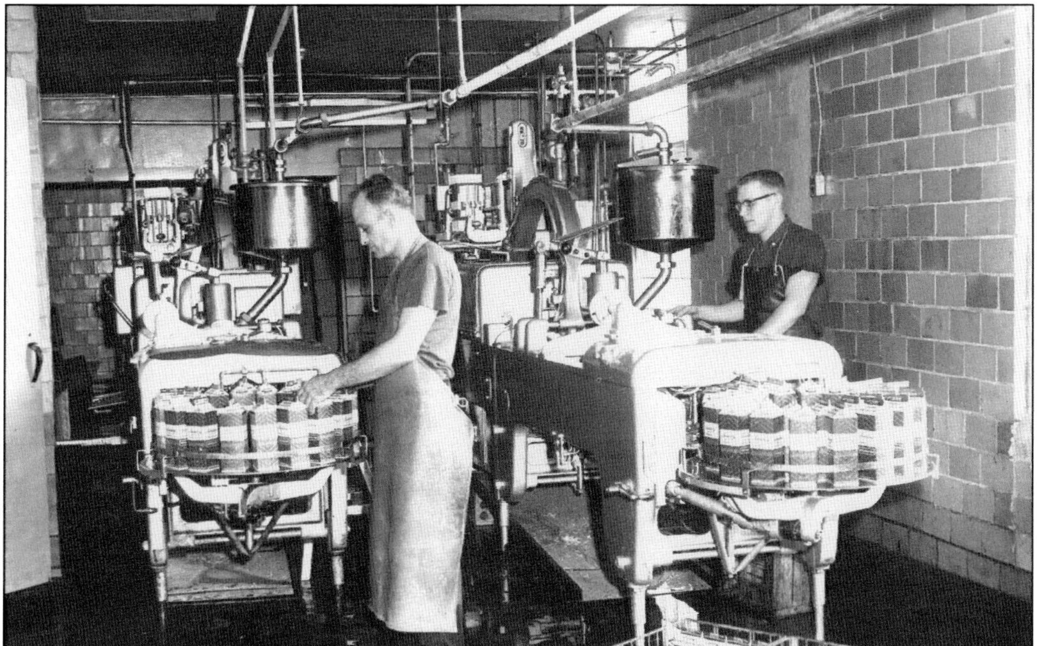
In this *c.* 1960 photograph, William Spaid (left) and Philip Wingard (right) are busy working at Sanitary Dairy. This dairy was among the first to use a square glass milk bottle, to offer homogenized vitamin D milk, to use refrigerated delivery vehicles, and the first to offer paper milk bottles for home and wholesale delivery. (Courtesy Curwensville-Pike Township Historical Society.)

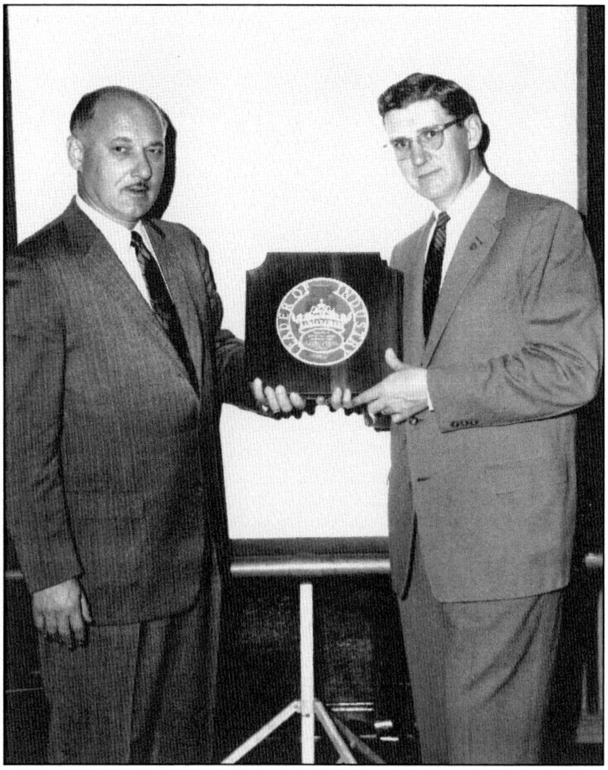

The Sanitary Dairy was awarded the Leader of Industry Award in 1957. John Kaiser presented it to Frank Hoffman, left, who operated the company for 40 years, at a special dinner held at the Park Hotel. Sanitary Dairy was the smallest dairy in Pennsylvania to receive this award. (Courtesy Curwensville-Pike Township Historical Society.)

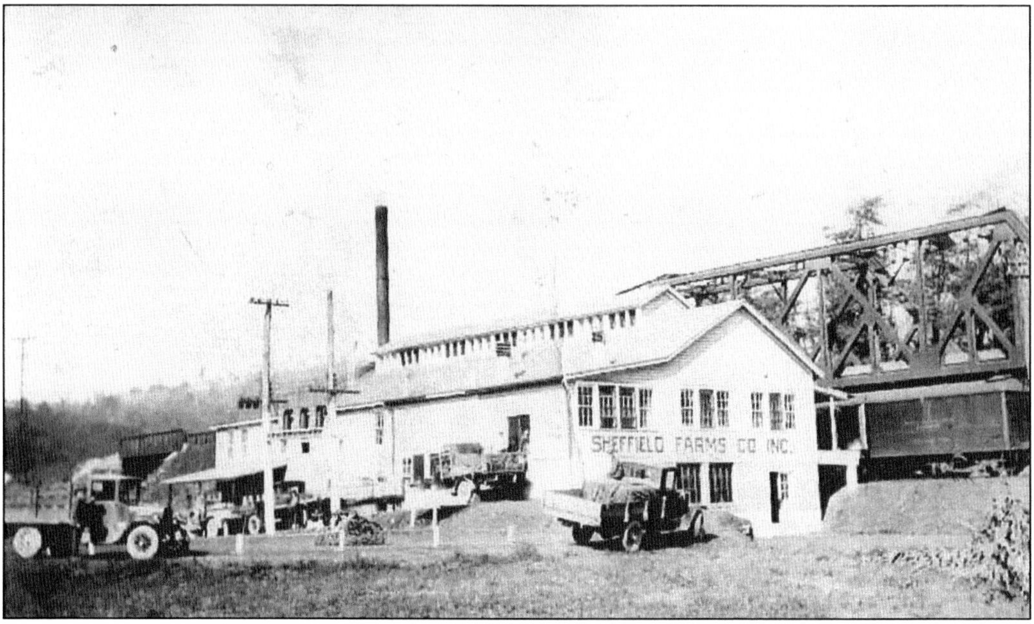

Prior to World War II, J. Hamer and William D. Tate rented the Sheffield Farms building on Meadow Street and started Clearfield Cheese. The supply for cheese during the war was so great, the company grew rapidly, becoming the third-largest processor of cheese in the country. Arnold Nawrocki, an employee for the company, invented the individually wrapped cheese slice. The Curwensville plant closed in 1988. (Courtesy Dan McDonald.)

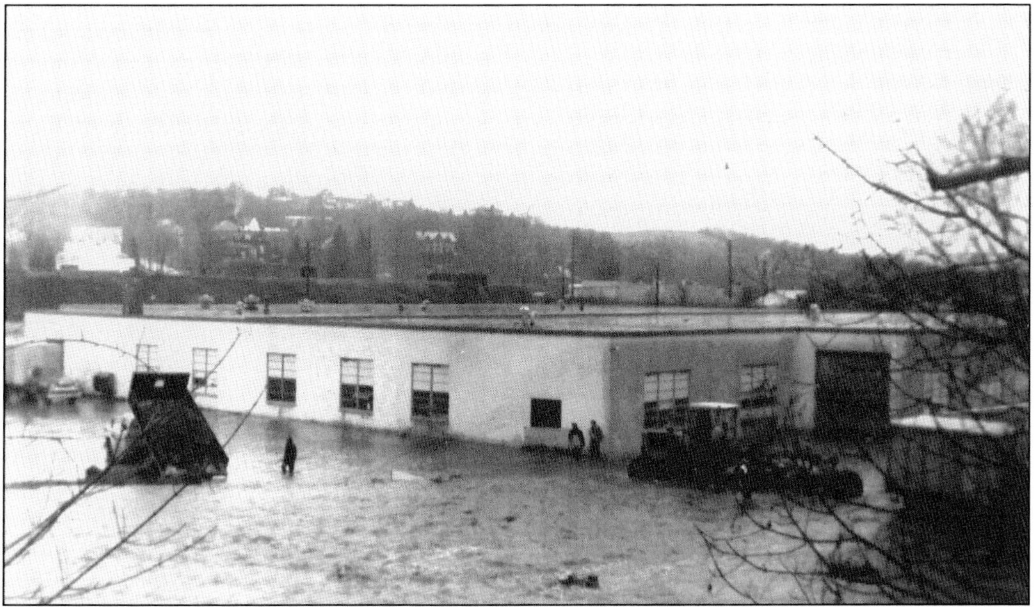

Kent Sportswear in Curwensville is surrounded by water in this c. 1960 photograph, in which a dike is being built to keep the waters of Anderson Creek away. Kent Sportswear was part of Bayer Clothing Group, which also had plants in Hyde and Fletcherville. They were once the largest producer of tailored men's apparel in the country. Unfortunately, most of the factory jobs were sent overseas in the 1990s. (Courtesy Deuwain Rickard Jr.)

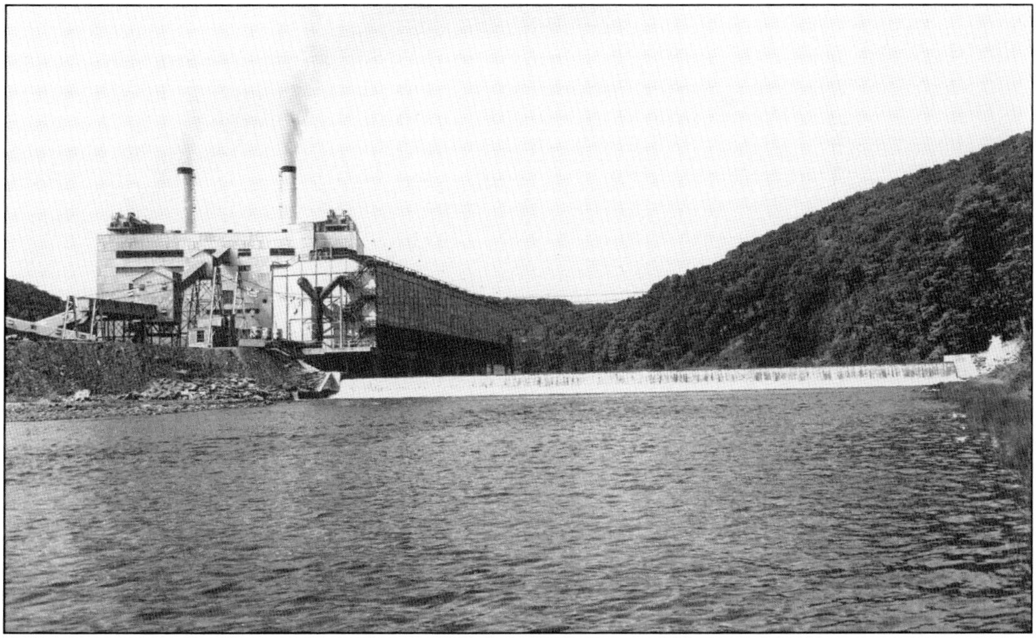

The Shawville power plant was built in 1954 and added two more units in 1960. The site was chosen because of its easy access to local coal. A third smokestack was later added to help cut down on local air pollution. The coal-burning electric plant was named in 2005 as one of the top 10 dirtiest in the country because of its high sulfur dioxide emissions. (Courtesy Clearfield County Historical Society.)

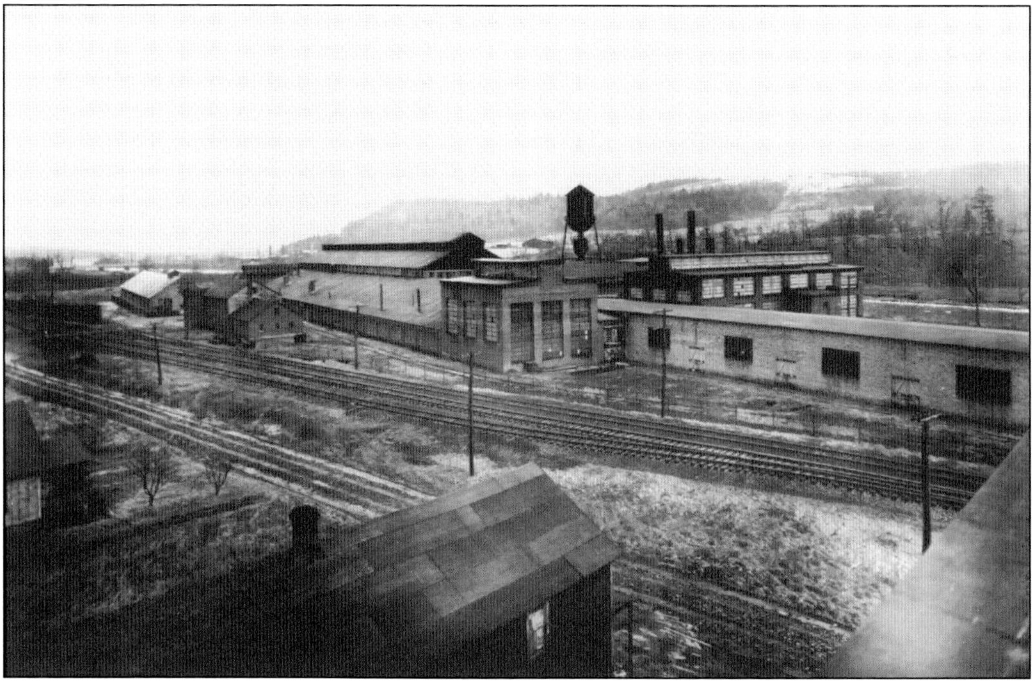

This site in Hyde, above, was originally a steel mill owned by Hyde Brothers. In 1909, it was taken over by the American Nickel Corporation, which is shown in this c. 1935 photograph. The company made a variety of items from kitchenware to tubing for fire extinguishers. In 1939, the same facility was used by the Airplane and Marine Instruments Company, which was later known as Dumont-Airplane and Marine. Below employees during the Airplane and Marine Instruments Company era are hard at work. Tafco, Inc. took over site in 1965. Today it is home to TMP Acquisitions. (Courtesy Clearfield County Historical Society.)

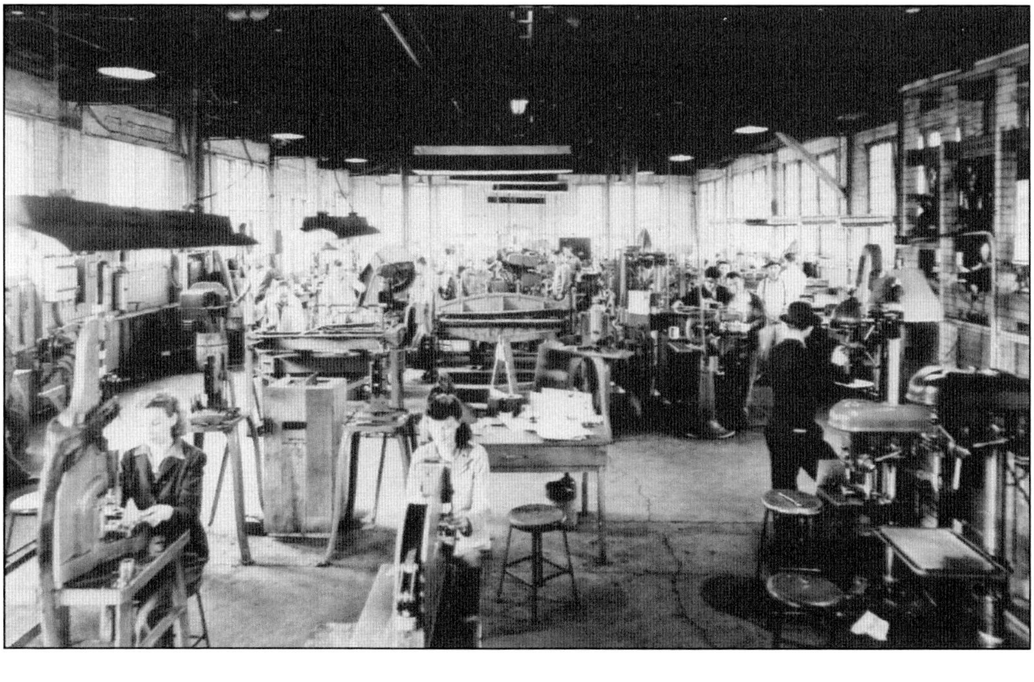

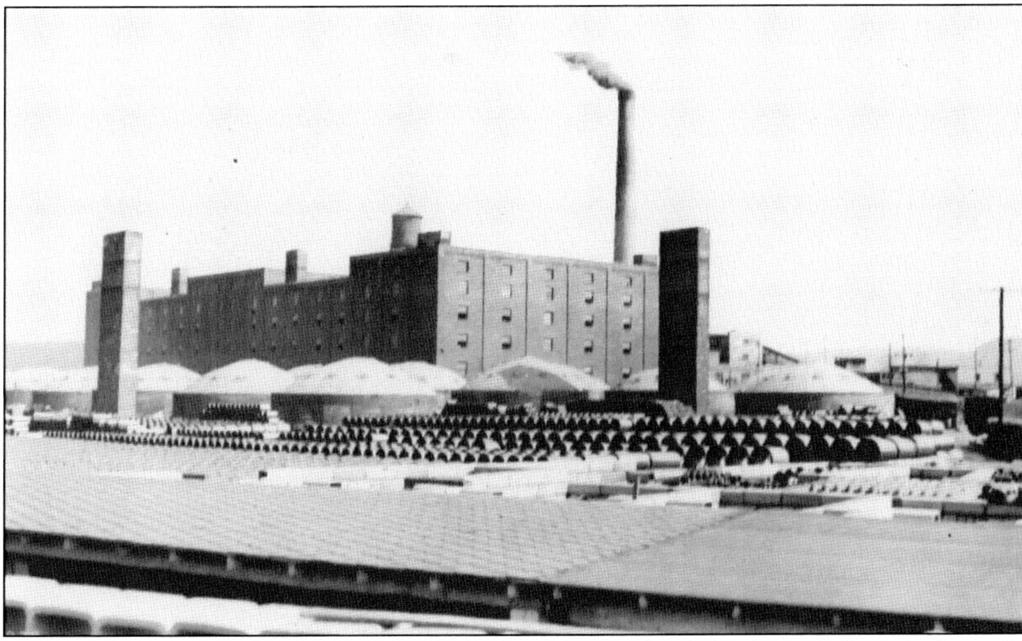

The Robinson Clay Product Company was located in Clearfield's East End near where the Clearfield Mall is now. The company began in Ohio in 1856 and expanded to several other plants, one being Clearfield in 1920. Company houses were conveniently located close by for its workers. It had its own clay mines located on the hill above the town. In the 1950s, a bucket line hung over Route 322 near Golden Rod, which transported clay from the mines to the plant. Below the line is a netting that kept falling clay from hitting passing cars. The plant, which manufactured clay pipes for water and sewer lines, closed in the 1960s. (Courtesy Clearfield County Historical Society.)

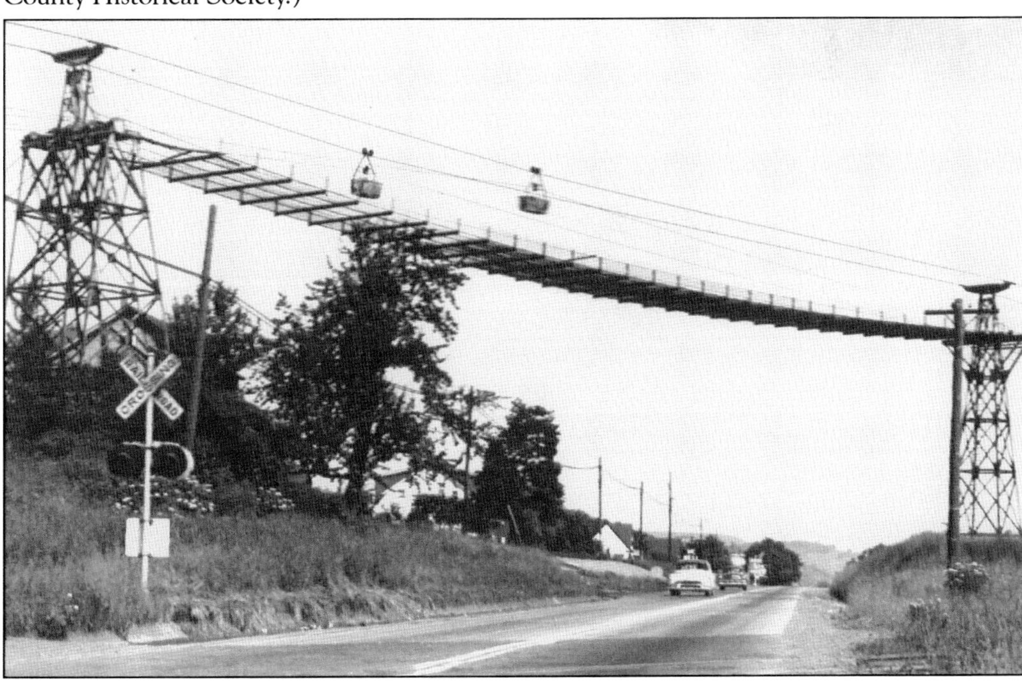

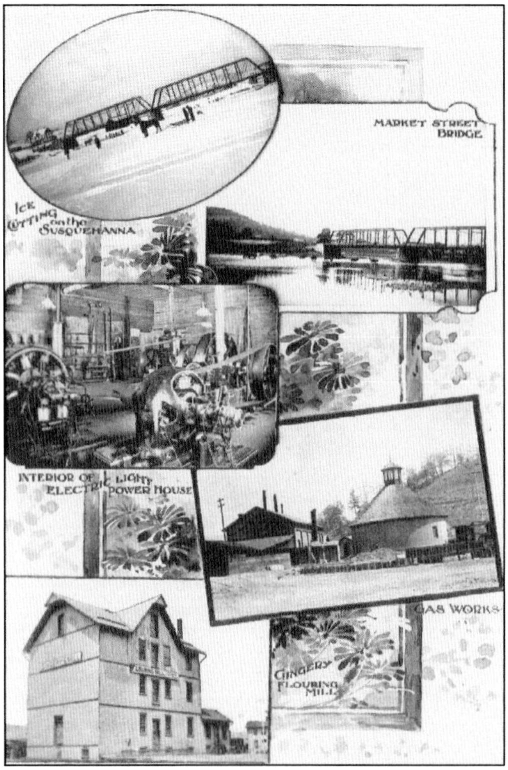

This postcard from 1895 highlights Clearfield's industries. At that time, ice cutting was a business with the river a main source of supply. The Electric Light Power House was located on Leavy Avenue, near where Mitchell Milling was until recently. The gasworks for the Clearfield Gas Light Company was in the area of CVS Pharmacy, as was a mill, which was home to Charles Heating Center until 2007. (Courtesy Clearfield County Historical Society.)

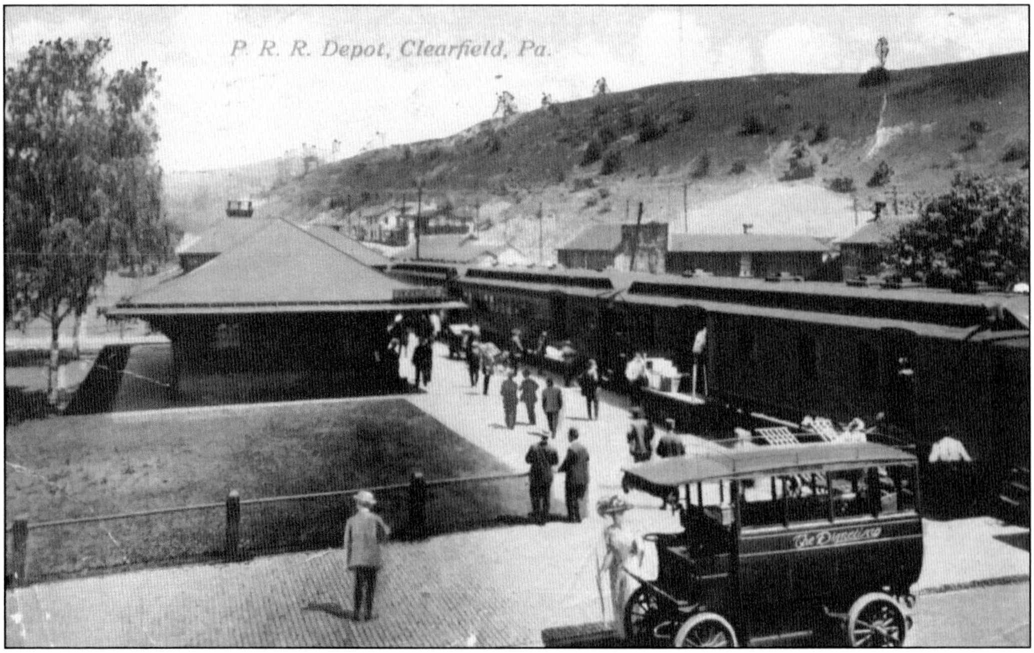

The Pennsylvania Railroad Depot in Clearfield was located on Third Street and is currently a Laundromat. A buggy waits to transport passengers a few blocks to the Dimeling Hotel. Many of the hotels provided transportation for customers. Others built near the railroad station, as did the St. Charles Hotel, located across the street. (Courtesy E. S. Shuck Estate.)

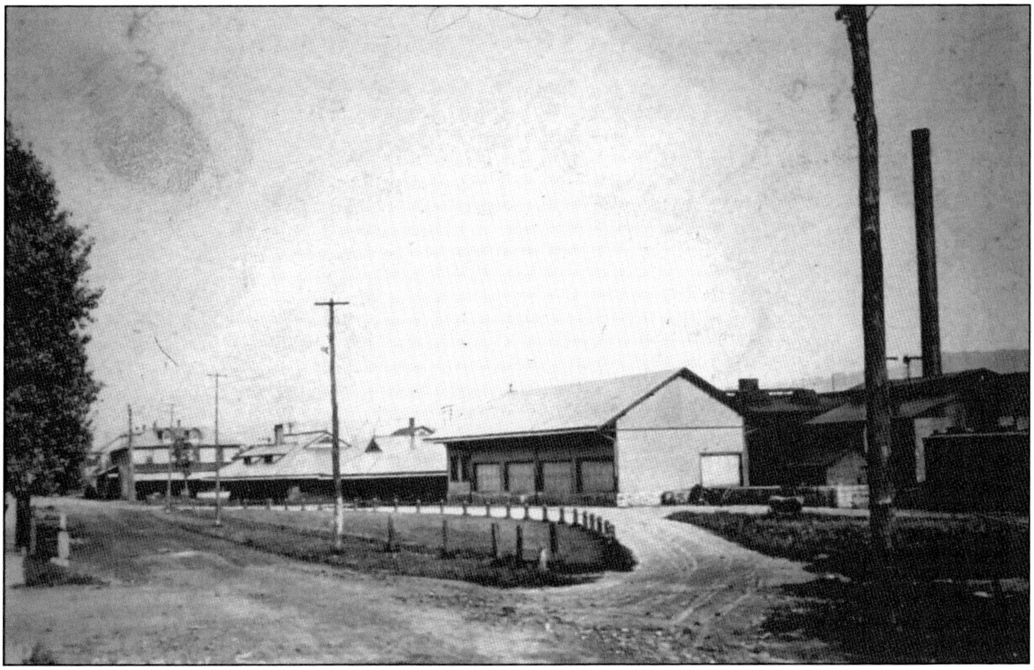

The Pennsylvania Railroad station on Meadow Street is now home to Curwensville Feed Store. The railroad was extended from Clearfield into Curwensville in 1874 as part of the Tyrone to Clearfield railroad. Among the contributors to this project were John Patton, Col. John Irvin, brothers John and James Irvin, and Samuel Arnold. In 1891, the line was extended to Grampian. (Courtesy Curwensville-Pike Township Historical Society.)

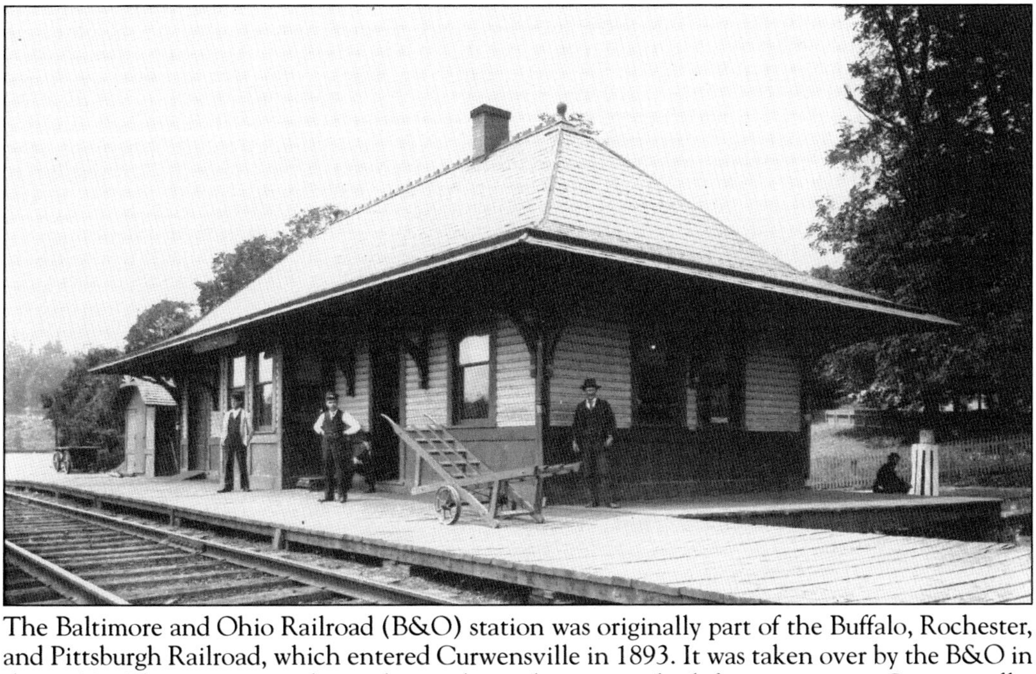

The Baltimore and Ohio Railroad (B&O) station was originally part of the Buffalo, Rochester, and Pittsburgh Railroad, which entered Curwensville in 1893. It was taken over by the B&O in the 1930s. This station was located near the underpass on the left as one enters Curwensville. (Courtesy Curwensville-Pike Township Historical Society.)

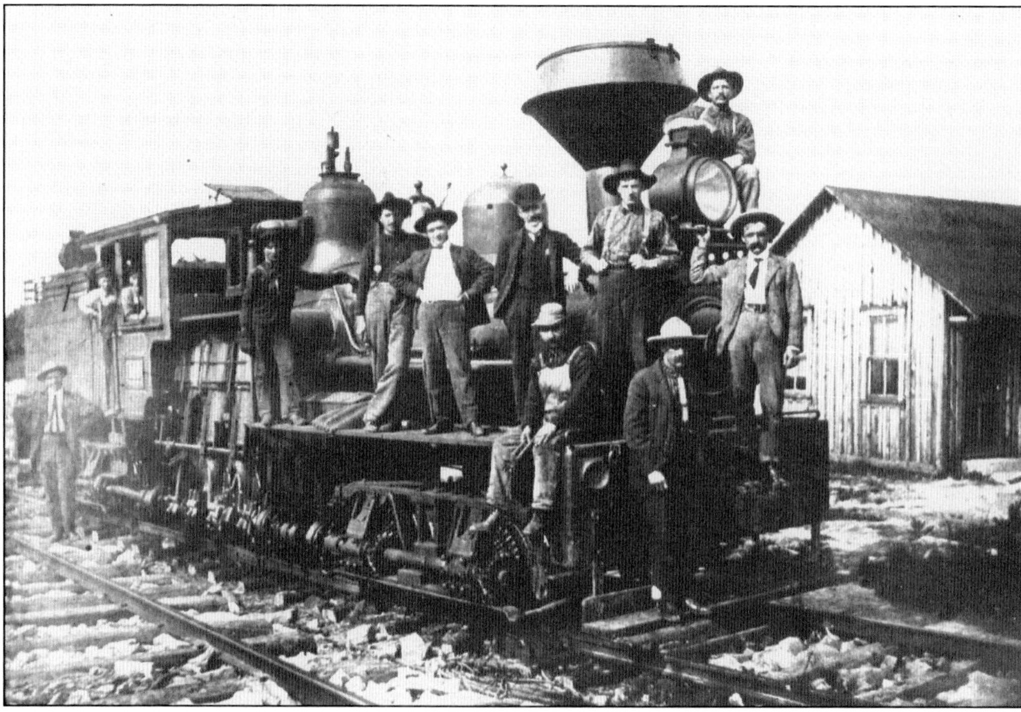

Above is the Conemaugh Stone Company locomotive No. 100, which was used on the Bloom Run Railroad around 1903. The five-mile line was built in 1902 to specifically carry stone from the Bloom Run Quarry. It ran from Grampian west, up Bloom Run, to the top of the mountain, and to the grand pit and quarry. The engine house was at Stronach. In 1908, the line was abandoned after the quarry shut down. Below a train loaded with stone blocks moves across the trestle at Stronach. Up to four flatcars were used in a single trip. The Bloom Run Quarry did not make any money in its short life. Reports are that its income in five years was only over $4,000 while loses were around $32,000. (Courtesy Clearfield County Historical Society.)

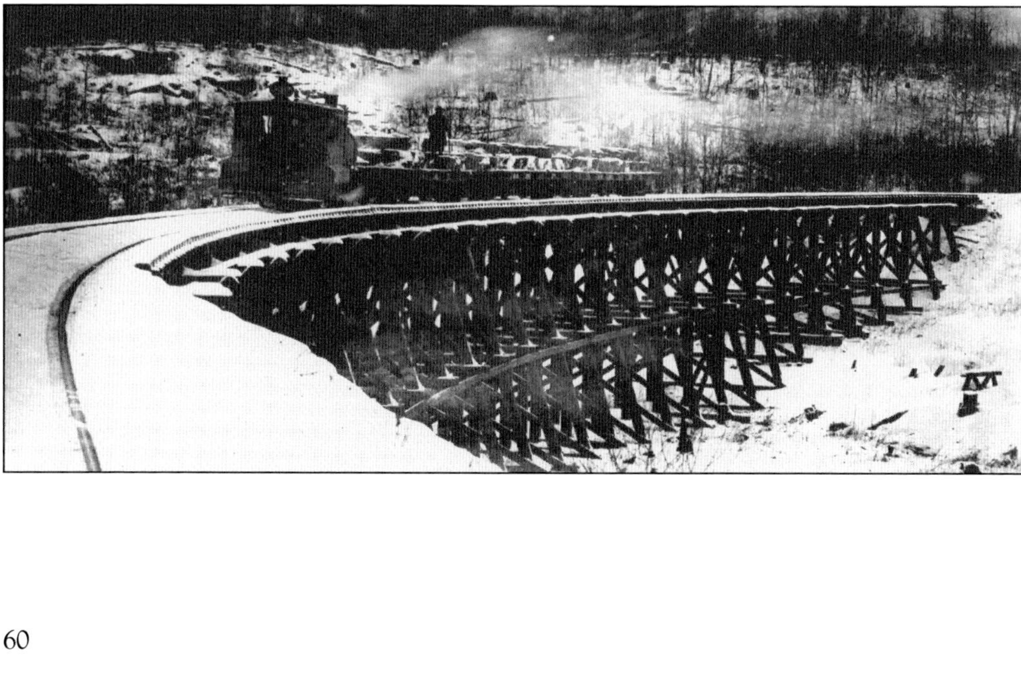

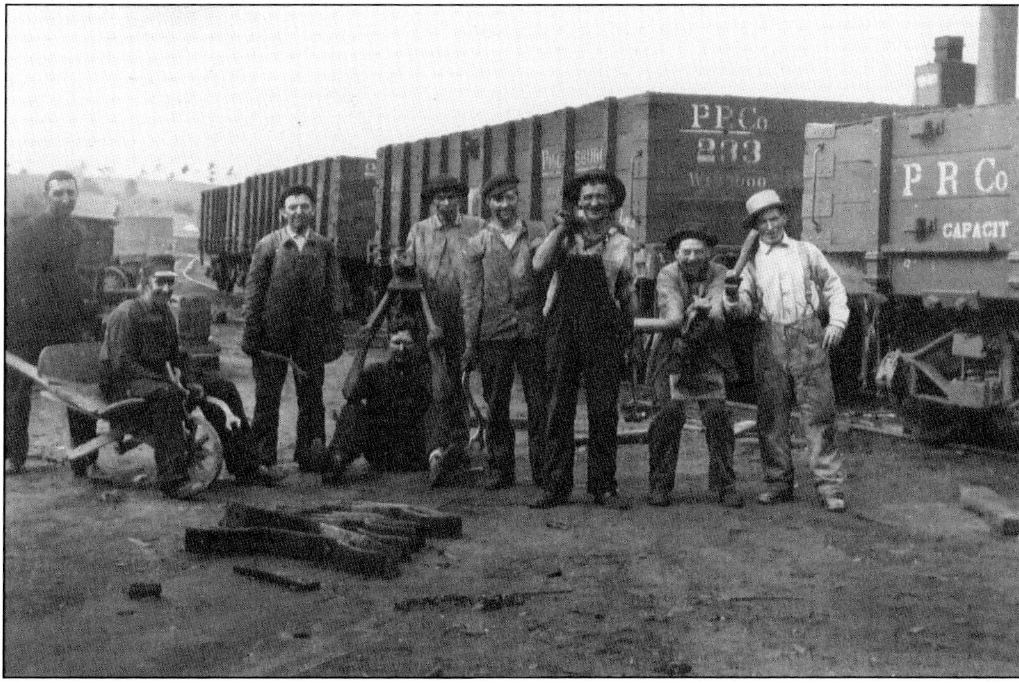

The crew of the *Alley Popper* poses in this undated photograph. On the wheelbarrow is Oscar Broberg. To the right of him are, from left to right, Albert Hiller, Martin Johnson (sitting), John McCrossin, John Edmunds, Frank Henderson, John Johnson and Dominick Costello. The *Alley Popper* was part of the Altoona to Philipsburg Connecting Railroad Company, which began that run in the late 1890s. (Courtesy Clearfield County Historical Society.)

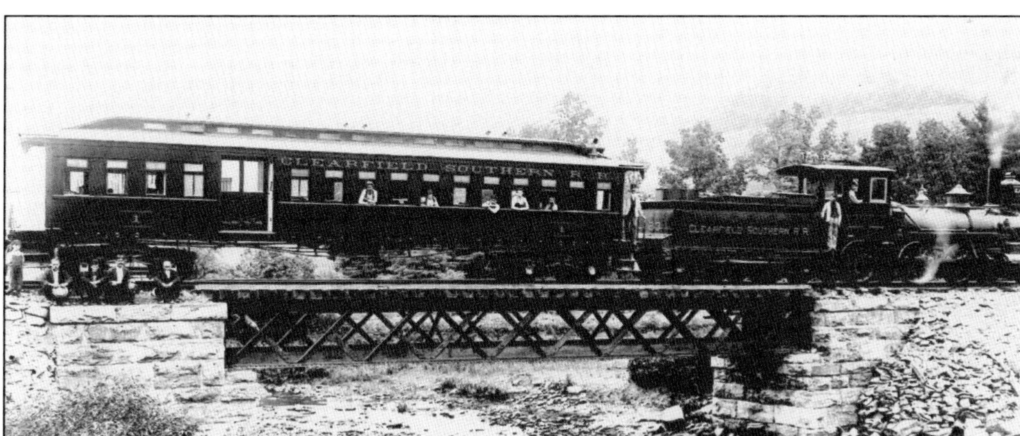

This Clearfield Southern Railroad train crosses the Little Clearfield Creek at Dimeling. This line ran to Faunce in 1900, was extended to Boardman due to the Potts Run Coal Company in 1901, and then to Irvona in 1904. The New York Central Railroad leased this road beginning in 1903. (Courtesy Clearfield County Historical Society.)

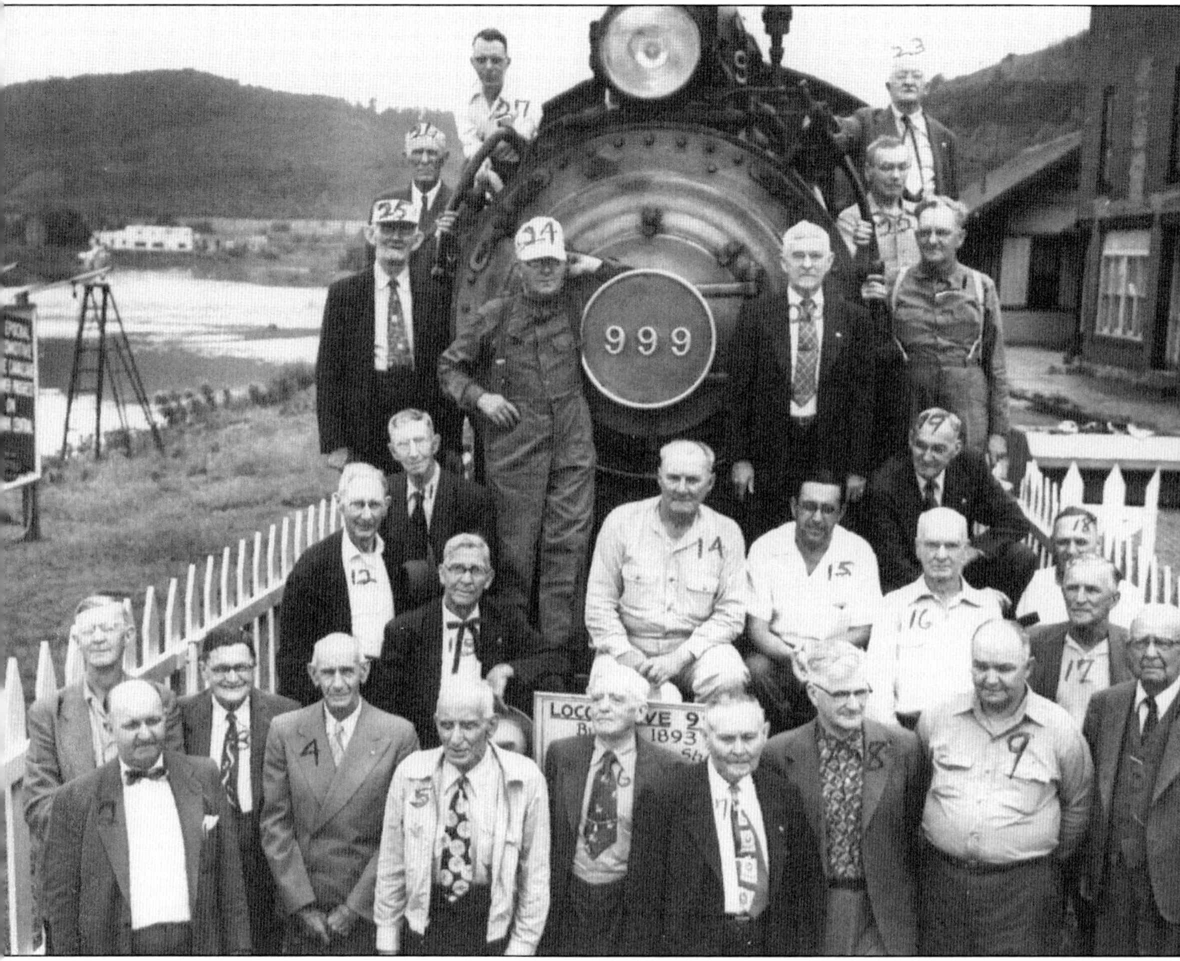

During the Clearfield County Sesquicentennial in 1949, these retired railroad men pose with locomotive 999, which set a world speed record. It was built in 1893 at West Albany Shops for $13,000. Seen here are, from left to right, (first row) Fay Ganol, E. P. Brown, Ira Smeal, W. H. Ziegler, Earl P. Carr, John Black (in front of sign), Jim Berry, Lloyd Wisner, John Henry, and Jewet Hills (second row; behind the sign) Dode Watson, Ed Wooster, Earl Hoover (sitting), Ray Baroni (sitting), Bob Lucas, Ray Miller, and behind him, Ray Smeal. In dark suits sitting on either side of train are, from left to right, Joe Harvey and Ed Reed. Standing on the train are, from left to right, Joe Breth, Ernest Ferguson, Eddie Lynch, John Savel (left of Locomotive 999), Harry Stewart (right of Locomotive 999), W. J. Hoover, Roy Williams, and Clarance Edmiston. (Courtesy Clearfield County Historical Society.)

Four

CLEARFIELD

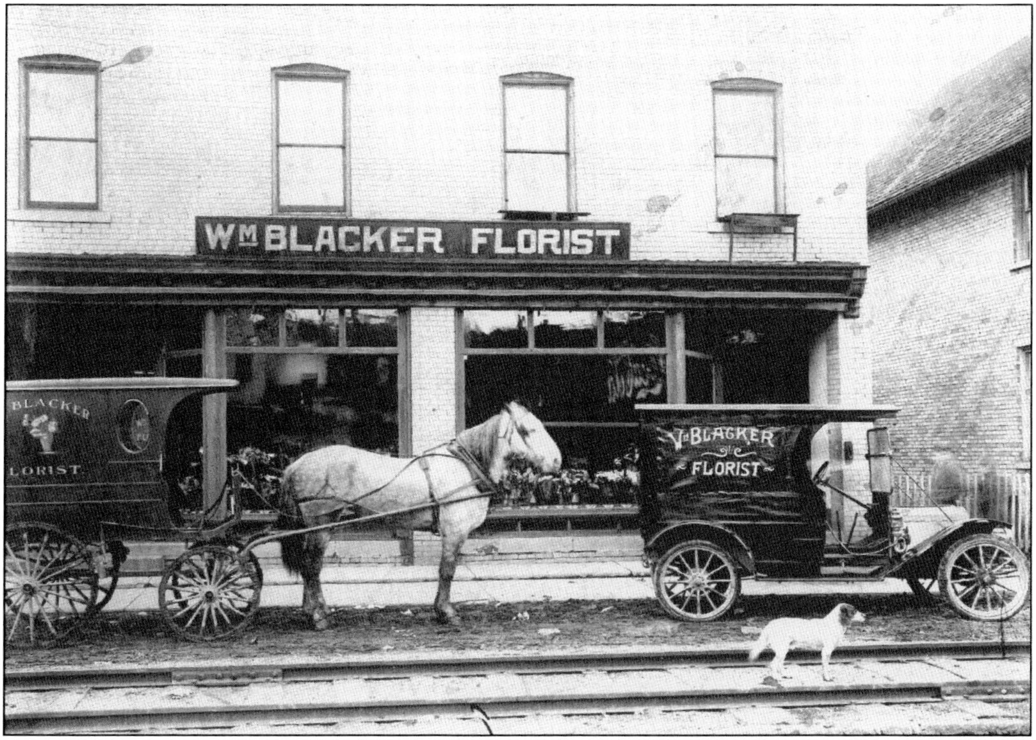

One of Clearfield's oldest retail establishments is Blacker Floral Shop, which began in 1900. Originally William Blacker Florist was located on North Third Street between Locust and Pine Streets. At one point in its history, deliveries were made by both horse-drawn carriages and "motorized delivery wagons." Today Blacker Floral Shop is still in business at 216 East Pine Street. (Courtesy Clearfield County Historical Society.)

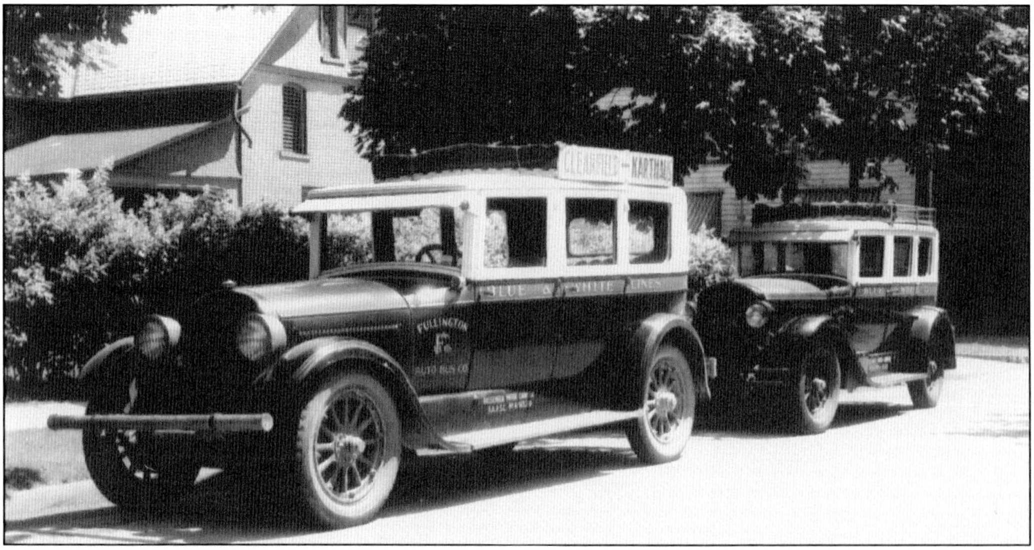

After beginning with a nine-passenger surrey wagon in 1908, Fullington Bus Company moved into the "auto bus" era. The bus above, left, ran from Clearfield to Karthaus around 1932, and the bus below ran from Clearfield to Tyrone in the 1920s. Over the years, Fullington Bus Company bought out its competition, Emerick Bus Lines of Bellefonte and Edwards Lake to Sea from Curwensville. Today the company remains family owned, is affiliated with Trailways, and runs its own tour service. J. Richard Fullington Sr. once admitted that his father did not own a car, and when it came time for his mother to give birth to him in 1918, his father took her to the hospital in a bus. (Courtesy Clearfield County Historical Society.)

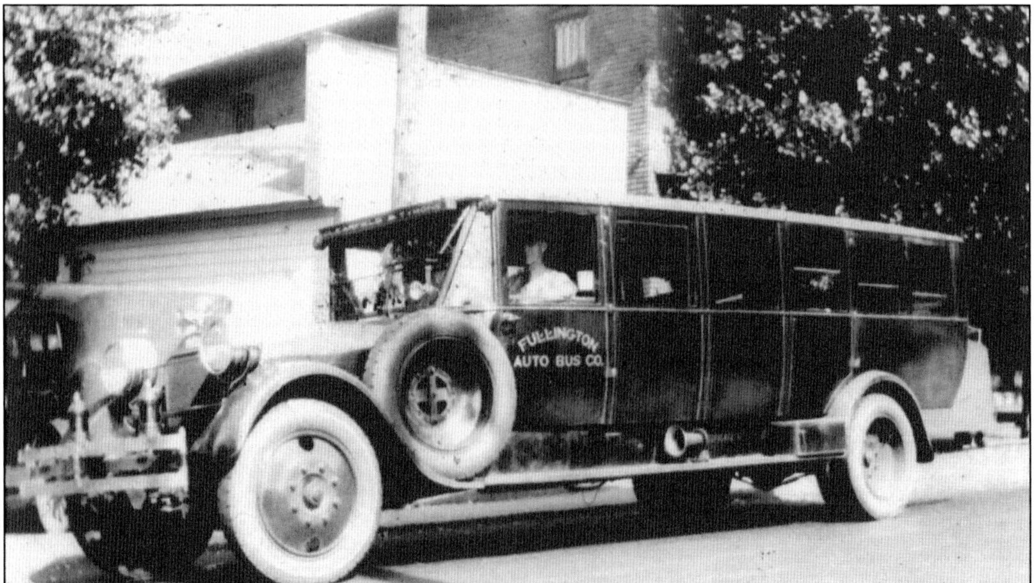

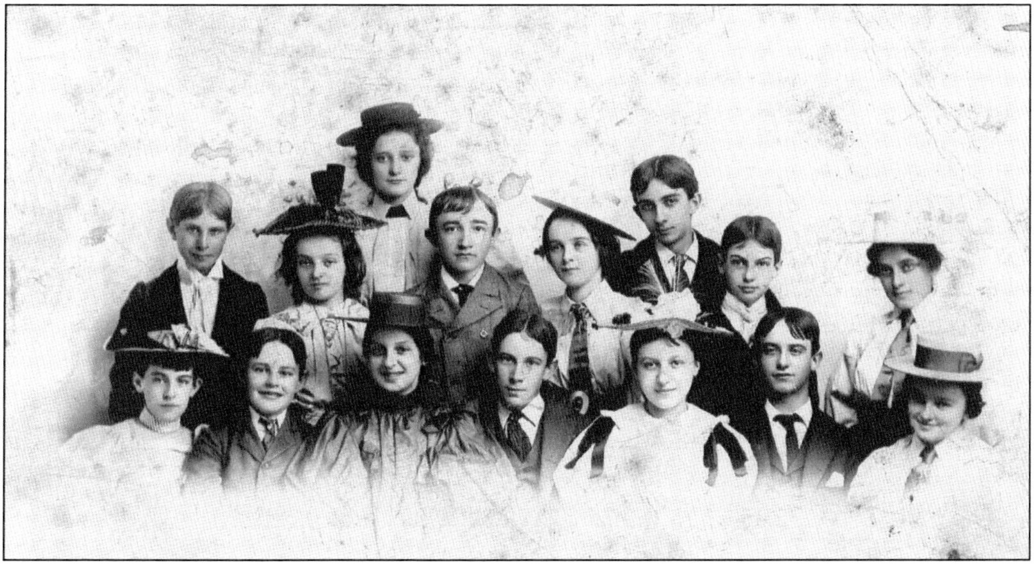

Clearfield High School students pose together in this photograph from July 1895. Although it is not identified as such, it is possible this was their graduating class. Seen here are, from left to right, (first row) Alice McQuown, Charlie Shaw, Edna Gable, Wallace Krebs, Sarah Bigler, Fred Ray, and Emma Biddle; (second row) Don McKinley, Jeanie Wallace, Lewis Irwin, Mame McQuown, Fred Reed, Robert Reed, and Fannie Irwin; (third row) Mattie Shaw. (Courtesy Clearfield County Historical Society.)

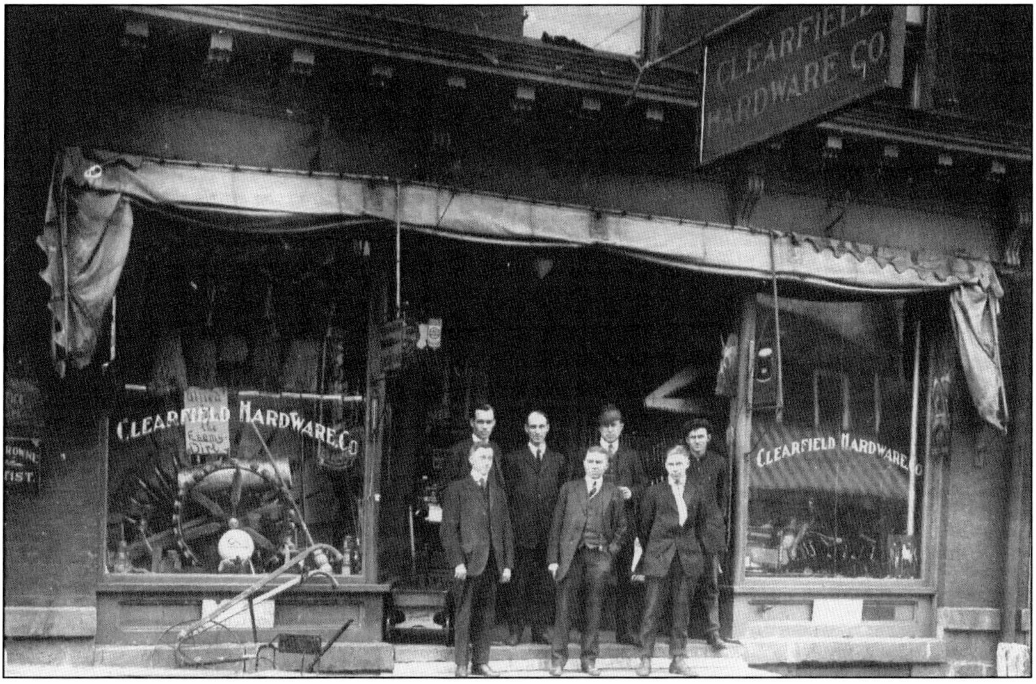

Clearfield Hardware, incorporated in 1910, was located at 125 Market Street. Seen here are, from left to right, (first row) ? Lawhead , bookkeeper; H. C. McCloud, salesman; and Bowman Weaver; (second row) Samuel Powell, president; G. Charles Hall, sales manager; Don Gingery, salesman; and Ira Jay. (Courtesy Clearfield County Historical Society.)

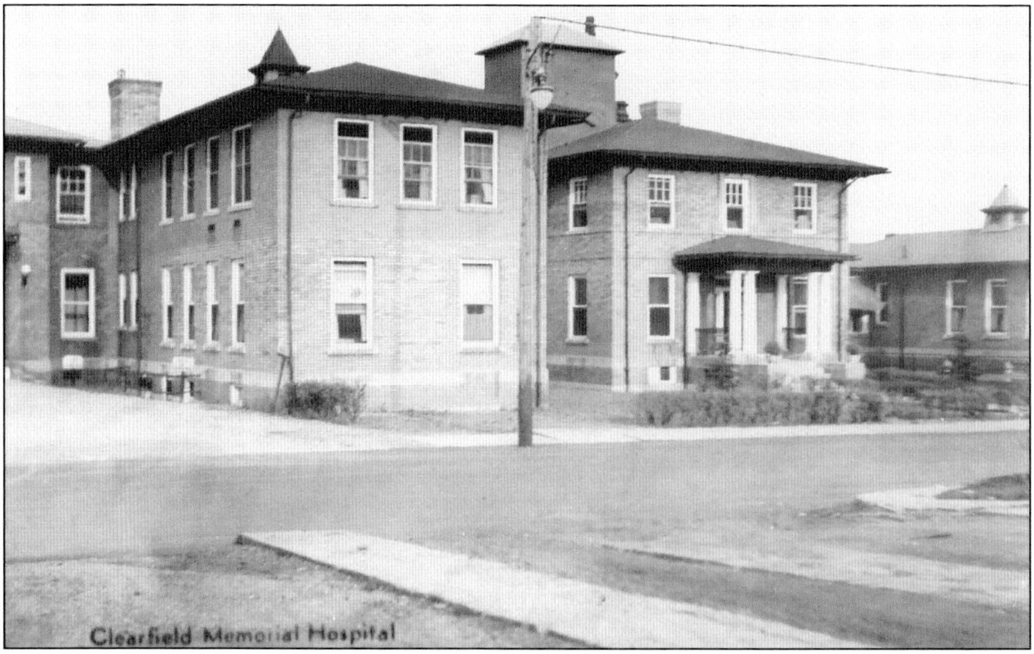

The Clearfield Hospital began on South Second Street in 1900. In 1904, the Mossop sisters donated land on Turnpike Avenue for a new hospital in memory of their brother Fred, who was once a director of the hospital. The above structure was built in 1906, and the current hospital at the same location was completed in 1949. (Courtesy Clearfield County Historical Society.)

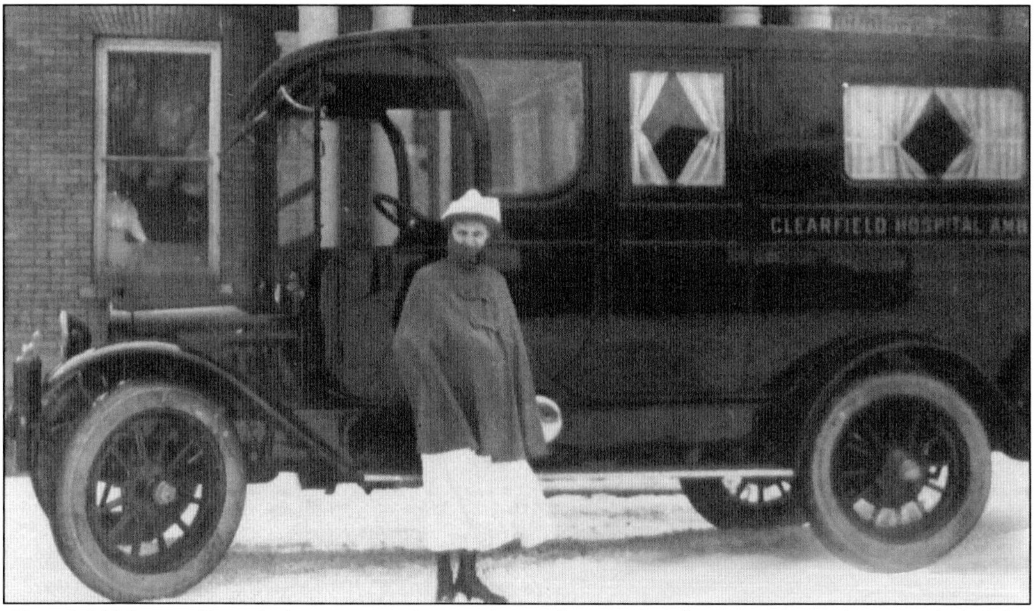

Clearfield Hospital's ambulance is ready to take its first trip with Margaret Wilson Bush (of the Clearfield Hospital School of Nursing class of 1917) eager to ride along. In June 1932, when the hospital's ambulance was out of service, a call came in for an elderly woman who had fractured her hip. Clearfield Fire Company No. 1 responded and has been providing emergency medical services ever since. (Courtesy Clearfield County Historical Society.)

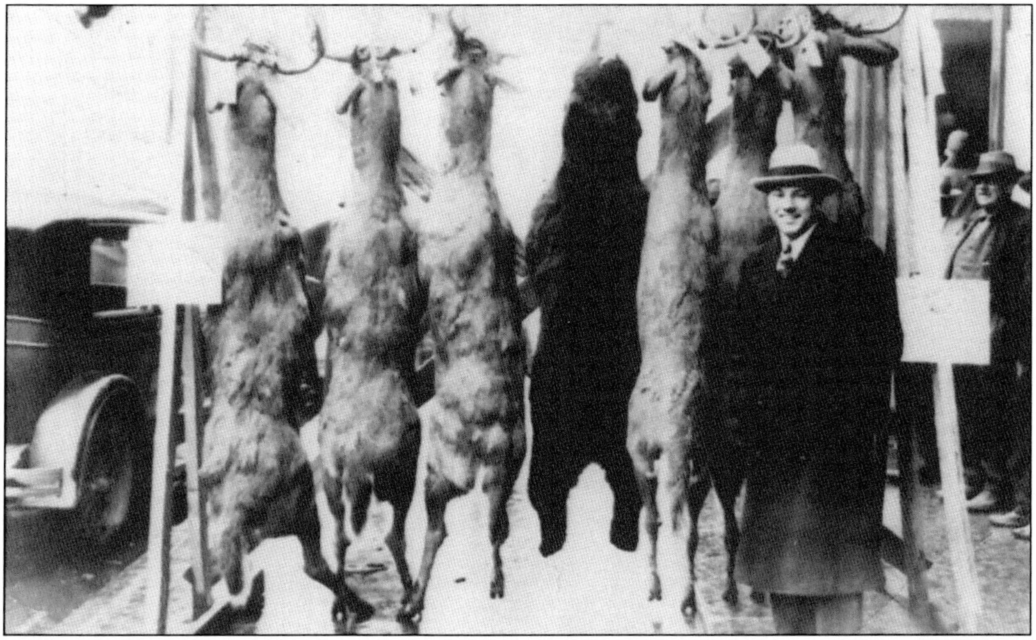

Guy Cowdrick poses with several deer and a bear in this *c.* 1929 photograph. Cowdrick killed the 10-point deer and the bear both on the first drive at Bee Hollow Camp in Lawrence Township that year. This picture was taken in front of Clearfield Hardware on East Market Street near the current location of County National Bank. (Courtesy Clearfield County Historical Society.)

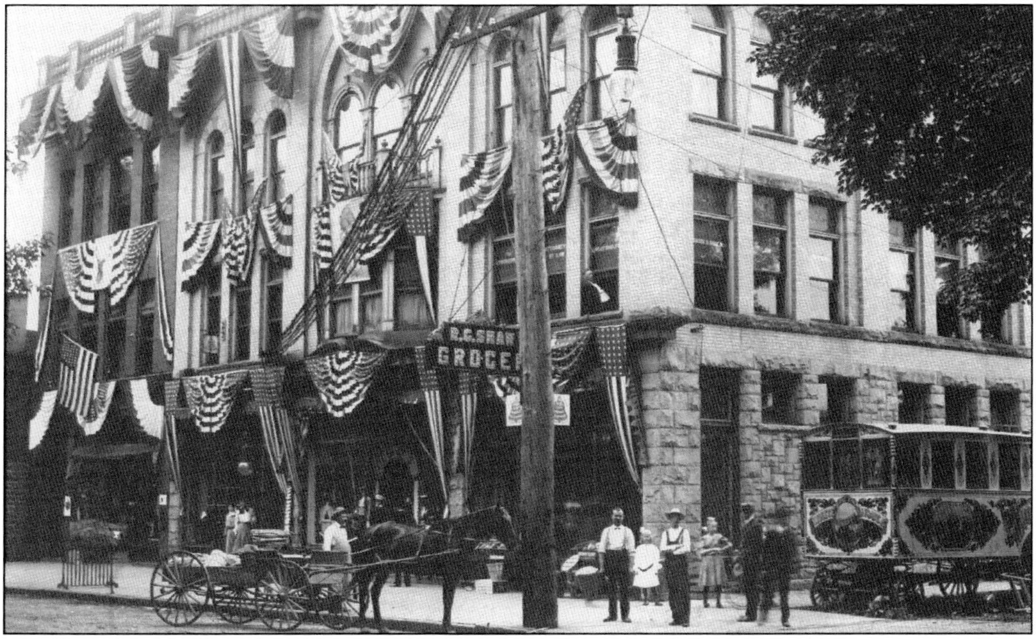

The Keystone and the Kurtz Brothers buildings on Second Street are decorated for Clearfield County's centennial in 1904. The Keystone building, which was constructed in 1900, was home to Flegal's Grocery Store. Today it houses Play at the Plate, the Shoe Tree, and the Republican Headquarters. The Kurtz Brothers building was built in 1901. (Courtesy Clearfield County Historical Society.)

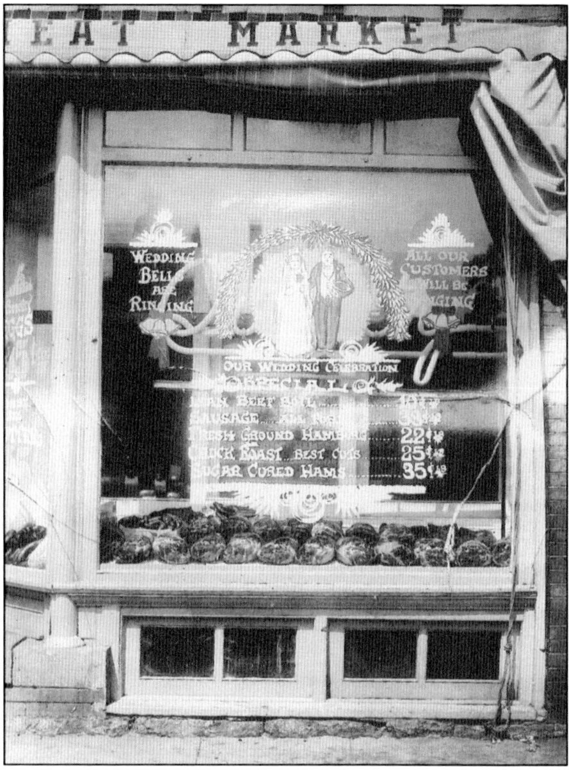

"Wedding bells are ringing! All our customers will be singing!" reads the window of the Quality Meat Market in Clearfield at 108 North Third Street around 1930. As part of the wedding celebration, several specials were offered, including fresh ground hamburger at 22¢ per pound. The shop was owned by Edward E. Boalich. (Courtesy Clearfield County Historical Society.)

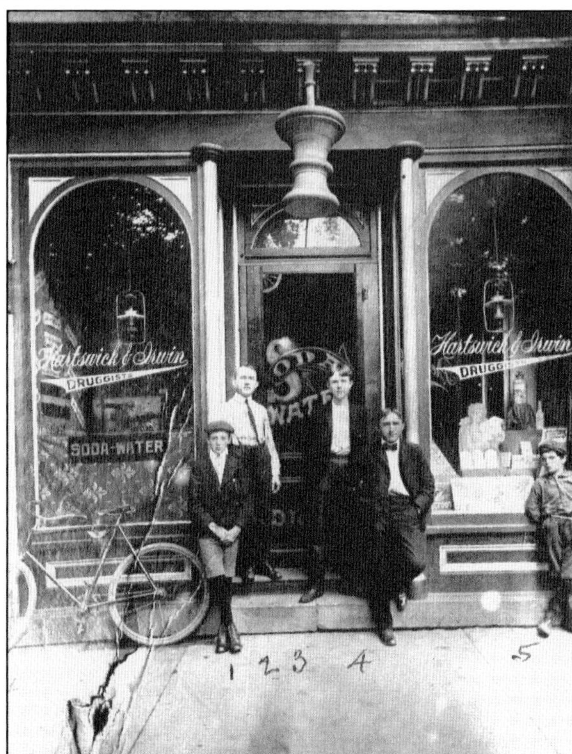

Hartswick and Irwin Druggists had its store at 26 North Second Street. The business began in 1865 as the successor to Hartswick and Huston. Seen here are, from left to right, William W. Wrigley, Ellis Irwin (owner), Sam Stewart, Lewis Irwin, and Hughey Brawley. This site is currently home to Jim's Sports Center. (Courtesy Clearfield County Historical Society.)

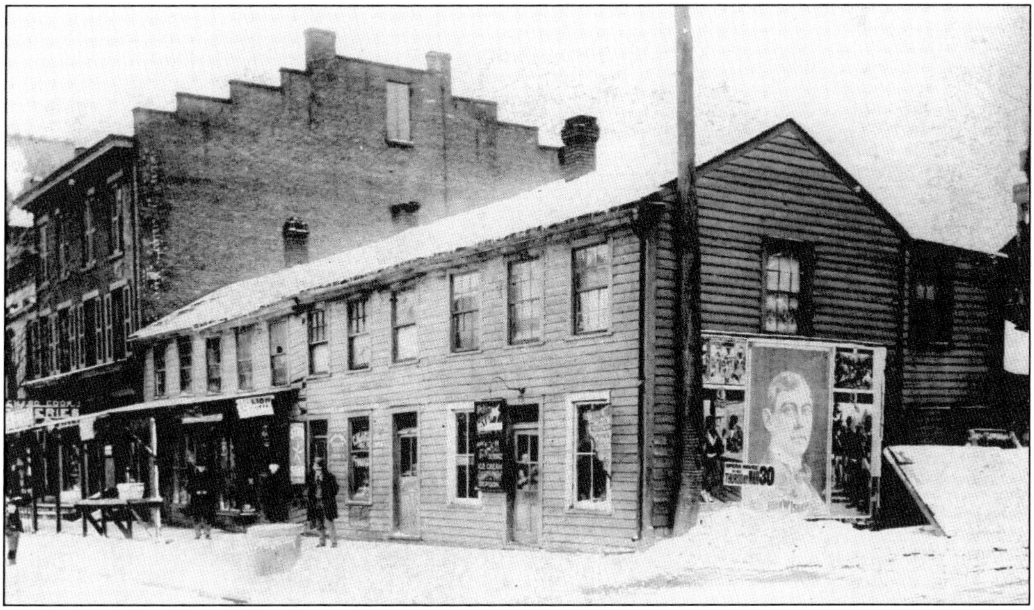

East Market Street in 1899 featured an interesting poster, right. It is a promotion for John W. Isham's latest show, which was performed at the opera house on March 30. According to a publicity article, the show "featured negro jokes, darkey dancing, and coon melodies." Isham is described as having "done more for the colored stage folk than any other manager." (Courtesy Clearfield County Historical Society.)

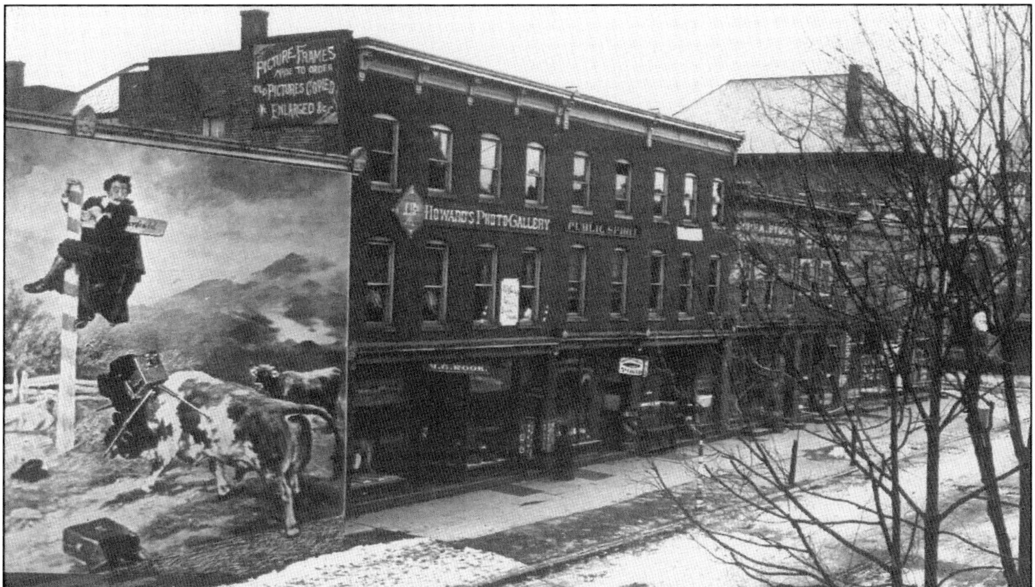

The Howard Photo Gallery was on Market Street between Second and Third Streets. Chan Howard started his business in 1892. This photograph appears to be an example of Howard Photo Gallery's expertise in trick photography, as it is not possible that a painting of this size ever covered part of this street. Also in the Howard Photo Gallery building is the office of the *Public Spirit*, a newspaper that was published from the 1870s to the 1920s. (Courtesy Clearfield County Historical Society.)

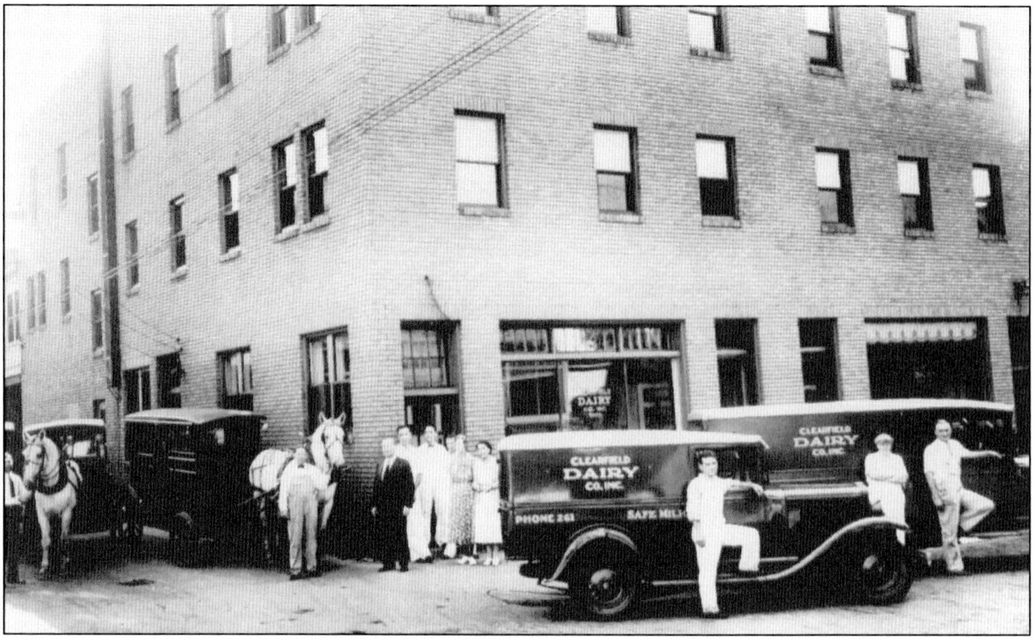

Clearfield Dairy operated on 213 Reed Street around 1929. Here drivers pose with both horse-drawn buggies and motorized Clearfield Dairy delivery trucks. The company, which started in the 1920s, was purchased by Sani-Dairy of Johnstown in 1979. This was one of many dairies once operating in Clearfield. Others included the Keystone Dairy and Miller Dairy. (Courtesy Clearfield County Historical Society.)

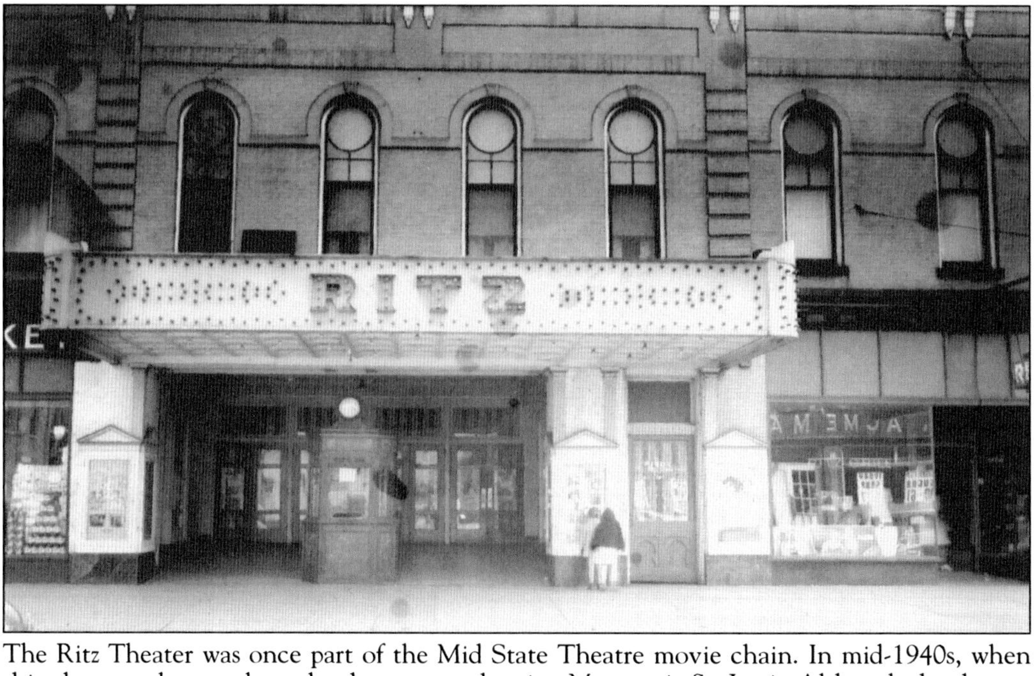

The Ritz Theater was once part of the Mid State Theatre movie chain. In mid-1940s, when this photograph was taken, the theater was showing *Meet me in St. Louis*. Although the theater is still active, it has changed quite a bit. Note the outside ticket office and the theater-long marquee. (Courtesy Clearfield County Historical Society.)

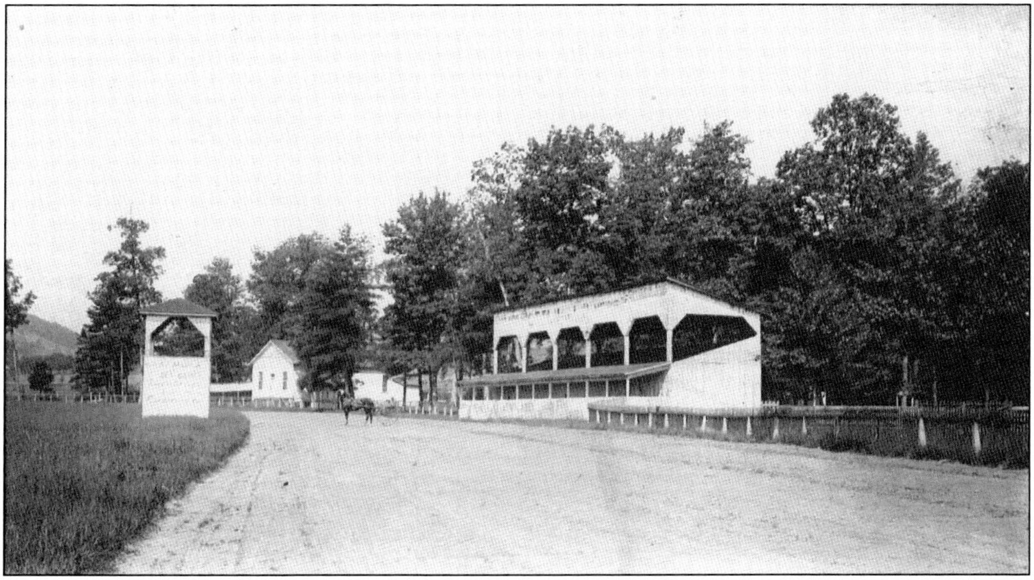

The track at the Driving Park, which is used for the Clearfield County Fair, is in what was once known as "West Clearfield." The advertisement on the booth at left reads, "Go to A. E. Martin for Best Goods in latest styles, lowest prices." This picture, showing a horse and driver and probably taken during the fair, dates from before the 1920s, when a new grandstand was built. (Courtesy Clearfield County Historical Society.)

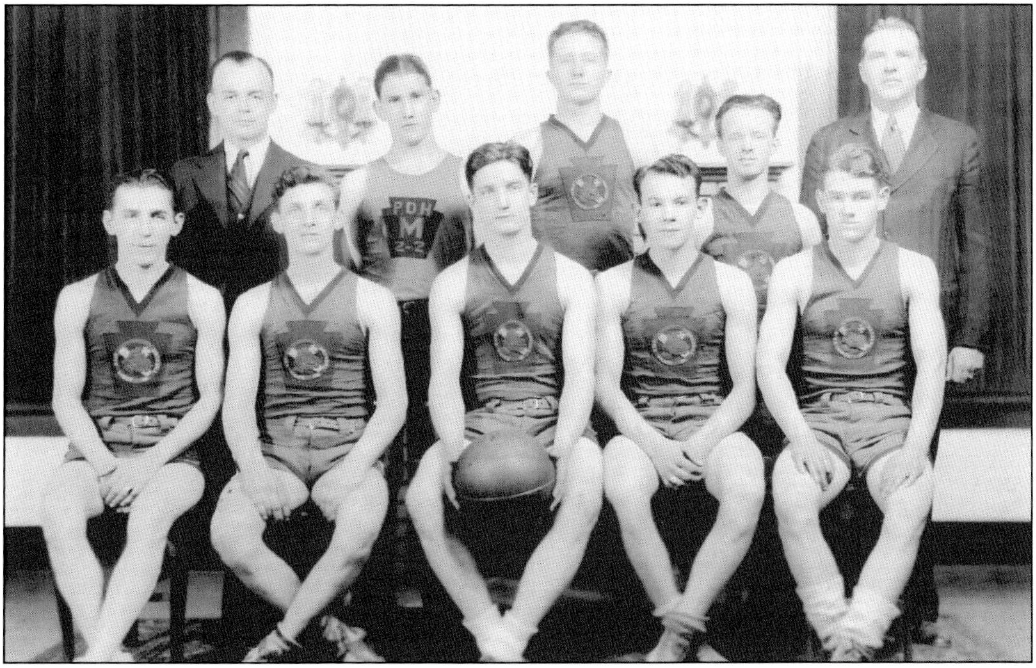

The YMCA City Basketball Champs for the 1928–1929 season pose proudly in this photograph. They are, from left to right, (first row, seated) Lester Shull, Elsworth Imdorf, Charles "Bud" Edmiston, Clarance "Brownie" Sensor, and George Shively; (second row, standing) Walter Flegal, Jack Westcott, George Gearhart, Albert "Pep" Undercoffer, and William A. E. Leitzinger. (Courtesy Clearfield County Historical Society.)

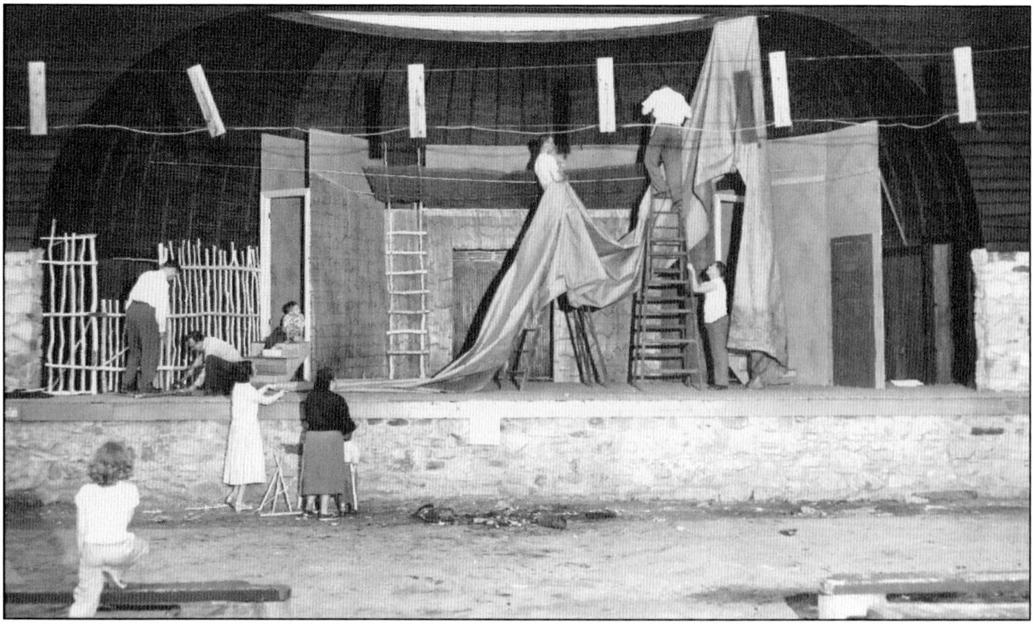

Preparations are made at the band shell at Elliott Park for the 1950 production of *We're No Angels* by the Old Town Players, who produced over 90 plays here before disbanding when the band shell was demolished. Some of the members of that group started producing plays in the St. John Lutheran Church and later founded Clearfield Arts Studio Theatre (CAST) in 1982. (Courtesy Clearfield County Historical Society.)

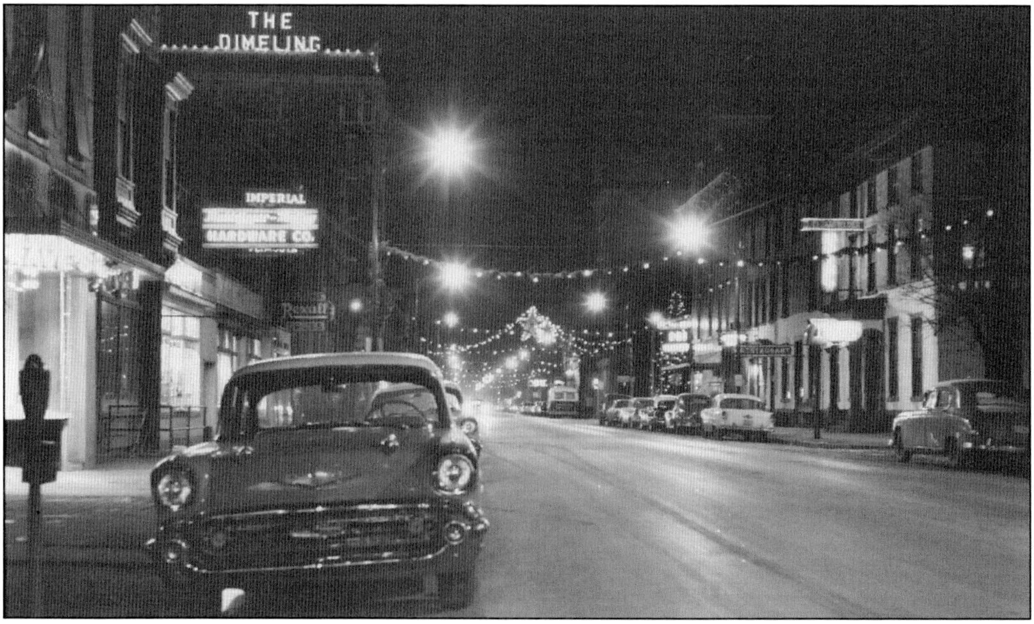

South Second Street around 1957 is decorated for the holiday season. Of particular interest is the lighted sign of the Dimeling Hotel. At this point in history, some businesses on the west side of the street were Prave's Dress Shop and Beauty Salon, Cecil R. Bloom drugstore and bus terminal, and the County National Bank. On the east side of the street was the Clearfielder Hotel Dining Room. (Courtesy Clearfield County Historical Society.)

Five

NEIGHBORS

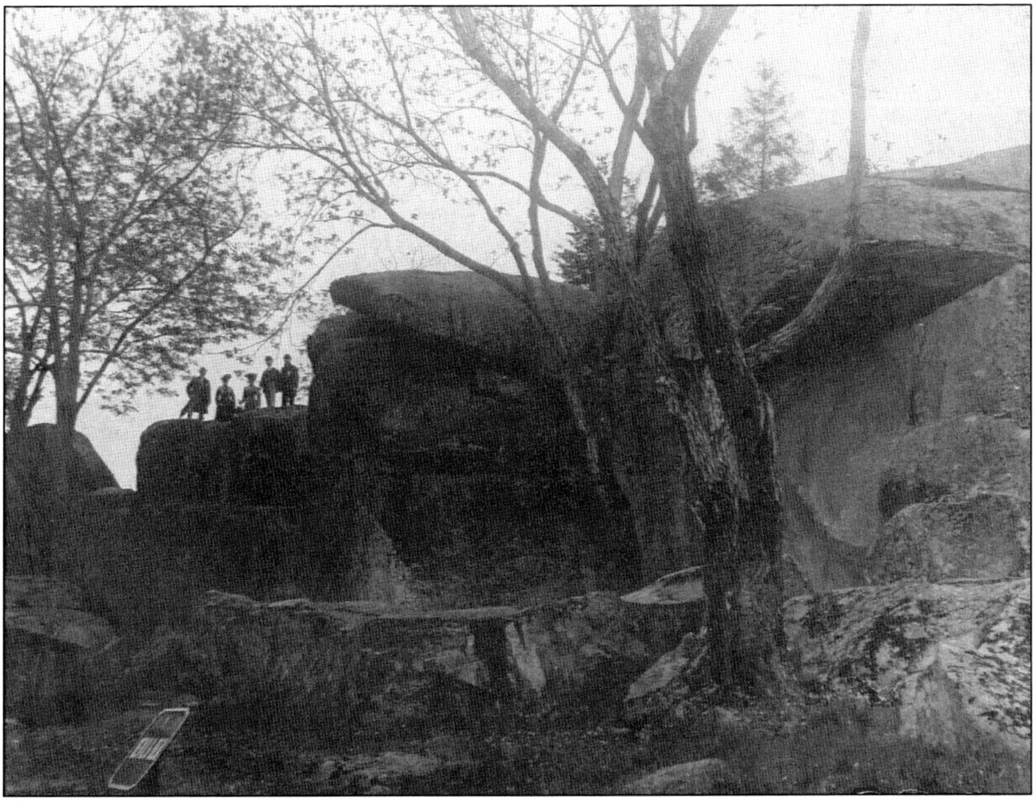

Bilger's Rocks in Bloom Township has always been a popular stop for visitors. Posing on the top in this *c.* 1900 photograph is Charles T. Kurtz (far left), founder of Kurtz Brothers. The rocks are 30 to 40 feet high and were used by Native Americans as shelter. A pavilion and a play area are some of the improvements made to the area by the Bilger's Rocks Association. (Courtesy Clearfield County Historical Society.)

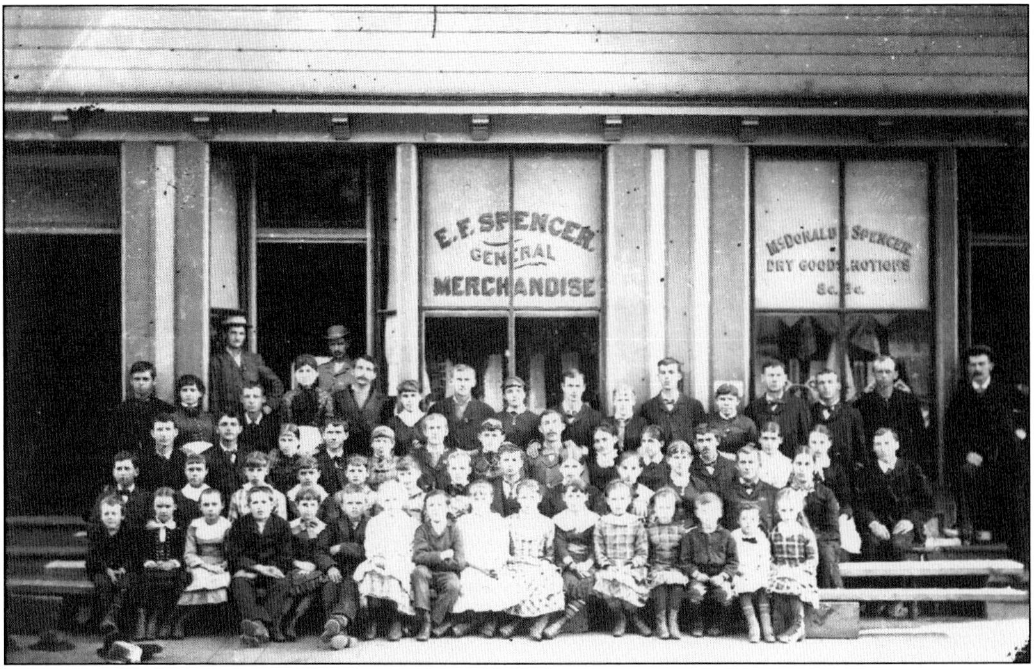

The E. F. Spencer and McDonald General Store in Grampian was the site of this portrait of the students of the normal school in Grampian around 1883. That is the teacher, Will McDonald, on the far right. The tradition of the corner store continues as this location is currently home to Sholes Grocery. (Courtesy Dan McDonald.)

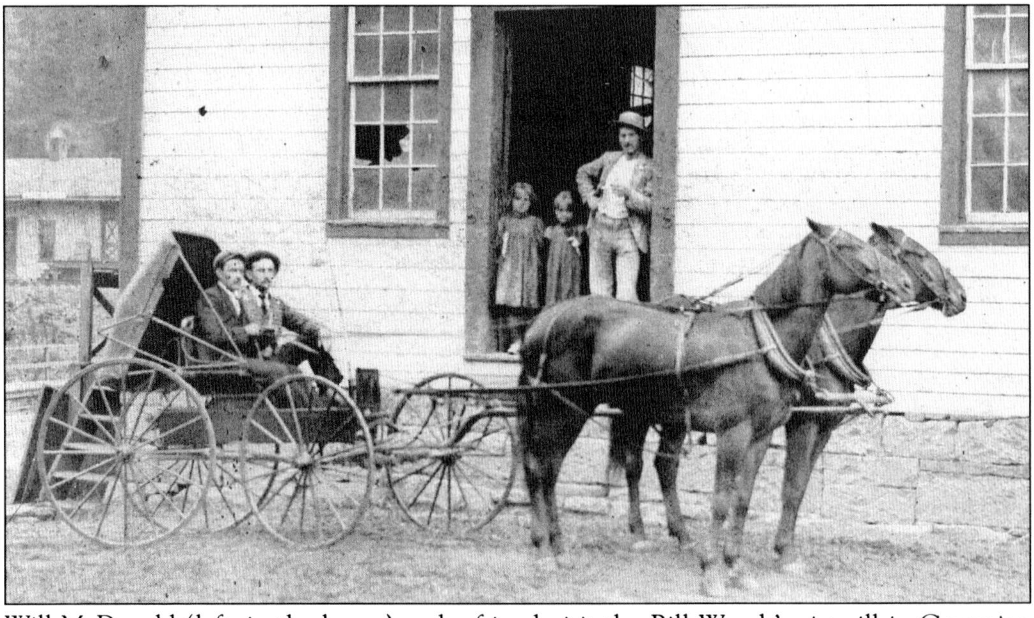

Will McDonald (left, in the buggy) and a friend visit the Bill Woods' gristmill in Grampian around 1885. Woods and his two daughters stand in the doorway. Grampian originally was called Pennville until Dr. Samuel Coleman moved to town. He said it reminded him of Scotland and renamed the area Grampian Hills. The name officially changed in 1895. (Courtesy Dan McDonald.)

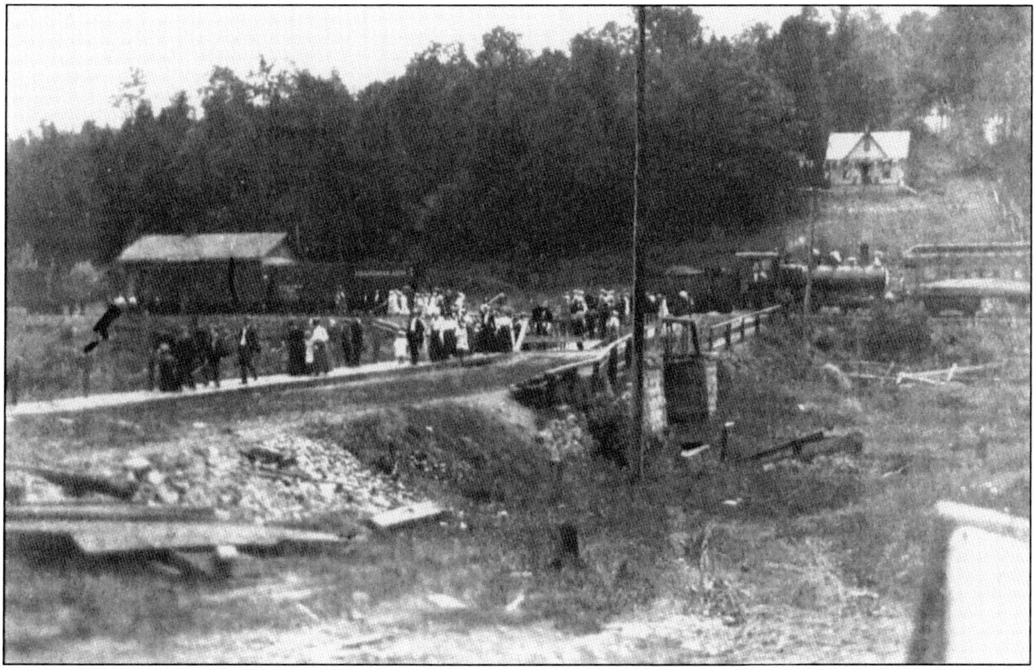

A train leaves passengers off at the Grampian station. The Pennsylvania Railroad line was extended from Curwensville to Grampian in 1892. Having a railroad stop helped put many communities on the map. This station was located just a block from the main intersection in town. (Courtesy Dan McDonald.)

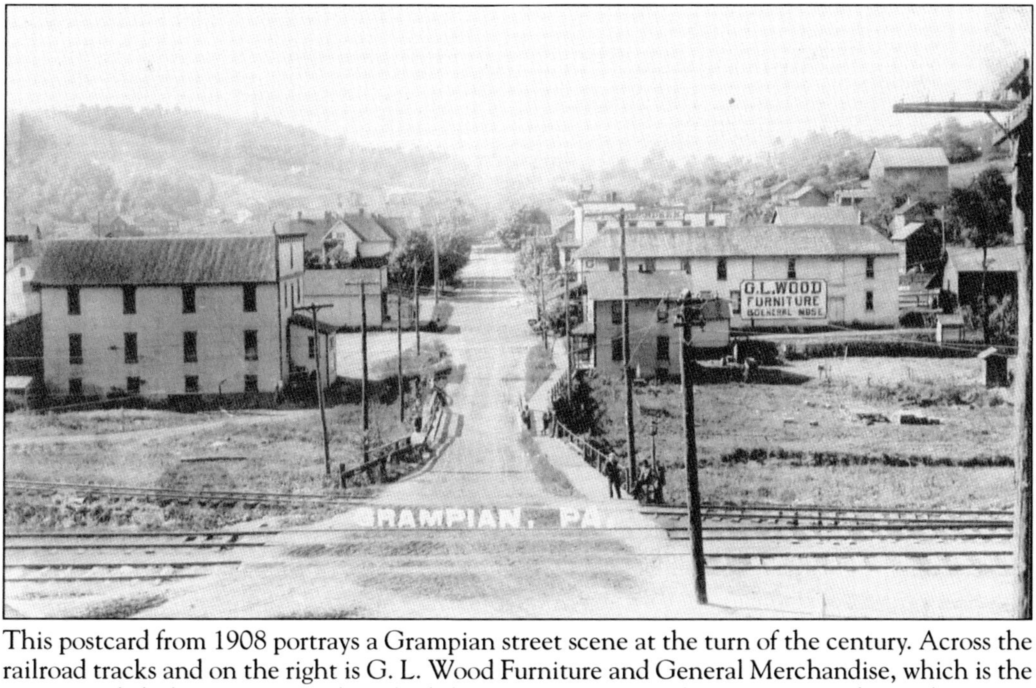

This postcard from 1908 portrays a Grampian street scene at the turn of the century. Across the railroad tracks and on the right is G. L. Wood Furniture and General Merchandise, which is the site now of Sholes Grocery, and on the left is the current site of Grampian Hardware. (Courtesy Dan McDonald.)

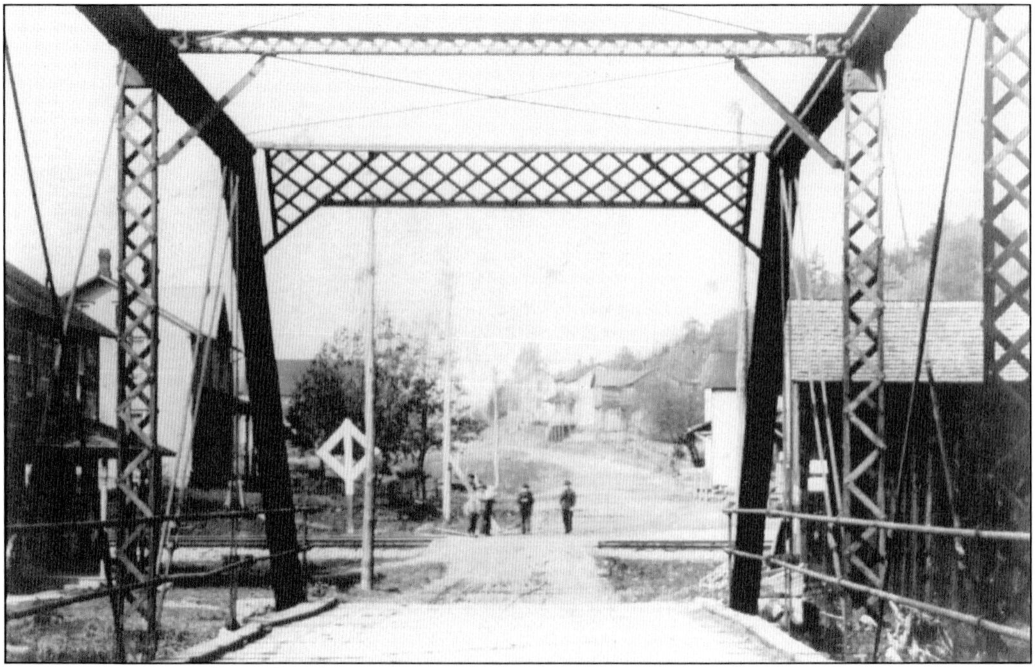

Olanta grew from the railroad line that came through this area in 1884. After a railroad station was added, other businesses followed. This view from the Olanta Bridge that looks from Knox Township into Pike Township shows the railroad tracks crossing the town. The Cathcart General Store can be seen as the white building on the right. The back of this postcard reads, "Harry of old lives in the house by the bridge. Mr. Cathcart in the big house. Here is Harry with baby Edith in his arms." Below is the Olanta Lutheran Church, which was destroyed by fire in 1986. It was rebuilt shortly after and stands in the same spot. (Courtesy Clearfield County Historical Society.)

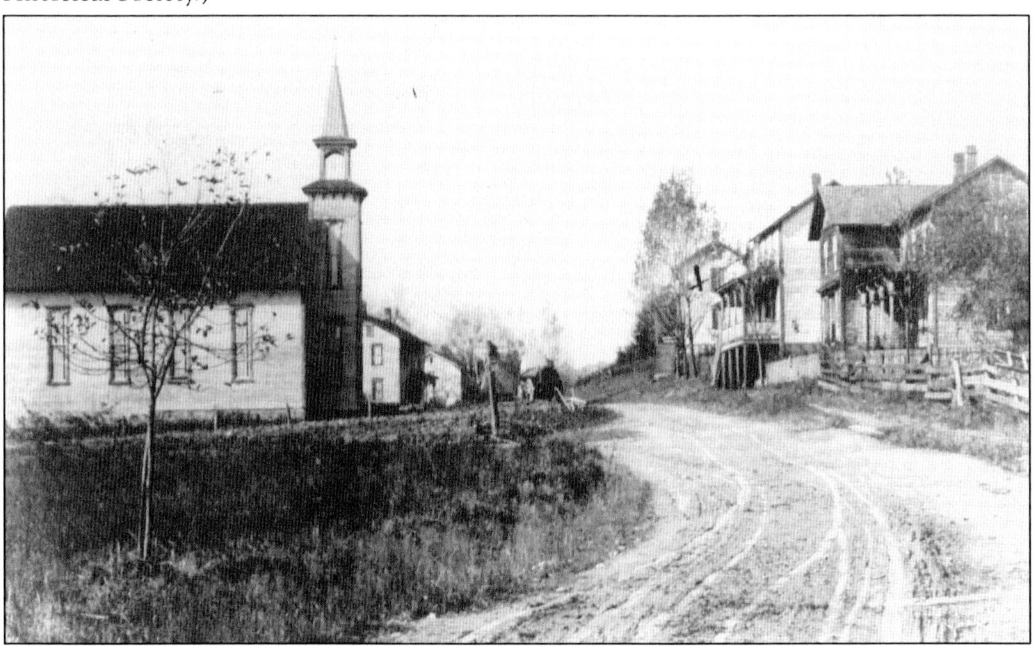

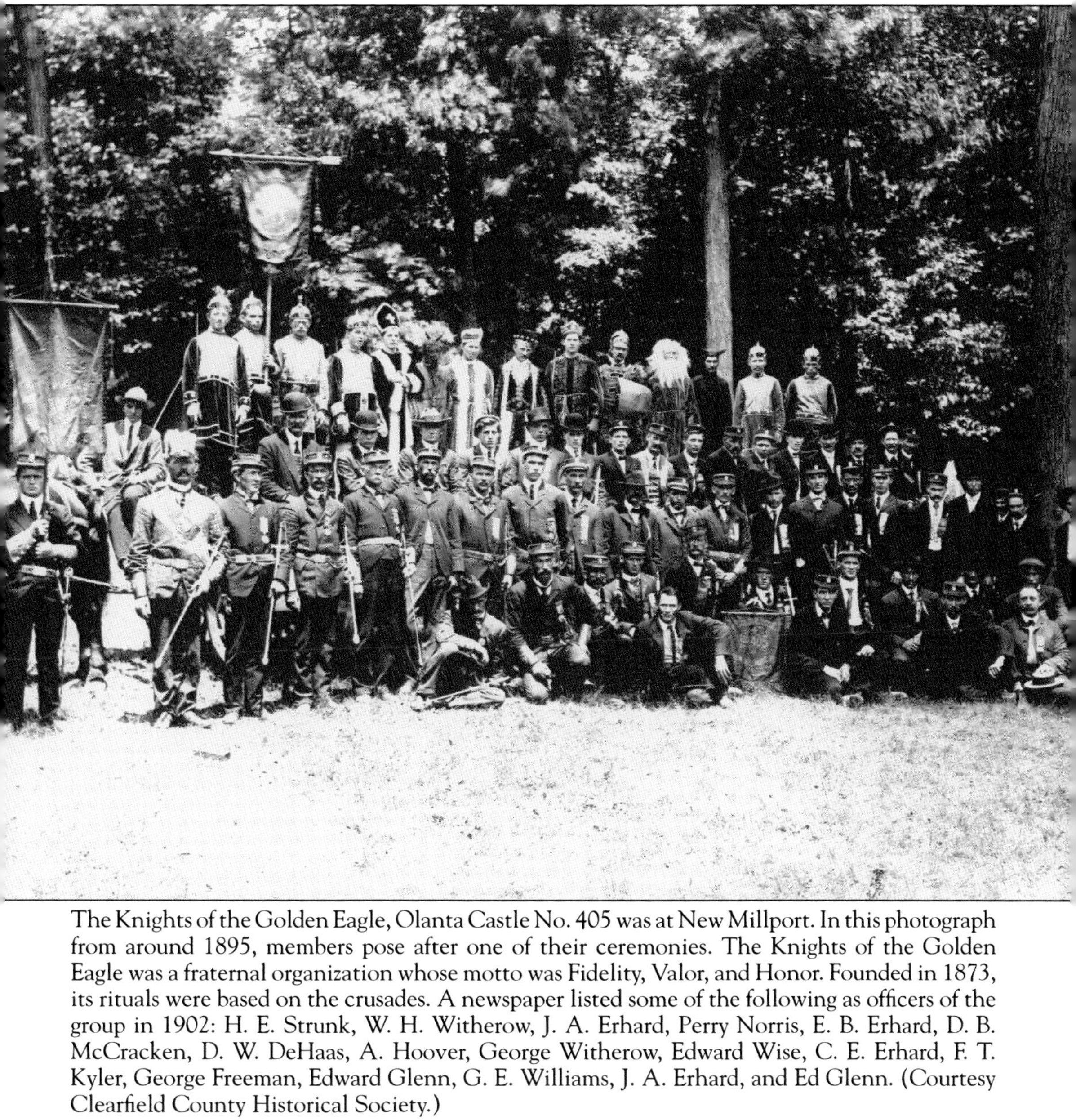

The Knights of the Golden Eagle, Olanta Castle No. 405 was at New Millport. In this photograph from around 1895, members pose after one of their ceremonies. The Knights of the Golden Eagle was a fraternal organization whose motto was Fidelity, Valor, and Honor. Founded in 1873, its rituals were based on the crusades. A newspaper listed some of the following as officers of the group in 1902: H. E. Strunk, W. H. Witherow, J. A. Erhard, Perry Norris, E. B. Erhard, D. B. McCracken, D. W. DeHaas, A. Hoover, George Witherow, Edward Wise, C. E. Erhard, F. T. Kyler, George Freeman, Edward Glenn, G. E. Williams, J. A. Erhard, and Ed Glenn. (Courtesy Clearfield County Historical Society.)

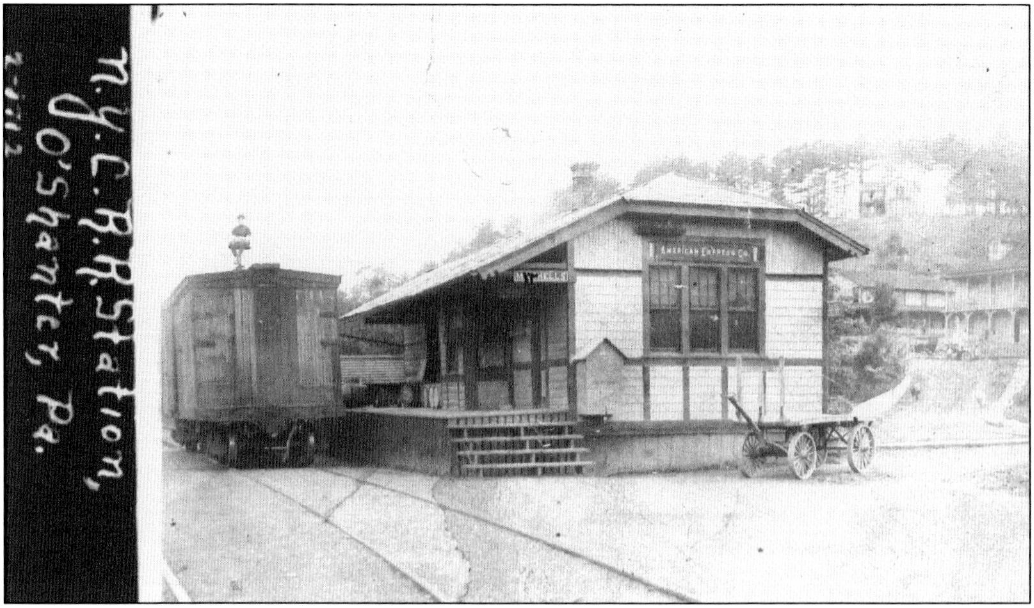

The New York Central Railroad station in O'Shanter helped bring this small coal town to life. At one point in its history, which began around 1882, it had two hotels, two stores, a post office, and a school. On the far right is the O'Shanter Hotel. The station was located near where the honor roll now stands. (Courtesy Clearfield County Historical Society.)

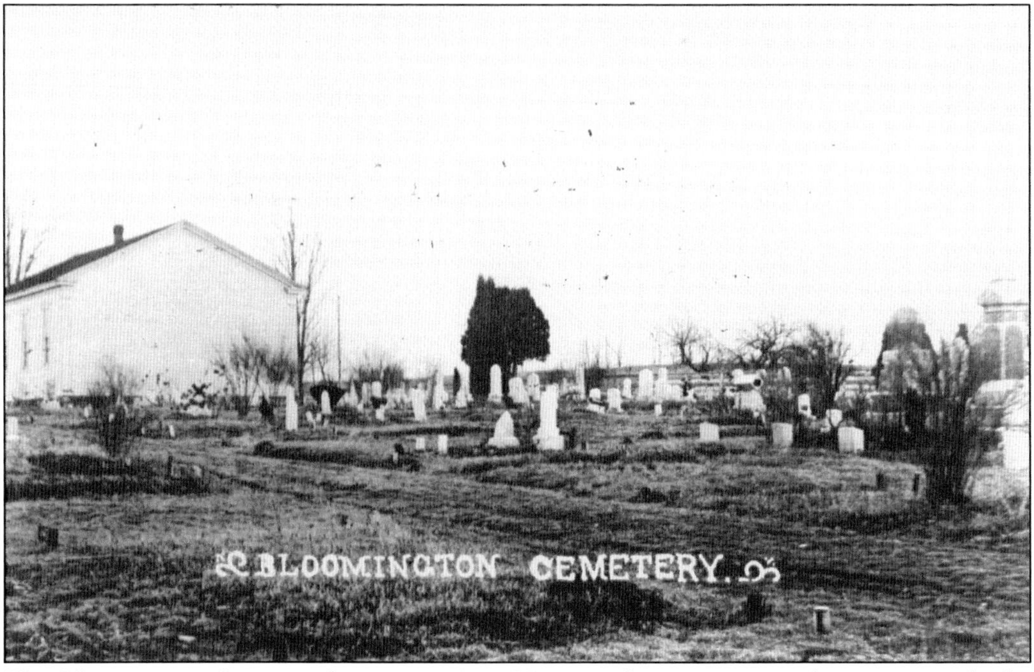

The Bloomington Cemetery began in 1844. Veterans from every war, beginning with the Revolutionary War, are buried here. The Lutheran church, left, which was built in 1851, was torn down in 1978. The cemetery now covers 15 acres and is run by the Bloomington Cemetery Association. Bloomington got its name from the large number of residents named Bloom. (Courtesy Clearfield County Historical Society.)

Two women in Curry Run around 1925 decide the road equipment is a nice place to pose for a photograph. Genevieve Dicky Nolan is on the left, and the other woman is unidentified. This scene is from the construction of Route 219 on Curry Run Hill when the first concrete road was put in. (Courtesy Jim Bennett.)

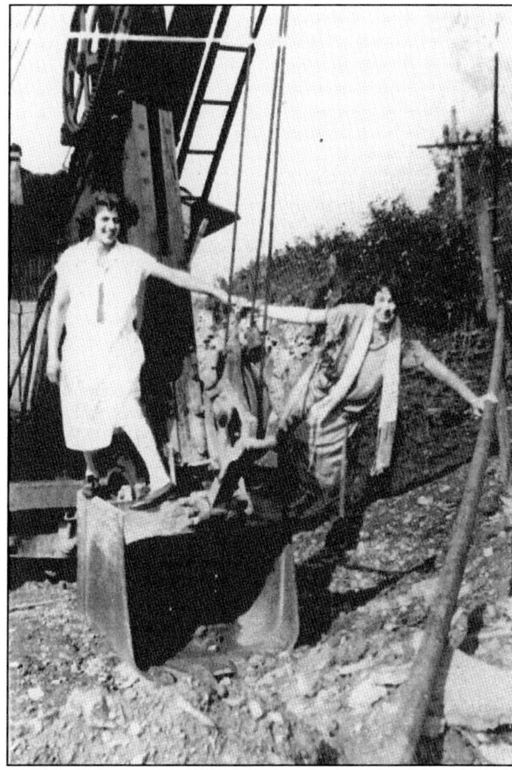

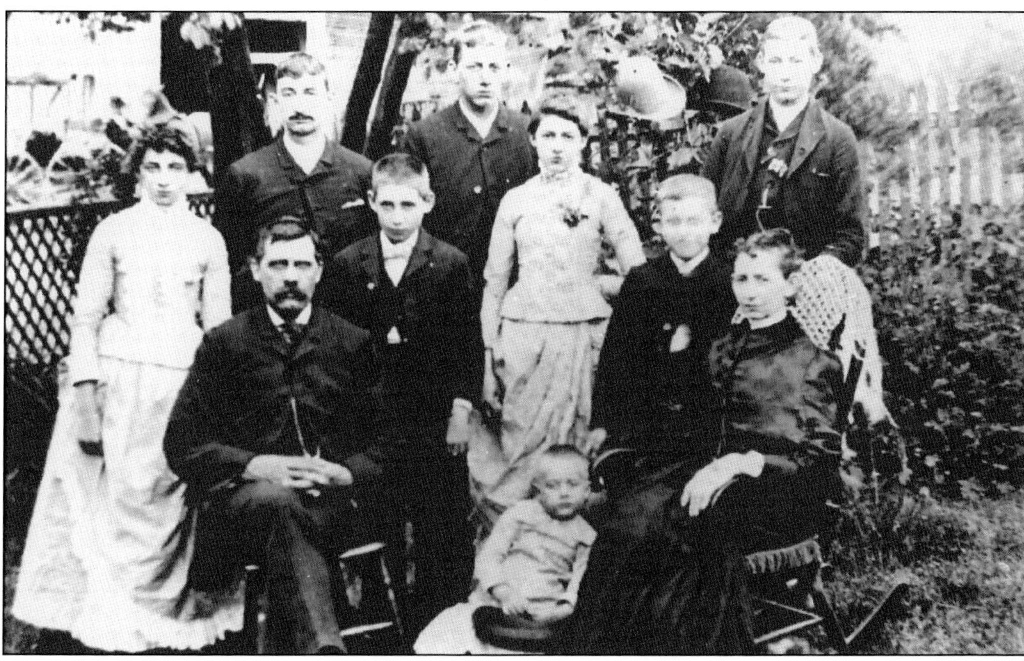

The Johnston family of Curry Run poses in this photograph from 1899. Seen here are, from left to right, are (first row, sitting) William, Allen, and Eliza; (second row) Maggie, Fred, Addie, and Ez; (third row) Harry, John, and Howard. A livery stable is visible behind them on the left. The Johnstons ran the Curry Run Hotel. (Courtesy Jim Bennett.)

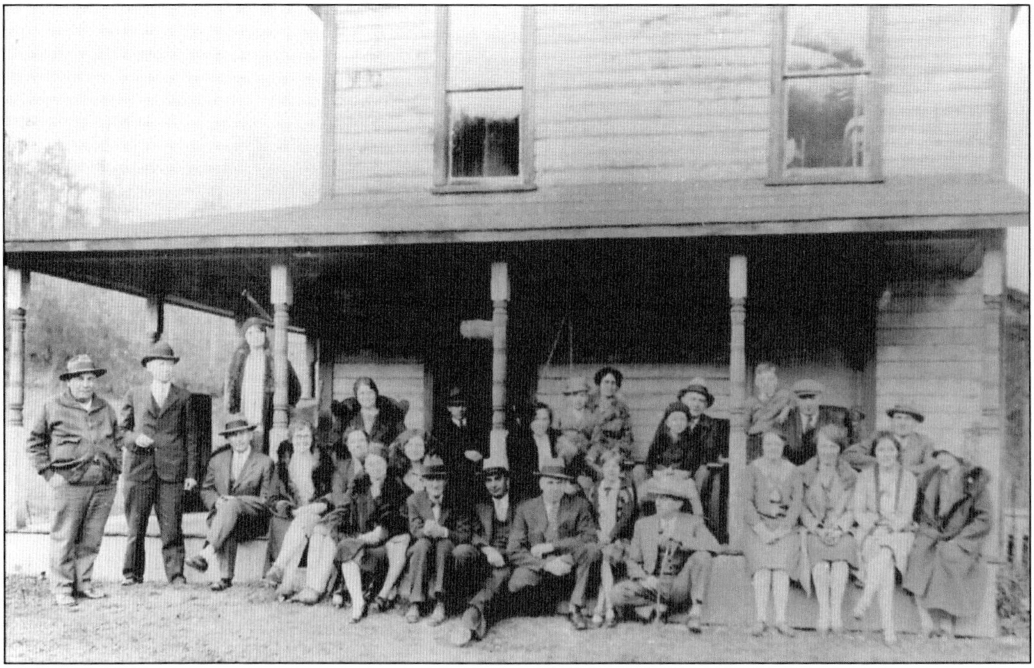

Members of the Cleary Rod and Gun Club in Curry Run pose in this *c.* 1928 photograph. Jack Cross, standing on the far left, took care of the camp. He died from a heart attack while fishing at Curry Run, and a headstone was placed at that spot but he is not buried there. Members included the Raymer, Cameron, Axtel, Larson, Kerr, Sutherland, Enkman, MacKintosh, Shomo, and Schell families. (Courtesy Jim Bennett.)

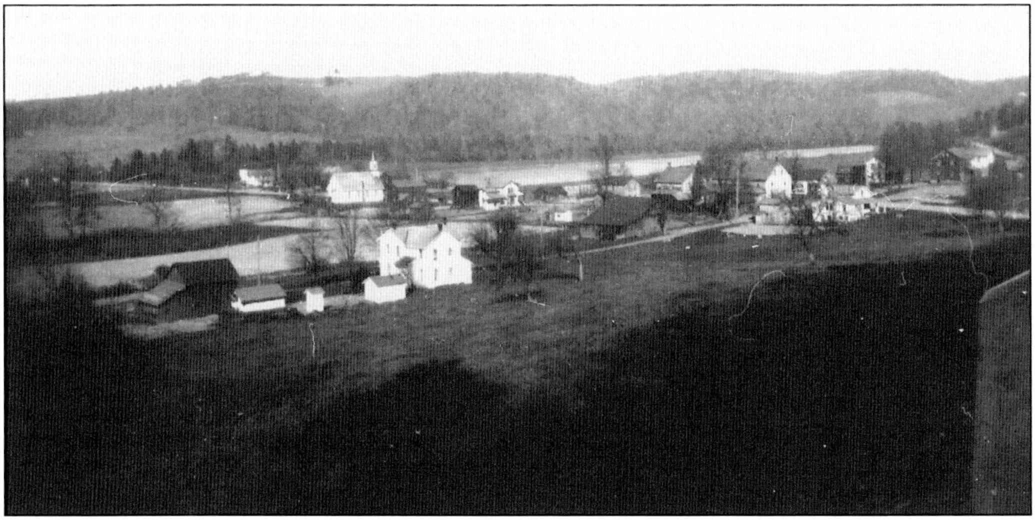

This photograph of Curry Run was taken prior to late 1936 when the Curry Run Methodist Church, the white building in the upper center, burned down. It was rebuilt in 1938 using stone. On the right is the livery stable and the hotel that William Betts built. The white house near the center belonged to the Johnstons who also ran the hotel. (Courtesy Jim Bennett.)

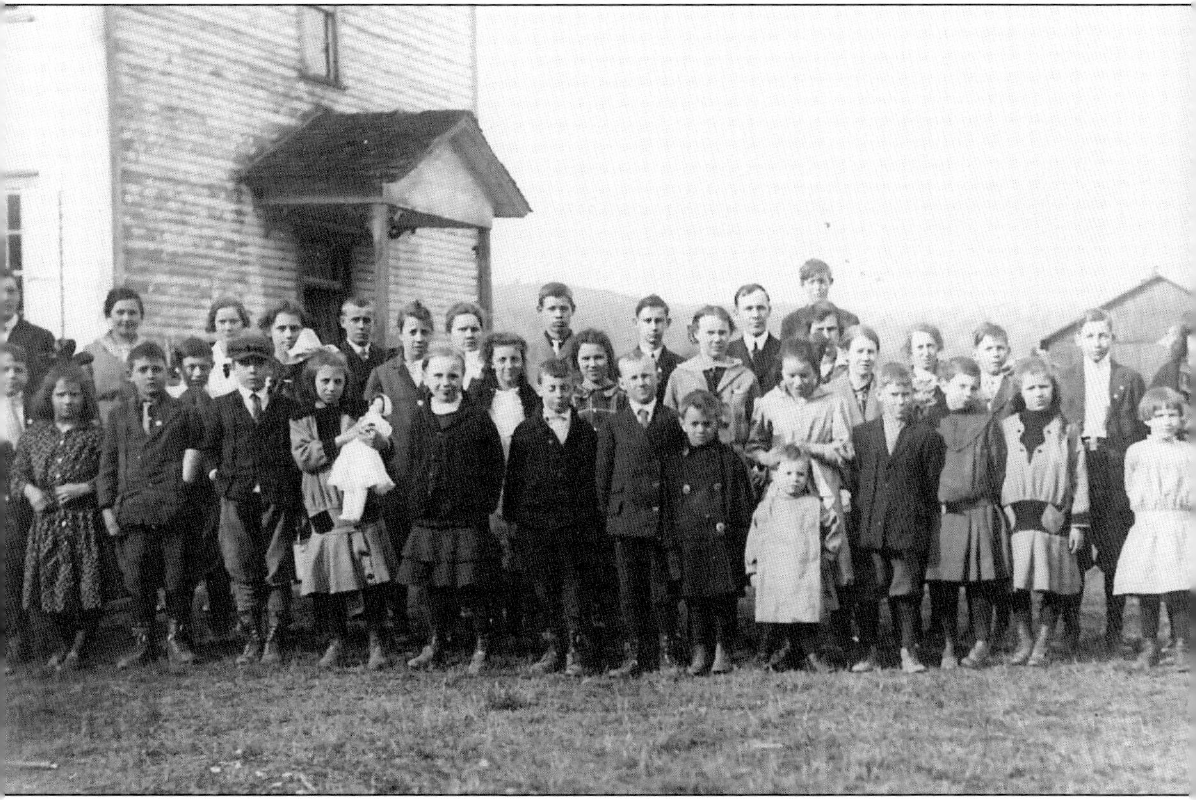

The Bower schoolhouse was used as both a church and school. Posing for this 1916 photograph are, from left to right, (front row) unidentified, Pauline Mitchell, Ford Johnston, Elkin Johnston, Eleanor Nolen, Mildred McDivitt, Earl McCracken, unidentified, Rance Thorp, Margaret Mitchell, Jean Mitchell (standing in front), Samuel Johnston, Frances Thorp, Genevieve Nolen, and Elizabeth Mitchell; (second row) Dayton Lines, Edwin Curry, Merla Thorp, Ruth McCracken, Lucy Mitchell, Emma McDivitt, Adda Johnston, Evelyn Johnston, William Curry, Clifford Johnston, and Hermie Nolen; (third row) Ferd Hullihen, Wilda Johnston, Virgie Johnston, Harry McDivitt, unidentified, Amos Tate, Owen Hatch, John McDivitt, and Eunice Lines; (fourth row) unidentified. Bower was located in Greenwood Township, along the river. Once it was a busy town with a sawmill, which floated lumber down the river to market. (Courtesy Jim Bennett.)

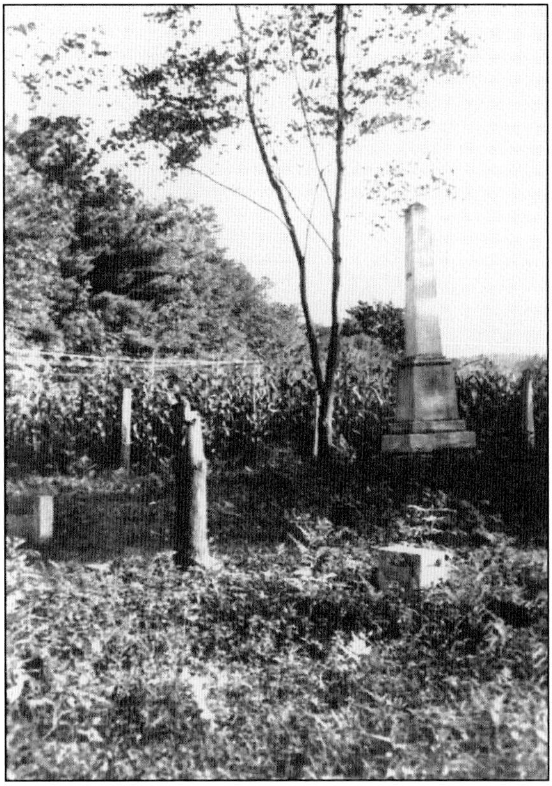

Another victim of the plans for the Curwensville Dam was the Bower cemetery. Most of its 97 residents went to the Mahaffey Cemetery or the Friends Cemetery in Grampian. Others were moved to the Watts Cemetery in Kermoor or to Lumber City. This site was approximately 15 miles upstream of the proposed dam site. Also relocated was the Ferguson Cemetery in Lumber City. (Courtesy Jim Bennett.)

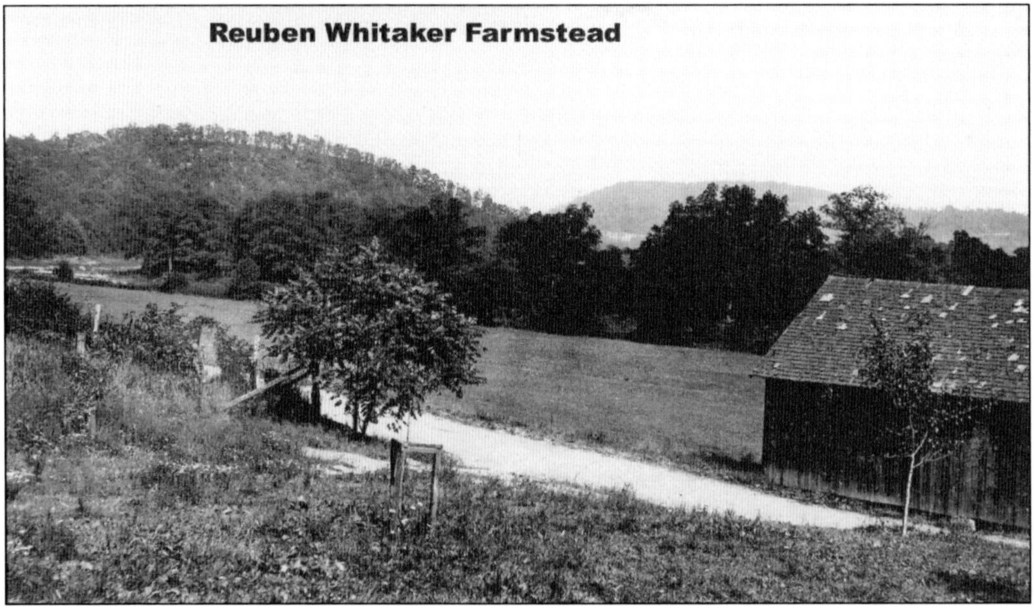

This c. 1917 photograph shows the Reuben Whitaker Farmstead in Lumber City, which was lost when the Curwensville Dam was built. Currently this area is underwater, with only the hill on the left still visible. Originally the river ran in the space between these hills. The dam's construction began in March 1963, and in November 1965, it began operating. The cost of the project was $19 million. (Courtesy Aletta Singley.)

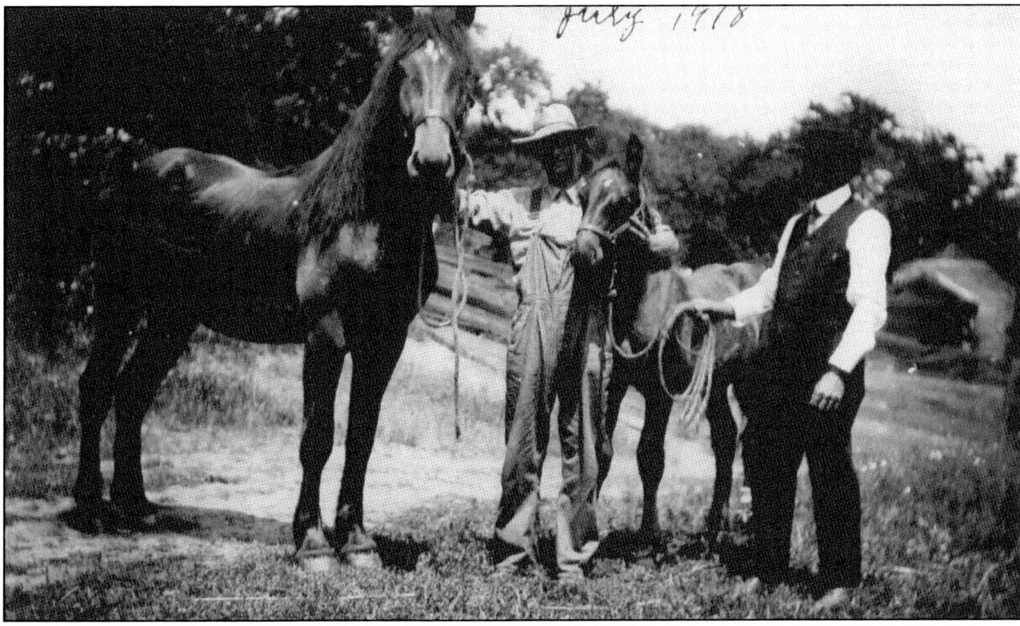

Joe Walker (on the left) and Reuben Whitaker pose with horses on the Whitaker Farm in July 1918. The horses were from racing stock and were capable of great speed. Whitaker raised hay to sell to the mines where it was fed to the mules. He also worked at the brickyard. (Courtesy Aletta Singley.)

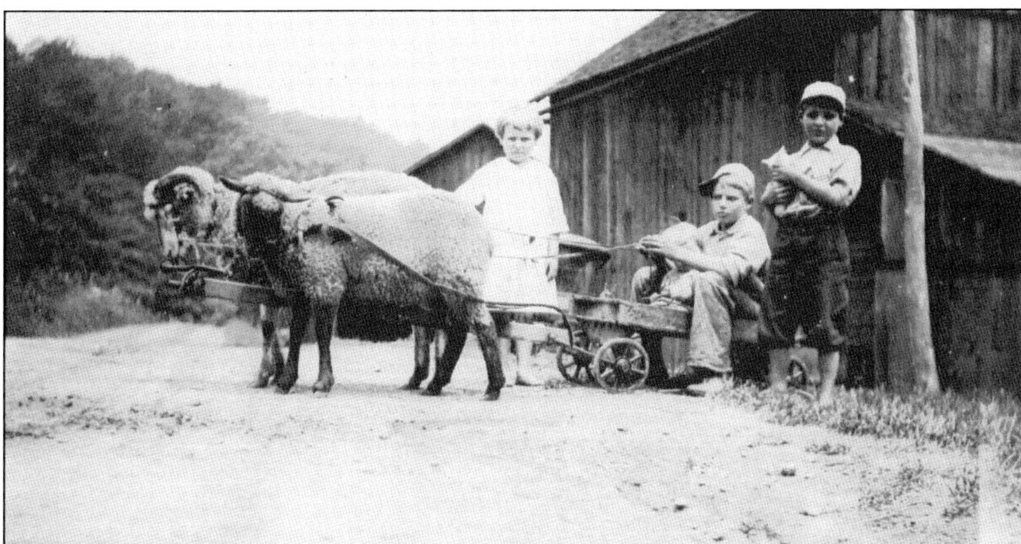

The Whitaker children play by harnessing sheep to a wagon on their farm in Lumber City around 1910. They are, from left to right, Zetta, Oralee (who is being held in the wagon), and Clair, while Fred stands by holding a kitten. The farm also had geese and horses. (Courtesy Aletta Singley.)

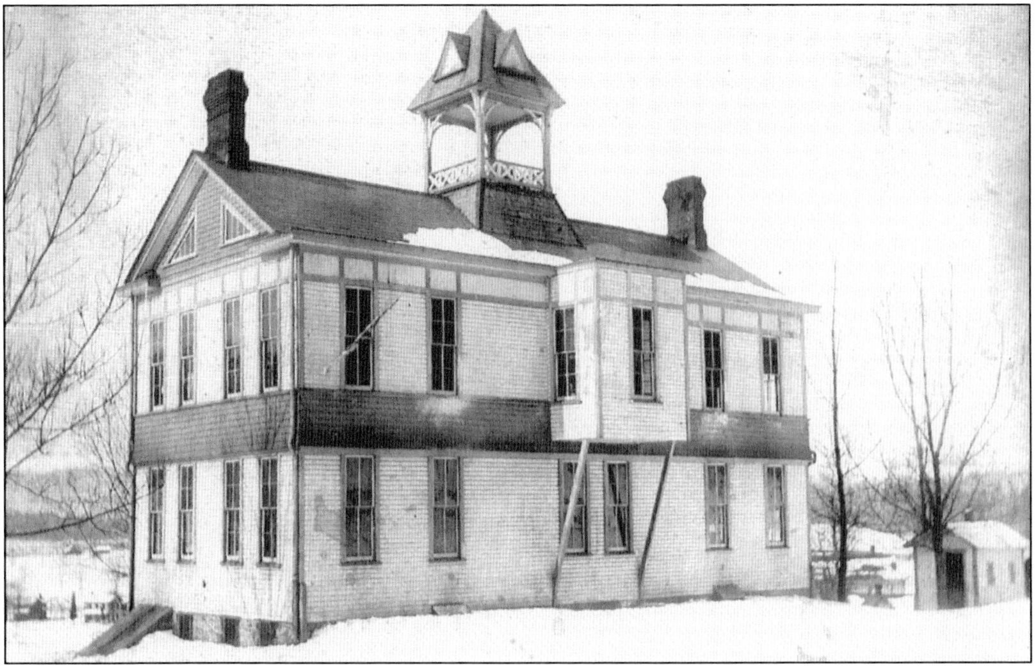

This back view shows the Mahaffey School, which was constructed around 1889. It was located along what is now State Route 36. It "had four rooms and was furnished with the latest improved desks and apparatus," according to a report from 1895. The school employed four teachers, a principal, and additional instructors. In 1917, it was replaced by new school. (Courtesy Clearfield County Historical Society.)

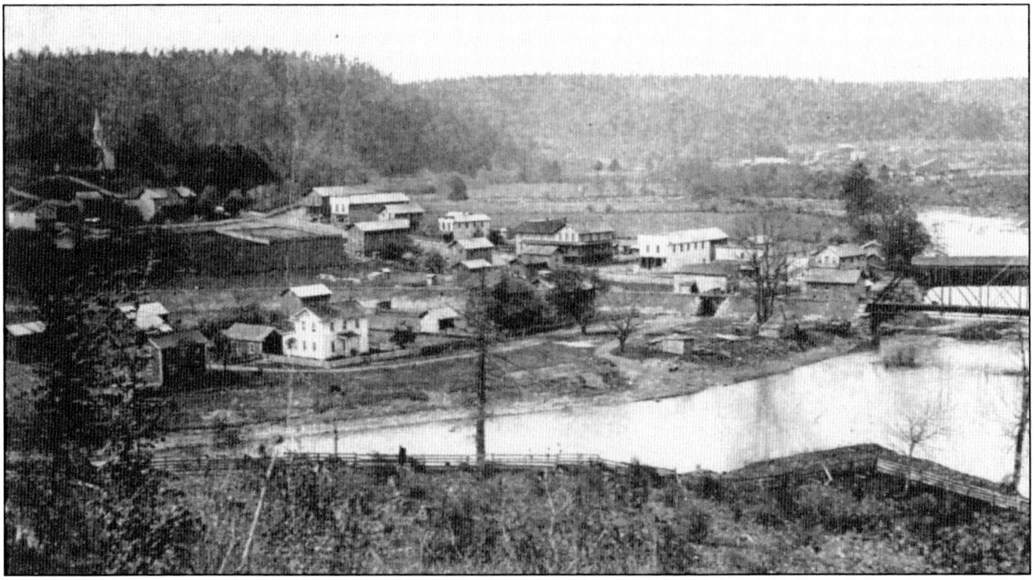

This photograph, thought to be the oldest of Mahaffey, shows the confluence of Chest Creek and the West Branch of the Susquehanna River. Also visible is the covered bridge, the railroad bridge (removed in 1984), and the Mahaffey House hotel (center), as well as on the far left, the Methodist Protestant Church, which burned down in 1984. This portion of town was once known as Franklin. (Courtesy Clearfield County Historical Society.)

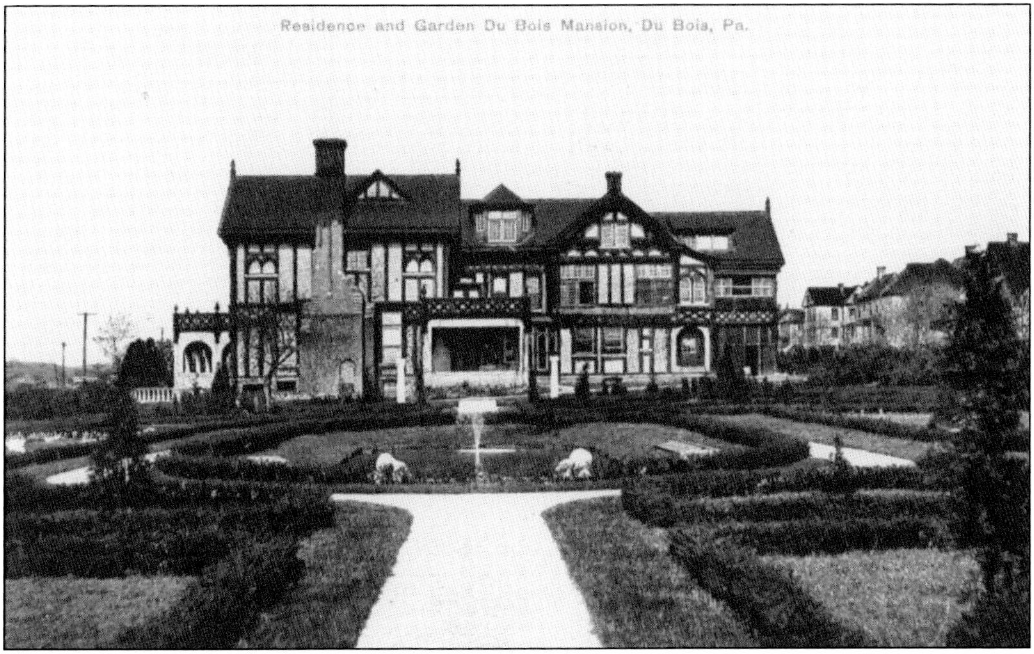

The DuBois Mansion and its beautiful gardens are portrayed on this postcard from 1909. The mansion, built around 1876, was remodeled by John E. DuBois and his wife, Willie. The mansion hosted many important events and dances in its ballroom. DuBois was the nephew of John DuBois, the founder of the town. (Courtesy Clearfield County Historical Society.)

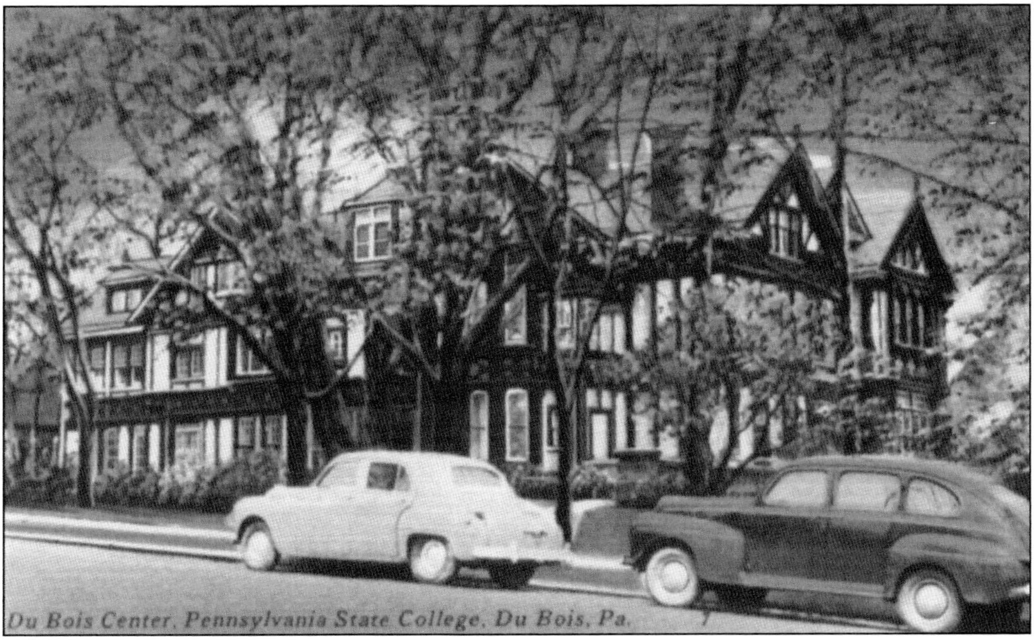

The DuBois family donated the mansion and four acres of land to the DuBois Board of Education, which was used for the DuBois Center in 1938. In 1958, the school became the DuBois Campus of the Pennsylvania State University. Unfortunately, this historic building was torn down in 1979. It was replaced by the Smeal Building. (Courtesy Clearfield County Historical Society.)

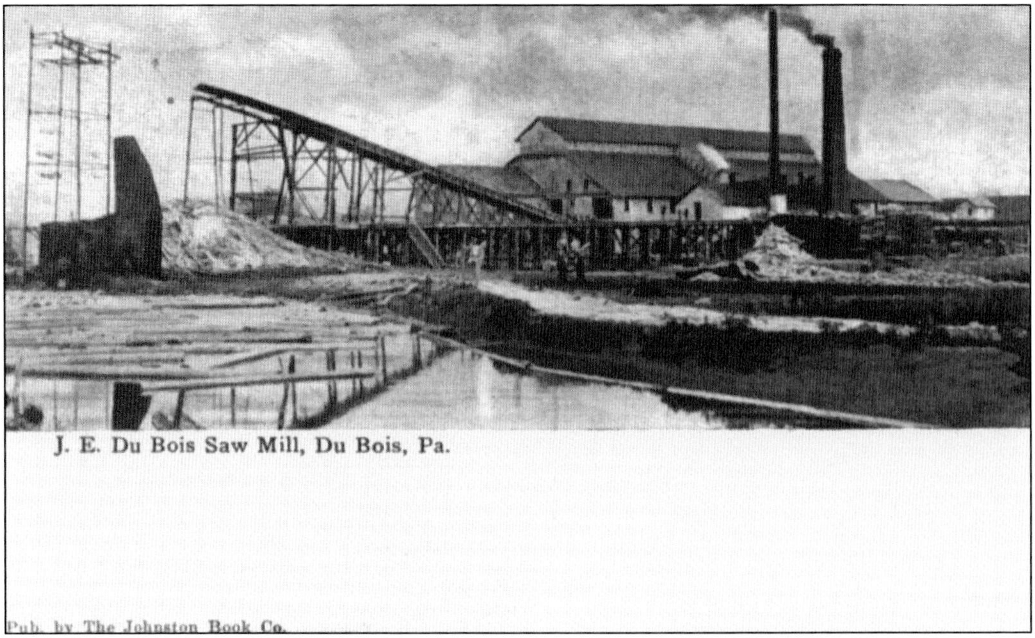

When the DuBois family came to the area they started a lumber business. This *c.* 1911 postcard shows the John E. DuBois sawmill, which was located in Beaver Meadows, near the old channel line of Sandy Lick Creek. Built in 1874, it was able to produce 120,000 board feet, 60,000 shingles, 40,000 lath, and 10,000 pickets a day. (Courtesy Clearfield County Historical Society.)

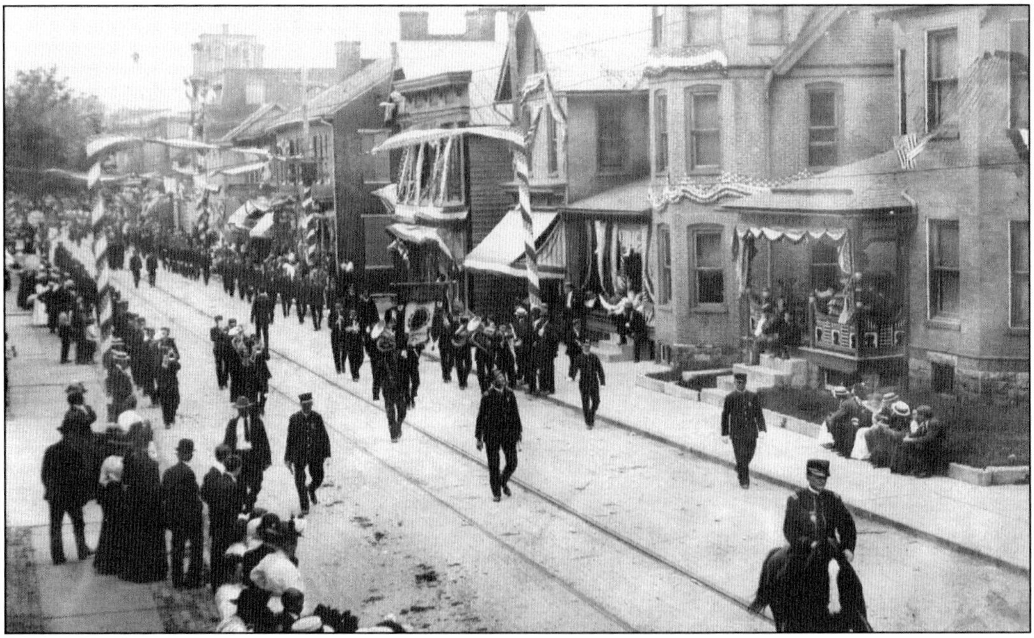

This DuBois parade moves down South Brady Street between East Long Avenue and East Washington Street around 1910. In 1888, a major part of the town was destroyed by a fire. A request for funds to rebuild was rejected by a Philadelphia committee. Local businessmen, including John DuBois, funded the rebuilding themselves. (Courtesy Clearfield County Historical Society.)

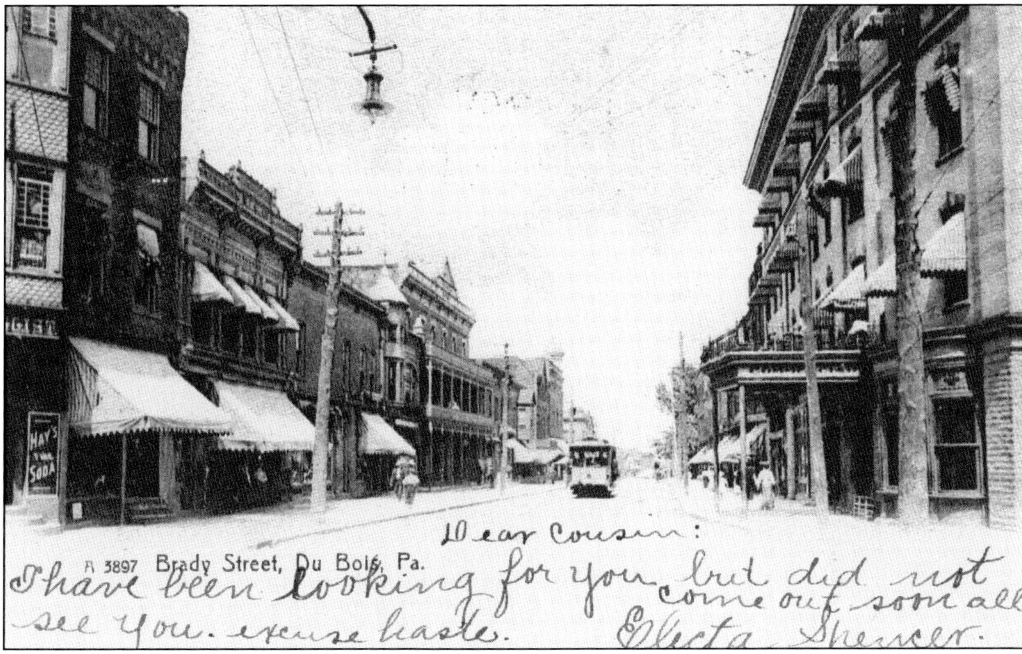

A trolley car moves down Brady Street in this postcard from 1906. DuBois had trolley cars from 1891 up until the 1920s. On the right is the Commercial Hotel, which was built in the 1890s and later became the General Pershing Hotel. It was owned by E. S. Shuck, who also owned the Dimeling Hotel in Clearfield. (Courtesy Clearfield County Historical Society.)

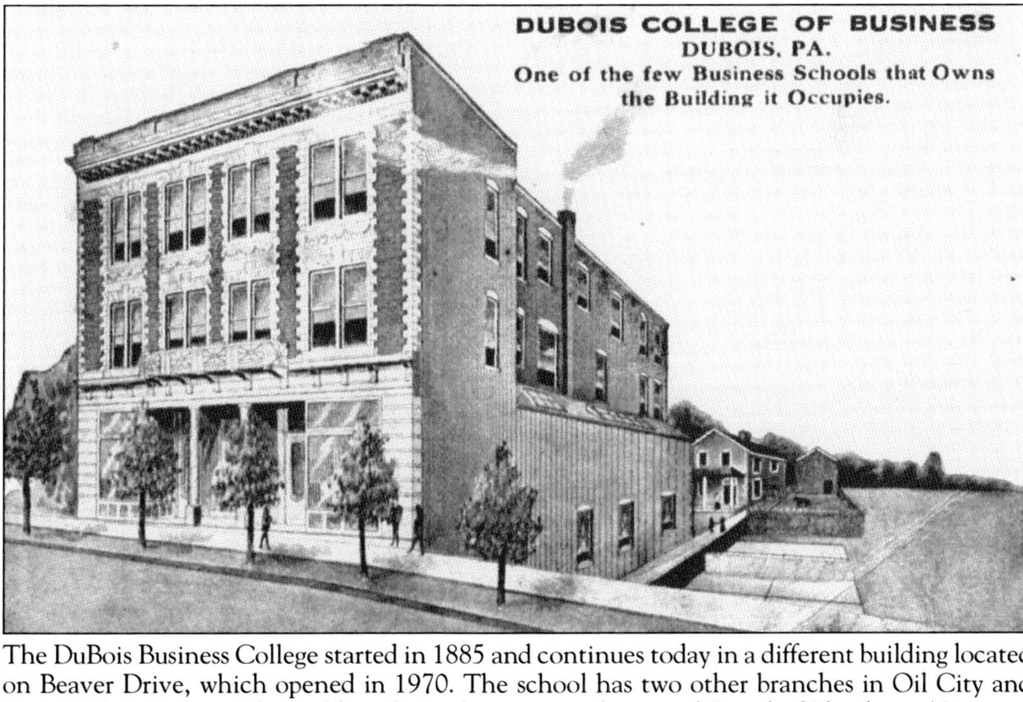

The DuBois Business College started in 1885 and continues today in a different building located on Beaver Drive, which opened in 1970. The school has two other branches in Oil City and Huntingdon County. The building shown here is now the site of Overdorf Plumbing. (Courtesy Clearfield County Historical Society.)

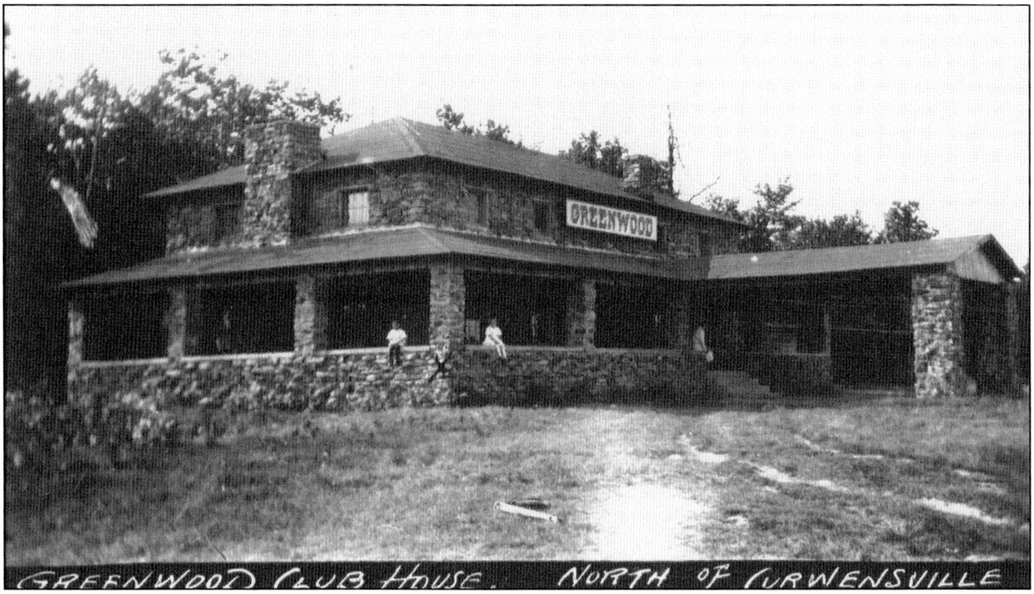

Greenwood Club House, shown here around 1923, features "Billy and Betty" sitting on the railing. The camp was established in 1921 after a group of businessmen from Curwensville purchased 100 acres and built this two-story building from the stone fences of the former Bloom farm. There was a United States weather station here in the 1930s. (Curwensville Pike Township Historical Society.)

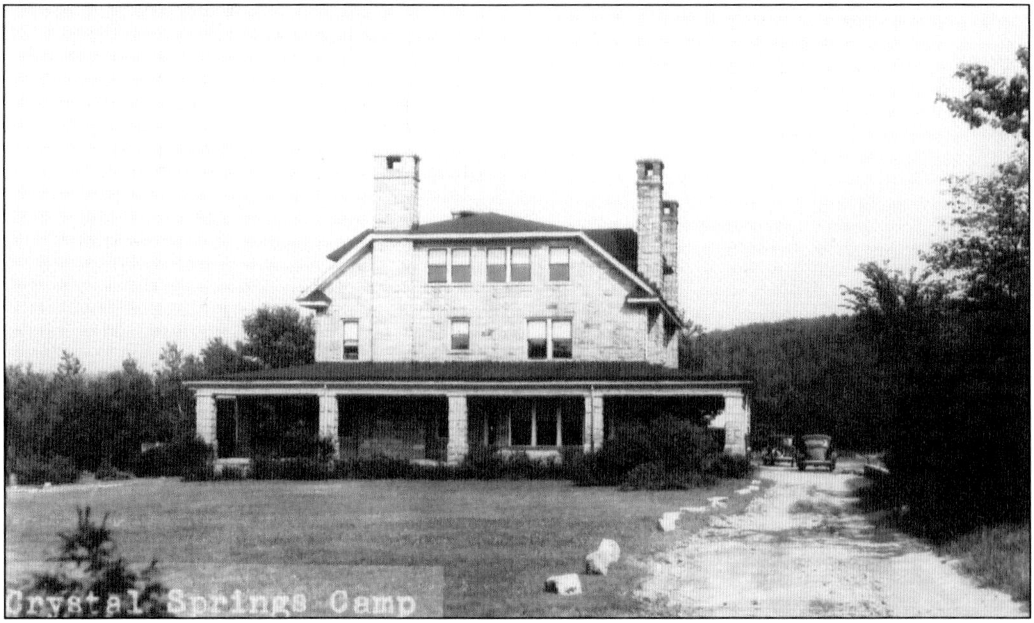

The Crystal Springs Camp, which was located on Penfield Mountain, was built by the Crystal Springs Rod and Gun Club in 1921. The structure was made of stone taken from the scene and the masonry work completed by stoneworkers from the Curwensville quarries. The building had three stone fireplaces, with living quarters on the second floor. It burned in 1974. (Courtesy Clearfield County Historical Society.)

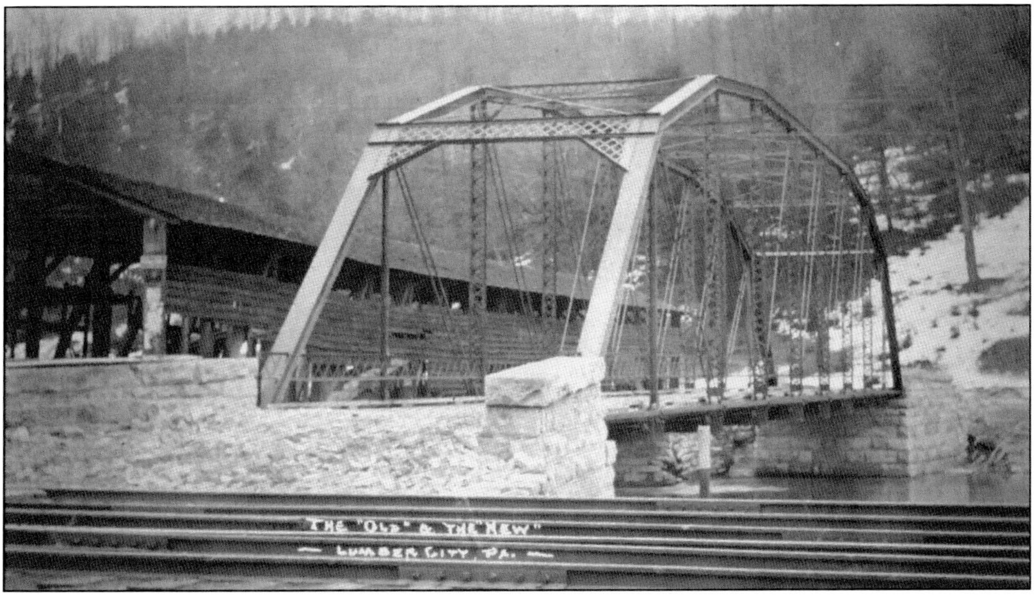

An old covered bridge sits next to its replacement at Lumber City on this c. 1902 postcard. At one point covered bridges were a normal site in the area, but in 2007, only one remains in the county at McGees Mills. Much of Lumber City was moved in the 1960s to make way for the Curwensville Dam. (Courtesy Curwensville-Pike Township Historical Society.)

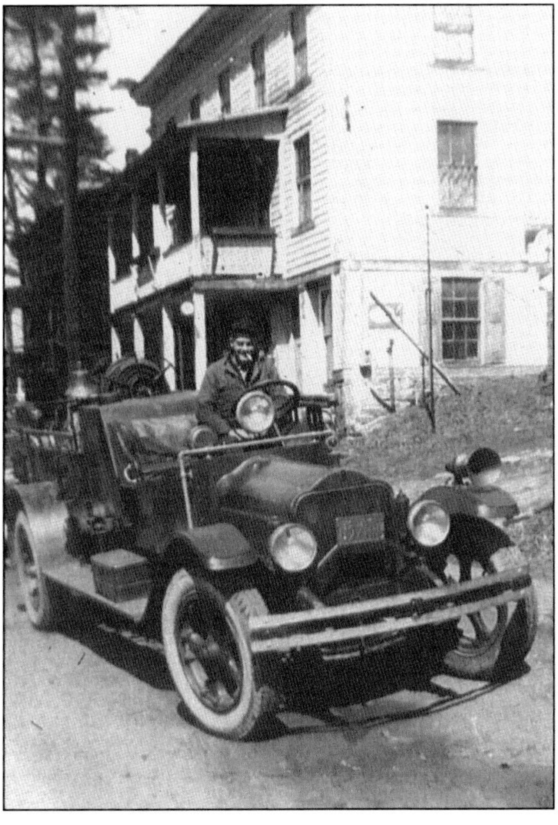

A man sits in Lumber City's LaFrance fire truck in this photograph from 1949. American LaFrance has been making fire equipment since 1832. Behind him is the local general store, which carried almost everything the residents needed. It was run by Goldie and Millard Wall. (Courtesy Lenore McDonald.)

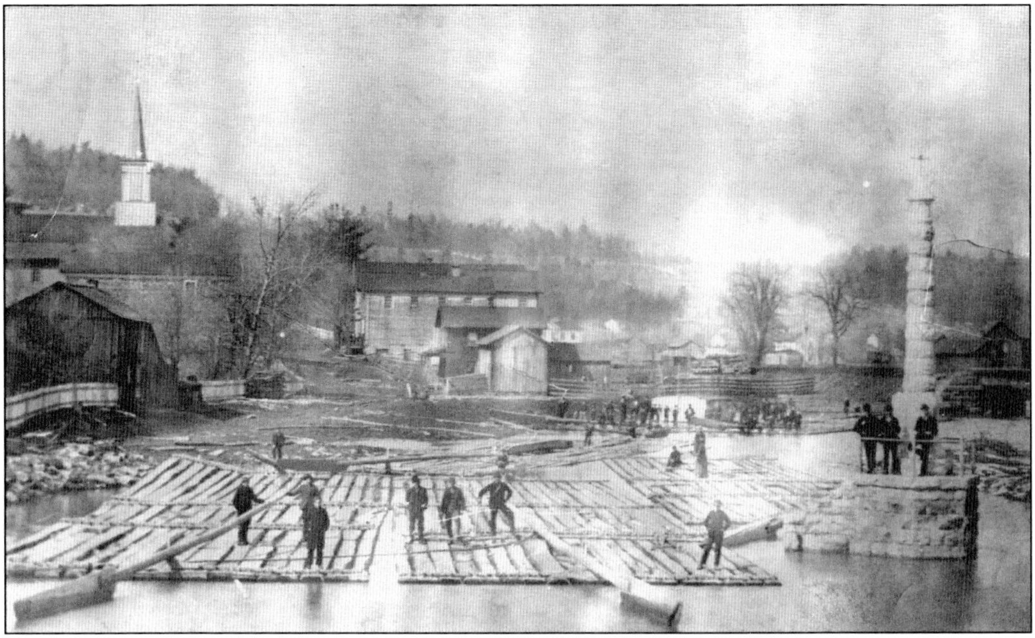

Men prepare a raft for a trip down the river at Cherry Tree. The monument (right), taking the place of the original cherry tree, marks the corner of the purchase of land William Penn made from the Iroquois in 1768. It also marks the corner of three counties, Clearfield, Indiana, and Cambria. Today the river runs on the other side of the monument. (Courtesy Clearfield County Historical Society.)

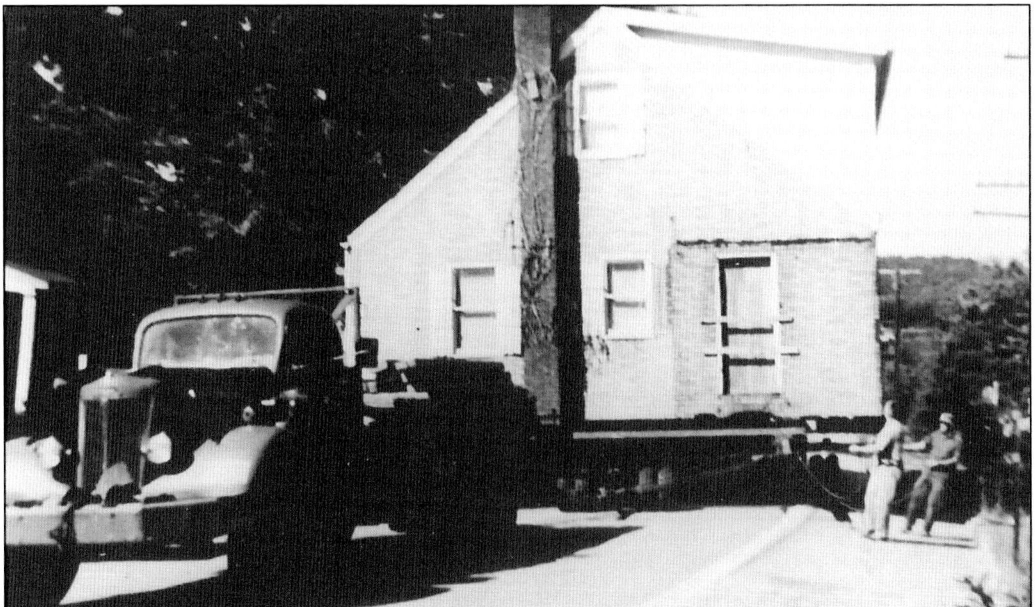

In 1962, the home of Eliza Johnston was moved to another part of Curry Run to make way for the new Curwensville Dam, which was authorized in the flood control act in 1954. Three homes were moved, and others in the flood plane were torn down. The dam was built in the mid-1960s. (Courtesy Jim Bennett.)

Six

DISASTERS

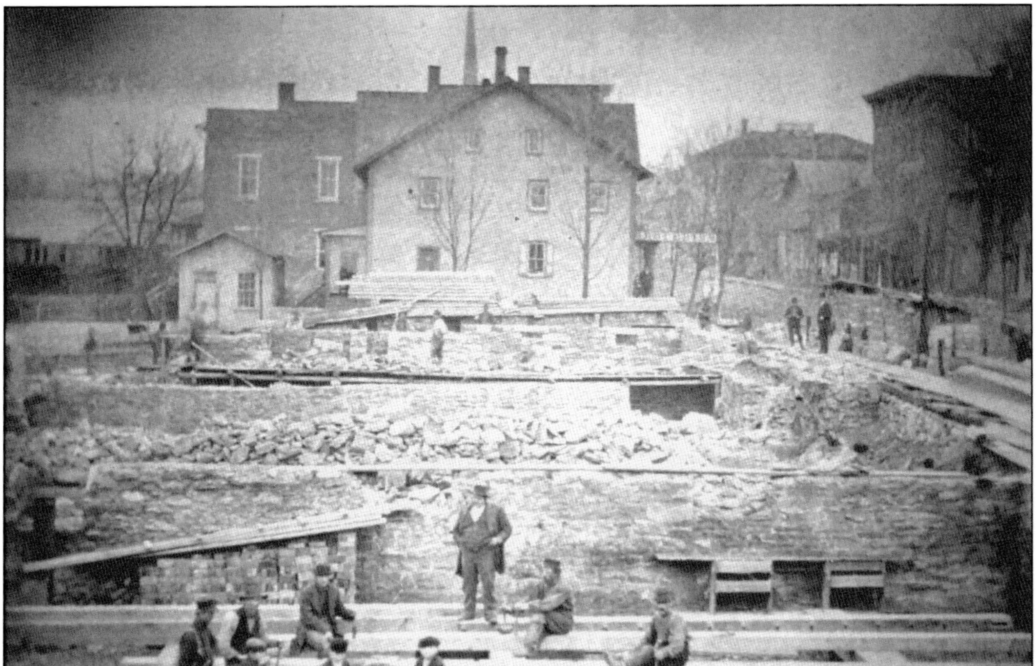

In October 1879, a tragic fire made headlines in Curwensville. It destroyed the Patton block at State and Thompson Streets, including the Curwensville Bank and the public library. The buildings were rebuilt shortly after and still stand today with businesses Kathy's School of Dance, a beauty shop, and a variety store. (Courtesy Curwensville-Pike Township Historical Society.)

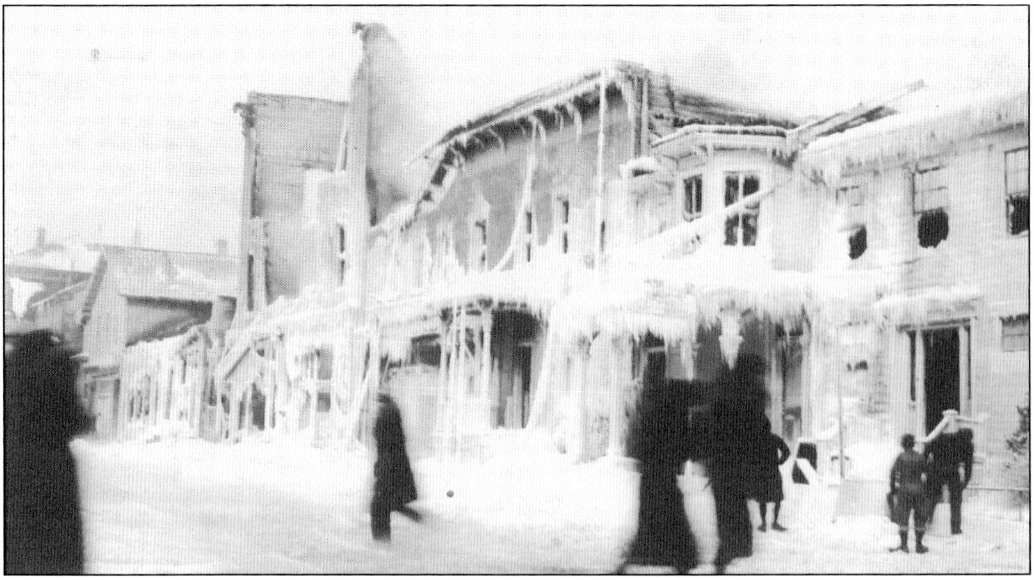

On January 25, 1936, another terrible fire struck Curwensville, completely destroying the Fullerton block. Among those lost were the Edmiston Store, Curwensville Herald office, Norris Barber Shop, A&P store, and Fred P. Robison's print shop and home. The fire started when a kerosene heater in the barbershop exploded. Temperatures were near zero or below that night, freezing the water left behind by the firefighting effort. (Courtesy Dan McDonald.)

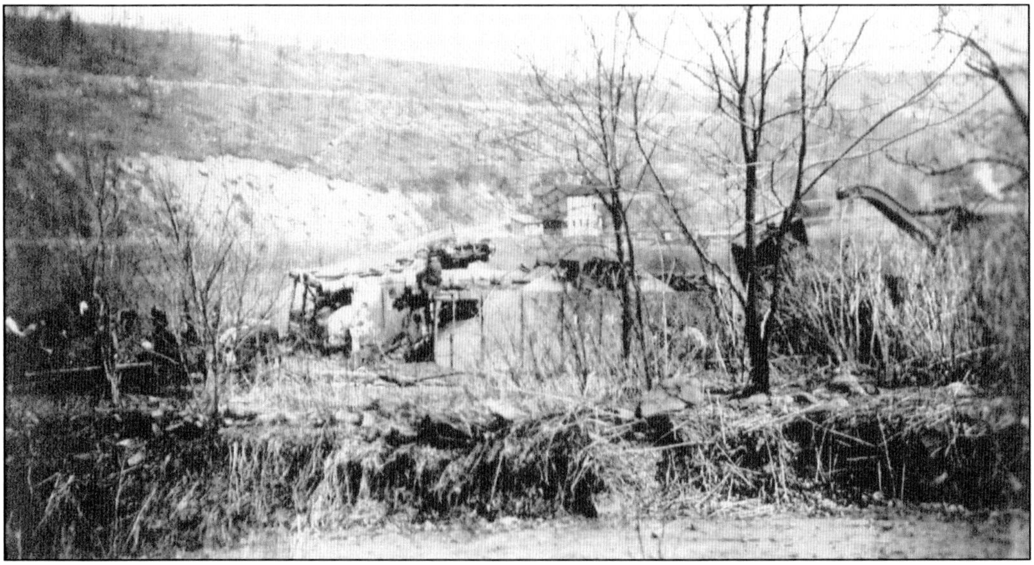

Bridgeport was the site of this train wreck on April 21, 1918. Also visible is the woolen mill in the center, which was run by Joe and Melinda Whitaker, who also took tolls for toll bridge. Bridgeport was given its name because of the large number of bridges in the town. (Courtesy Aletta Singley.)

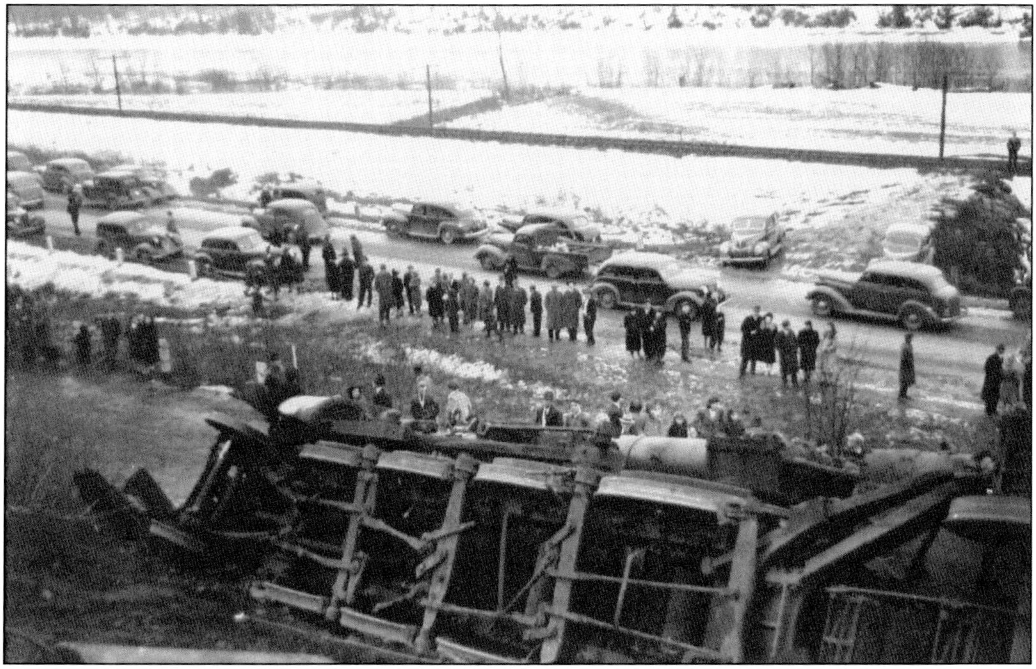

In 1941, at Arnoldtown, just outside Curwensville, this New York Central Railroad train engine slipped off the track and down over the bank toward the road, which is now Route 879. In the above image, curious spectators stop their vehicles in an attempt to view the overturned engine. Below is a view looking from the engine back toward the tracks. The original New York Central Railroad was formed in 1853. In 1869, it became the New York Central and Hudson River Railroad Company before returning to the New York Central Railroad name when it incorporated in 1914. (Courtesy Clearfield County Historical Society.)

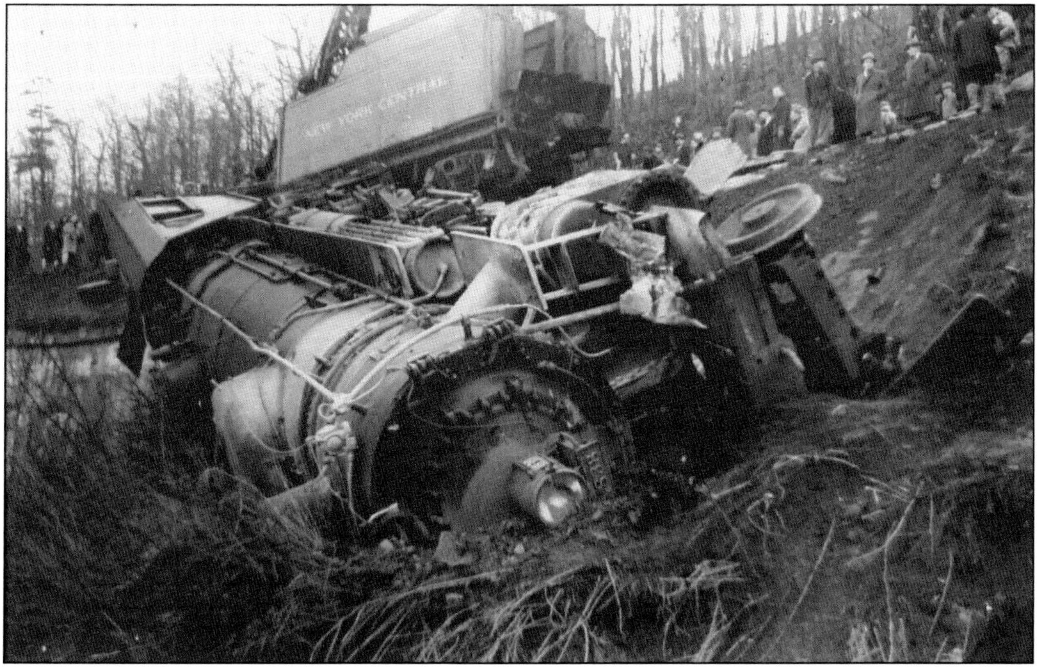

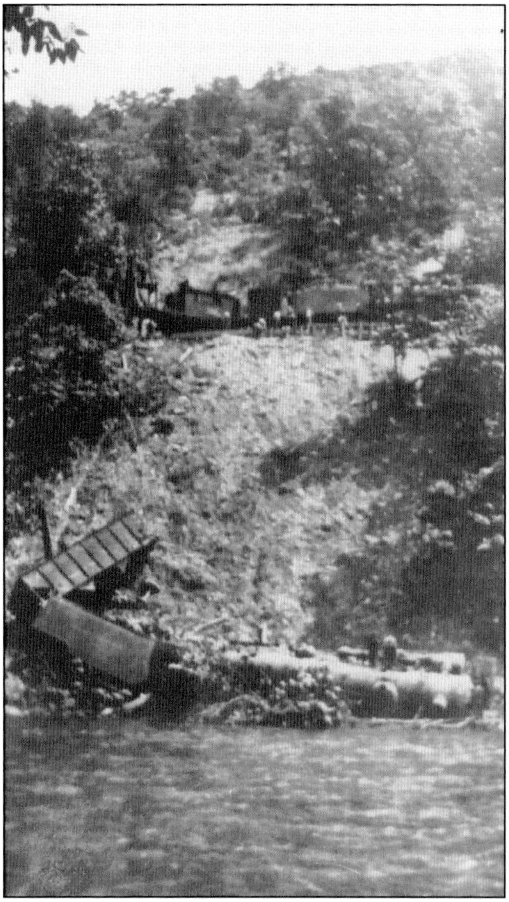

This New York Central Railroad train derailed from the Clearfield Southern Railroad line and fell over 50 feet down an embankment all the way into Clearfield Creek in 1924. The train is visible above, lying in the water as people from the bank above look on. In the image below, railroad workers pose with the wreckage of the engine. The train was traveling across the line that runs between Dimeling and Madera that was added in the early 1900s and derailed not far from the Narrows near Curwensville. The New York Central Railroad leased this railroad line beginning in 1903. (Courtesy Clearfield County Historical Society.)

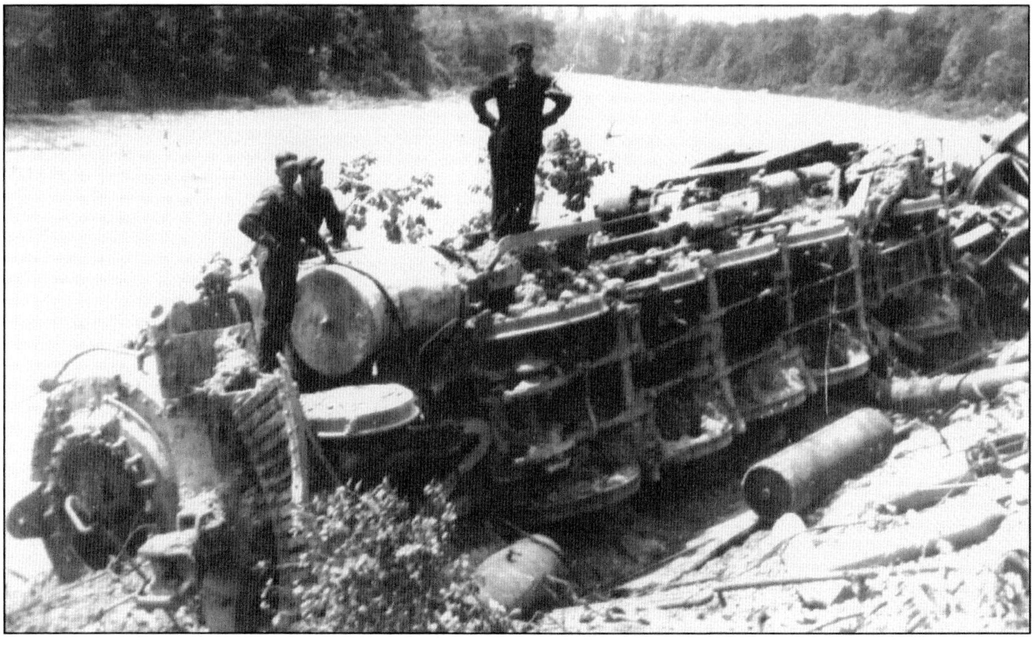

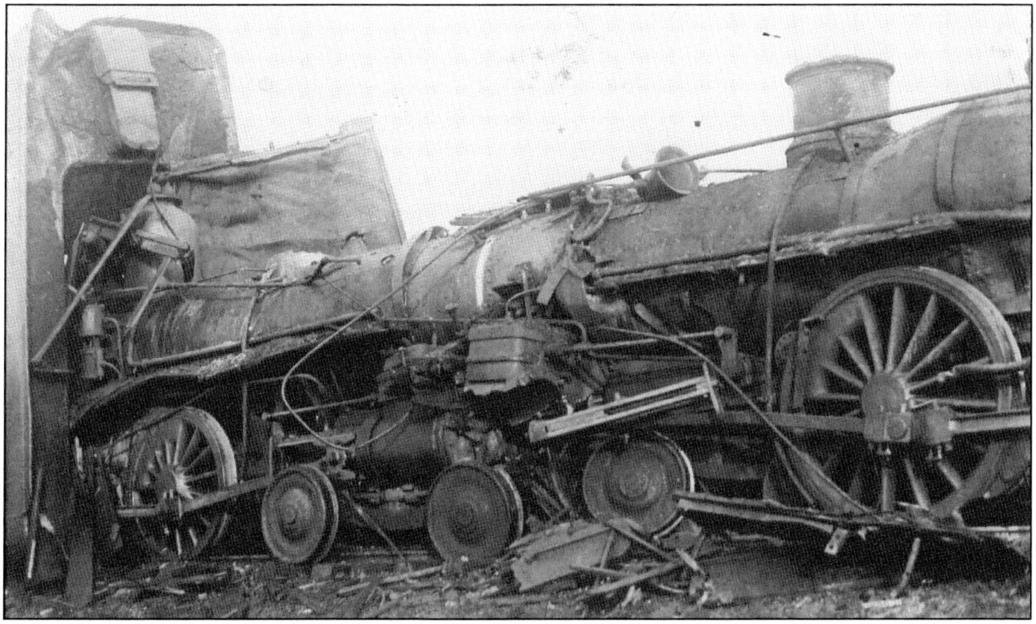

In 1914, the Alley Popper Railroad staged a train wreck for one movie that ended up being stock footage for many other films. The original film was called the *Valley of Lost Hope*. The wreck involved two trains rushing toward each other from a mile apart and crashing with a tremendous roar. (Courtesy Clearfield County Historical Society.)

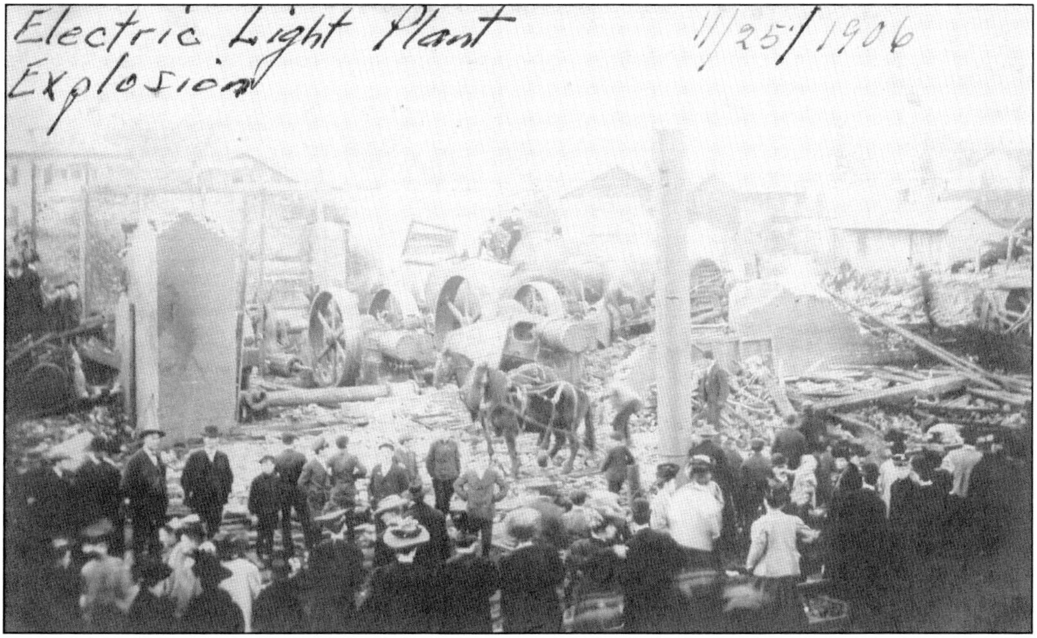

Churchgoers at St. Francis in Clearfield were startled by the sound of an incredibly loud explosion during mass on November 25, 1906. A boiler at the nearby Central Pennsylvania Light and Power Company plant had exploded, destroying the plant and the neighboring Smith's Mill. Smith's Mill later became Michell Milling, which was located on Leavy Avenue. (Courtesy Clearfield County Historical Society.)

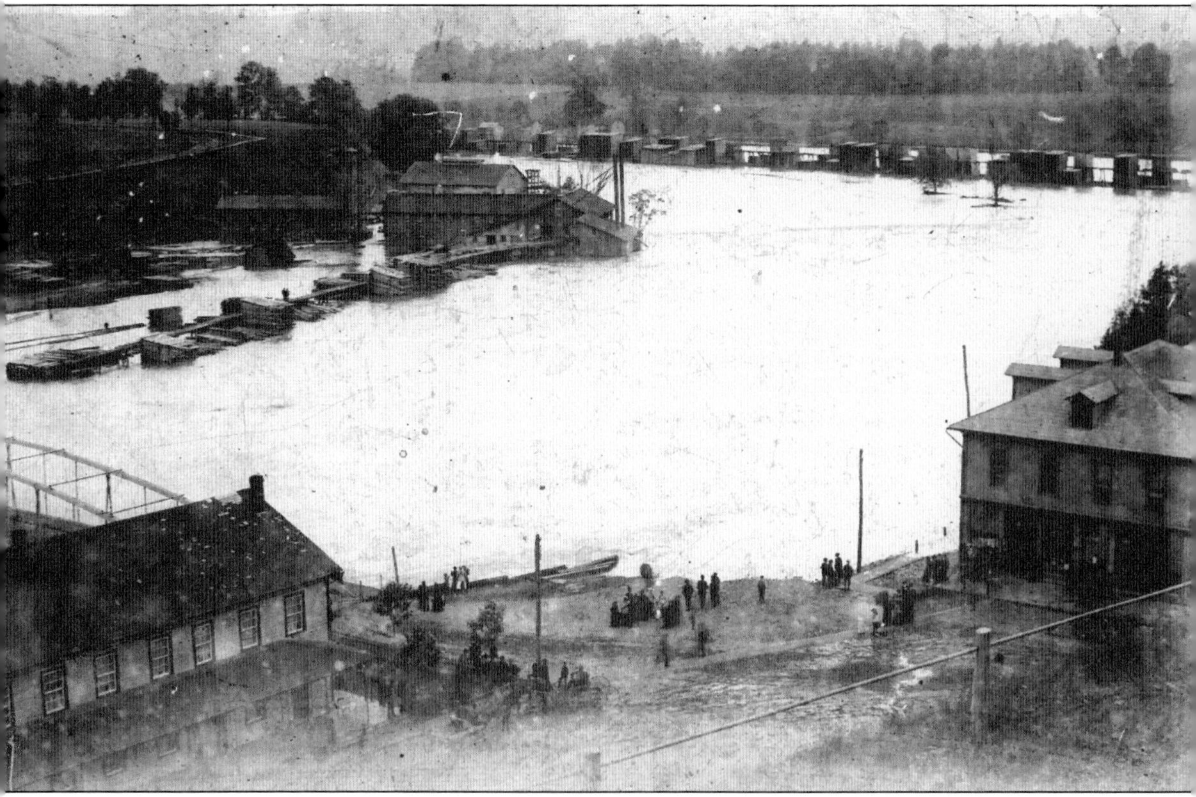

Johnstown was not the only town hit by a flood in May 1889. Curwensville also suffered, as seen in this photograph of the bridge to Irvin Hill, the Susquehanna House (left), and the corner store (right). The lumber mill across the west branch of the Susquehanna River is covered with water as the townspeople look on. Most business was suspended for the day. A dam at Arnold's Mill in Bridgeport gave way, allowing all types of debris, including logs, pigpens, outhouses, and fences, to travel down the river. This collection of wreckage hit the Walnut Street Bridge, took it out, and then crashed into the Filbert Street Bridge, which also was damaged. The debris continued until it struck the railroad bridge to the Big Mill. The railroad bridge held, saving both the covered bridge and the iron bridge above. The damage was estimated at $75,000. (Courtesy Curwensville-Pike Township Historical Society.)

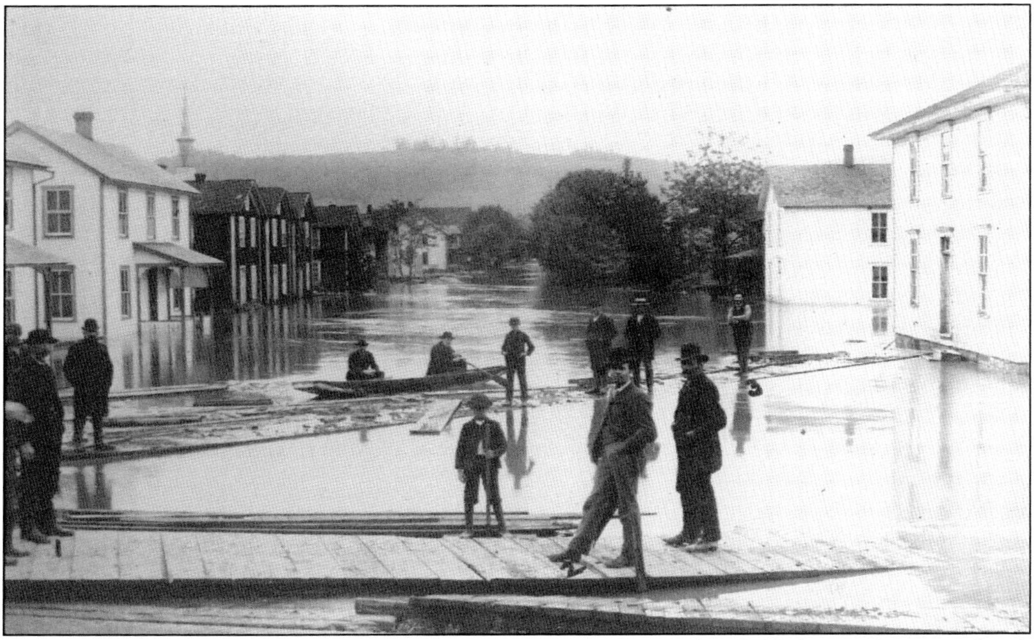

Water fills Cherry Street looking west from Fourth Street in Clearfield during the 1889 flood. George Gulich (marked No. 1) is on the far left, Clark Tate (No. 2) is standing near center, with one leg in front of the other, and the man furthest on the right behind the others is Charles Halford (No. 3). The other men and the boy are not identified. (Courtesy Clearfield County Historical Society.)

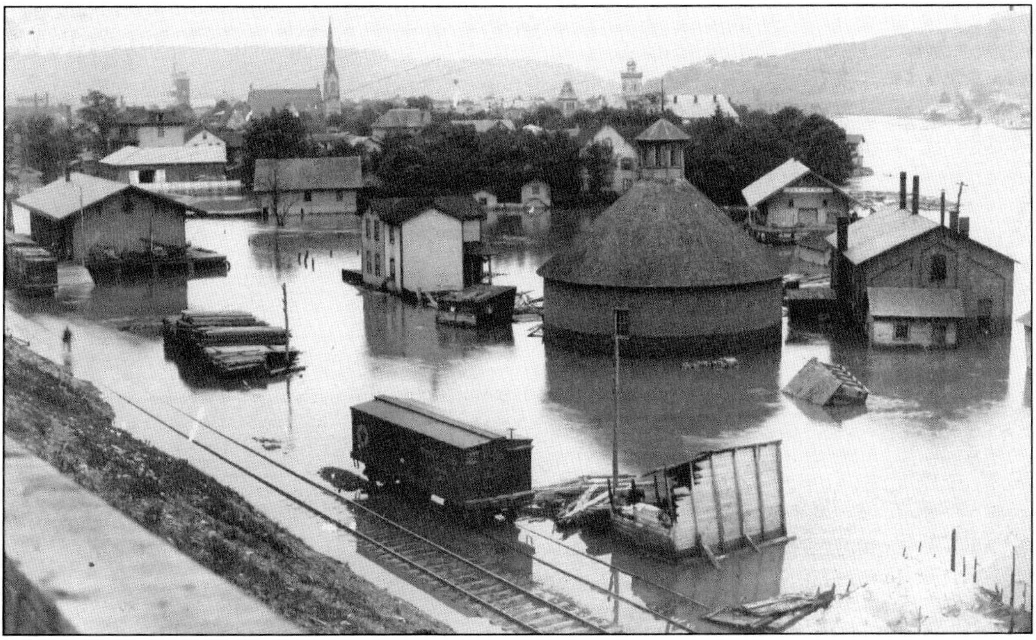

This view of Clearfield during the 1889 flood shows the area at the bottom of the hill where CVS Pharmacy is now located. On the far left is the Pennsylvania Railroad station, a grocery store building that was last used as Charles Heating Center, and the round building is the gasworks. (Courtesy Clearfield County Historical Society.)

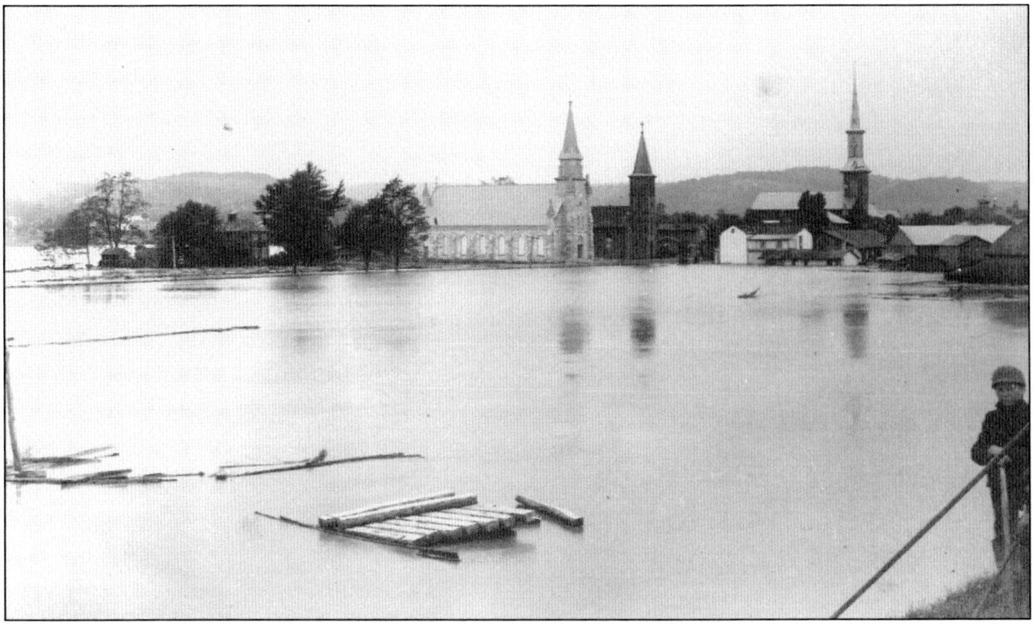

During the 1889 flood, Clearfield had two St. Francis churches. The "new" and current building is the first church on the left, with the old one next to it. The Trinity United Methodist Church is the one with the tallest steeple on the right. The new church was damaged by the floodwaters just months before it was dedicated on September 22, 1889. (Courtesy Clearfield County Historical Society.)

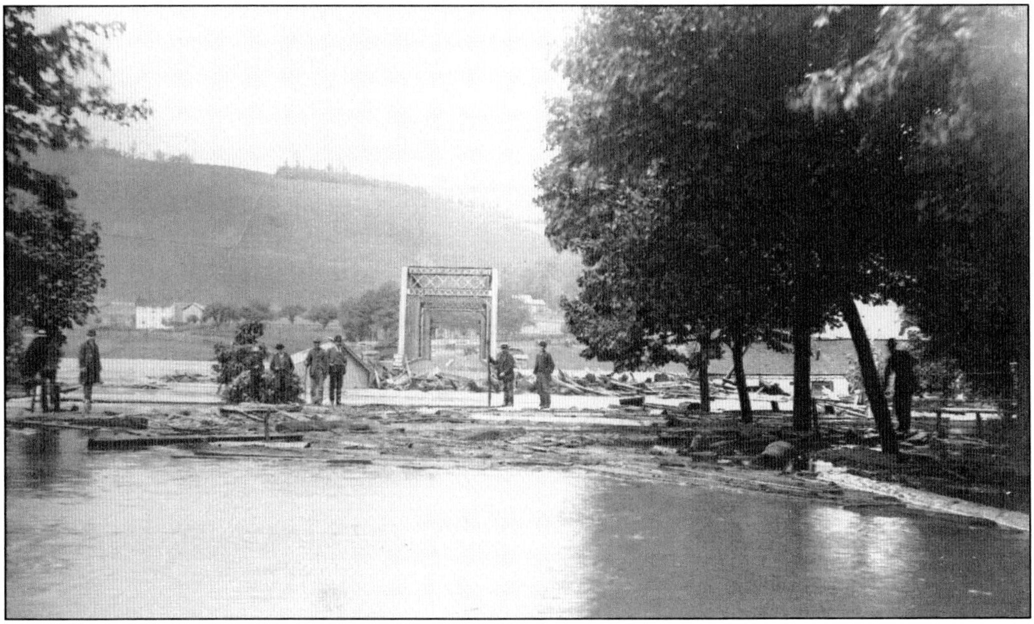

The Market Street Bridge in Clearfield is the only familiar sight in this photograph from May 1889. The river rose almost to the plank floor of the bridge, which is 24 feet above the low watermark. The flood was caused by over 33 hours of rain. When the water receded, all sorts of debris, including wood, shingles, and railroad ties, were visible. (Courtesy Clearfield County Historical Society.)

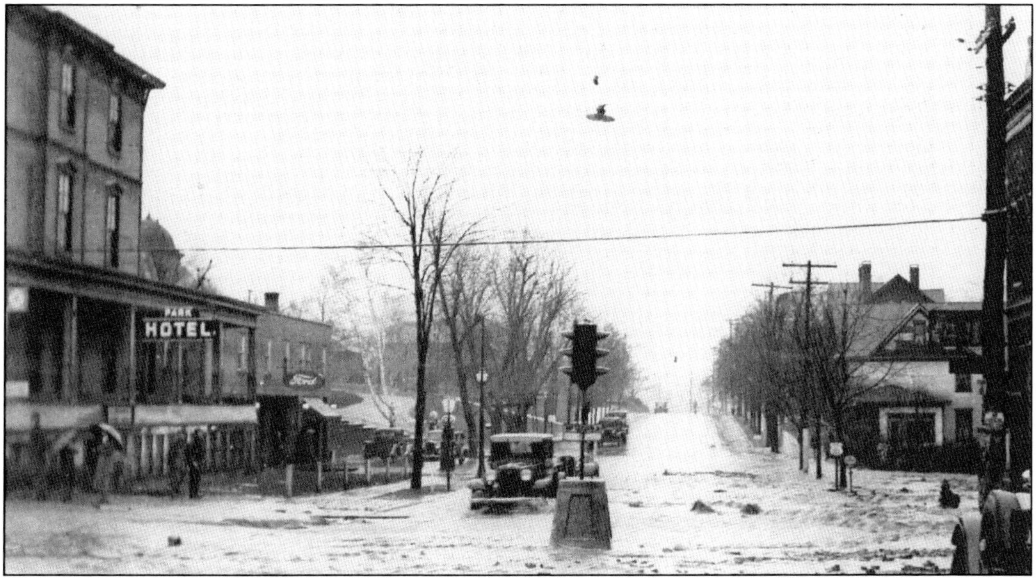

Water rushes through the streets of Curwensville on March 17, 1936, during what became known as the St. Patrick's Day flood. The Park Hotel and a Ford dealer are on the left. Note the traffic light in the middle of the intersection of State and Filbert Streets. (Courtesy Curwensville-Pike Township Historical Society.)

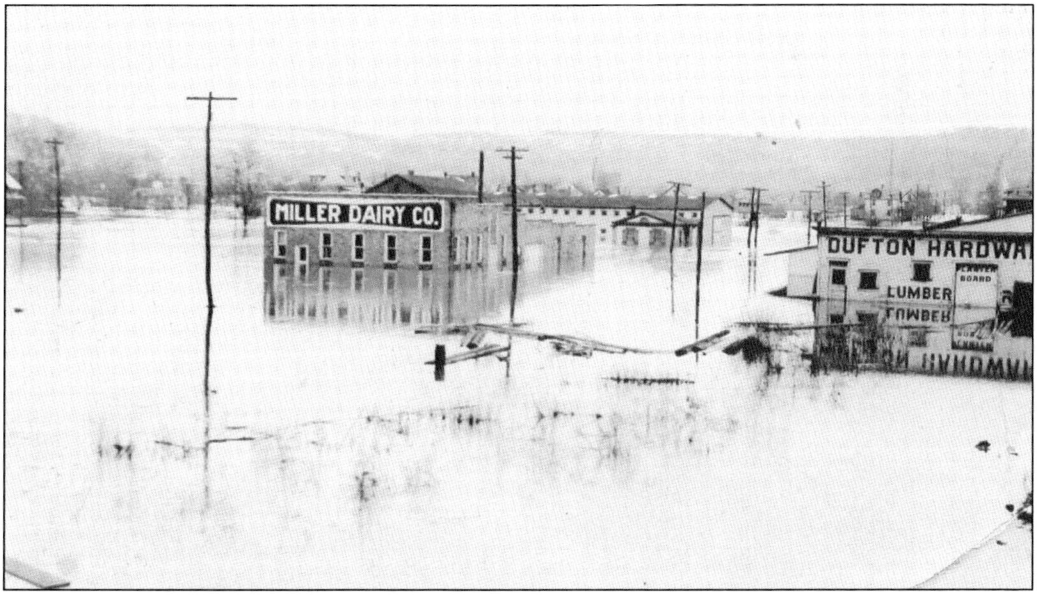

Miller Dairy and Dufton Hardware's lumberyard on West Second Avenue in Clearfield are surrounded by water in this photograph taken during the 1936 flood. Clearfield's floodwaters in 1936 were 18 inches higher than the ones in 1889. Miller Dairy was operated by Charles Mapes and his sister Gussie Bailey. The company was sold to Sanitary Dairy in 1975. The Dufton Hardware building is now home to Agway. (Courtesy Clearfield County Historical Society.)

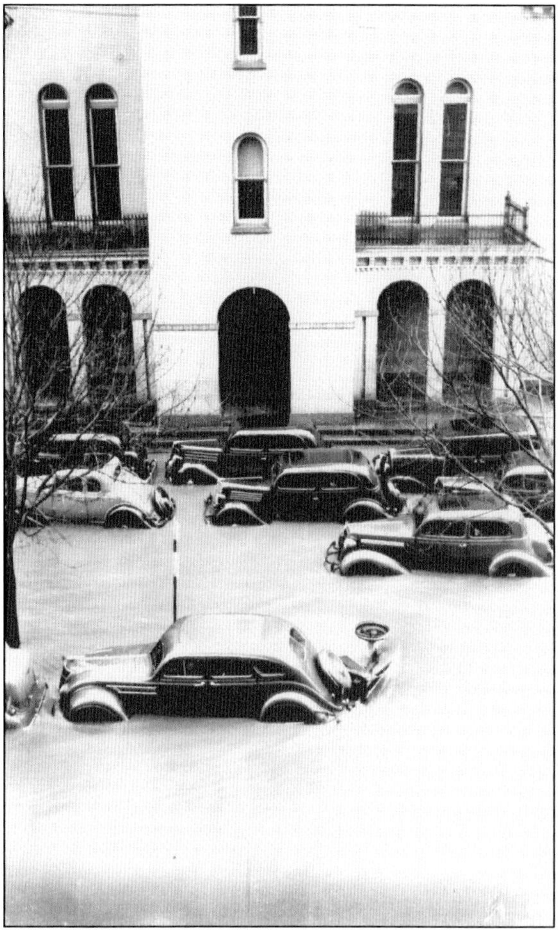

The view from the Dimeling Hotel in Clearfield on March 17, 1936, was not a pretty one. The above cars are stranded on Second Street in front of the Clearfield County Courthouse. The view below of Second Street looking toward the Presbyterian church is no better. Many of those stranded downtown by the flood found refuge in the Dimeling Hotel, the courthouse, and the YMCA, which is the dark building on the right. The Dimeling's owner, E. S. Shuck, used every available bed, cot, and crib. Because the furnace was flooded, a roaring fire was kept going in the lobby fireplace. Also the big coal ranges in the kitchen were kept busy supplying hot meals. At its peak, the water was within inches of the lobby floor. (Courtesy E. S. Shuck Estate.)

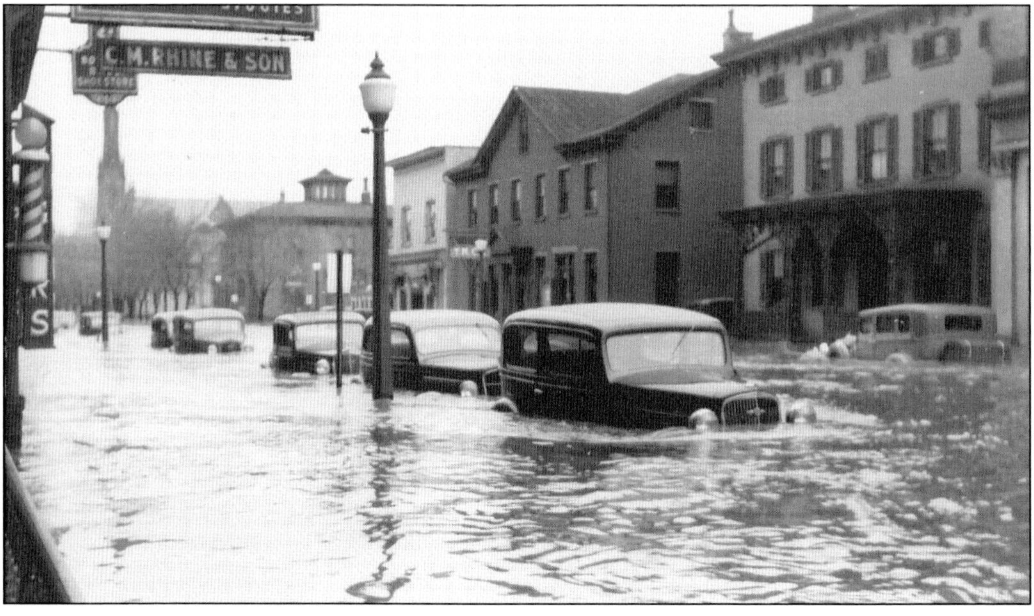

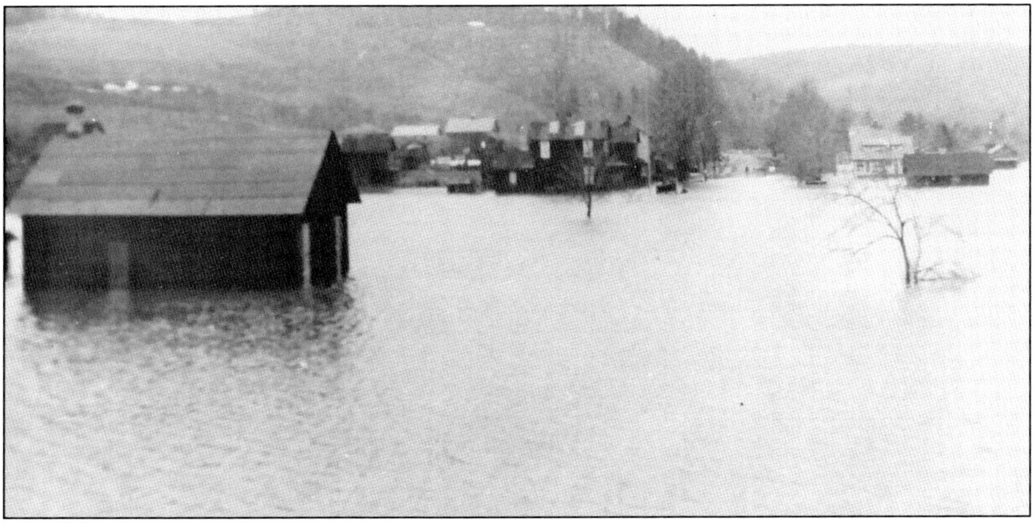

Parts of Bells Landing were subject to floods, and 1936 was no exception. This view, looking toward town, was taken from the railroad trestle. As part of the Curwensville Dam flood control project, the government purchased several homes here. When the dam was built in the 1960s, the days of devastating area floods ended. The dam more than paid for itself when Hurricane Agnes hit Pennsylvania in 1972. (Courtesy Jim Bennett.)

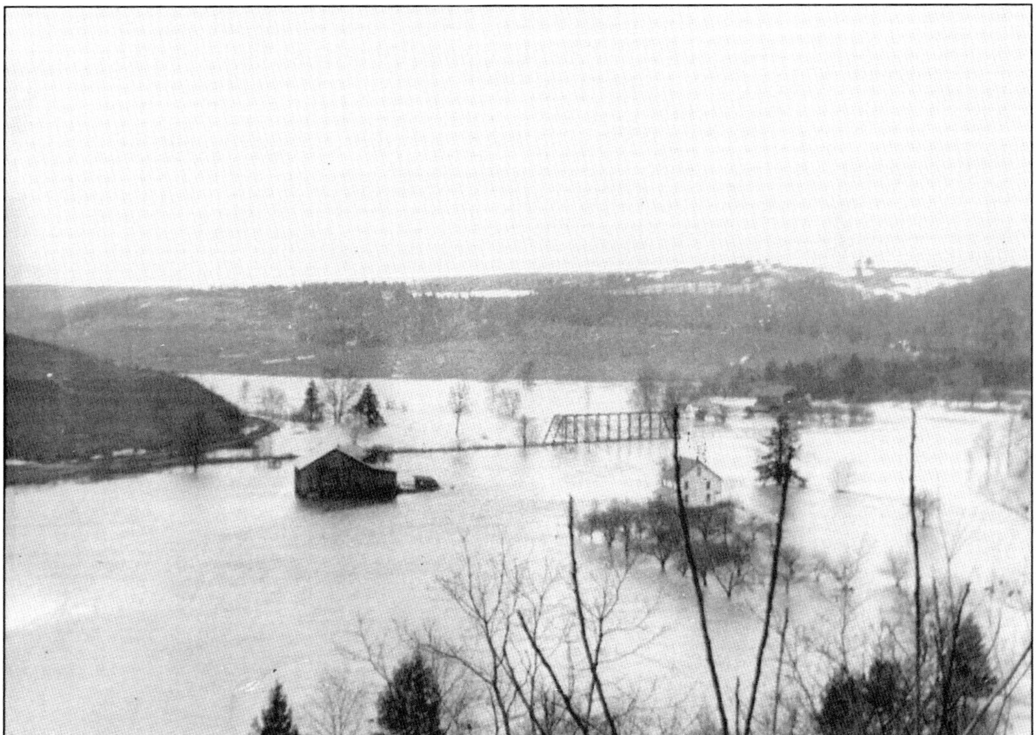

Curry Run was also damaged in the 1936 flood. Here the logging railroad bridge barely rises above the water and the barn of the Nolan Farm is visible near the center. During the flood, the family moved the cows to the upper part of the barn, which is where they stayed until the water receded. (Courtesy Jim Bennett.)

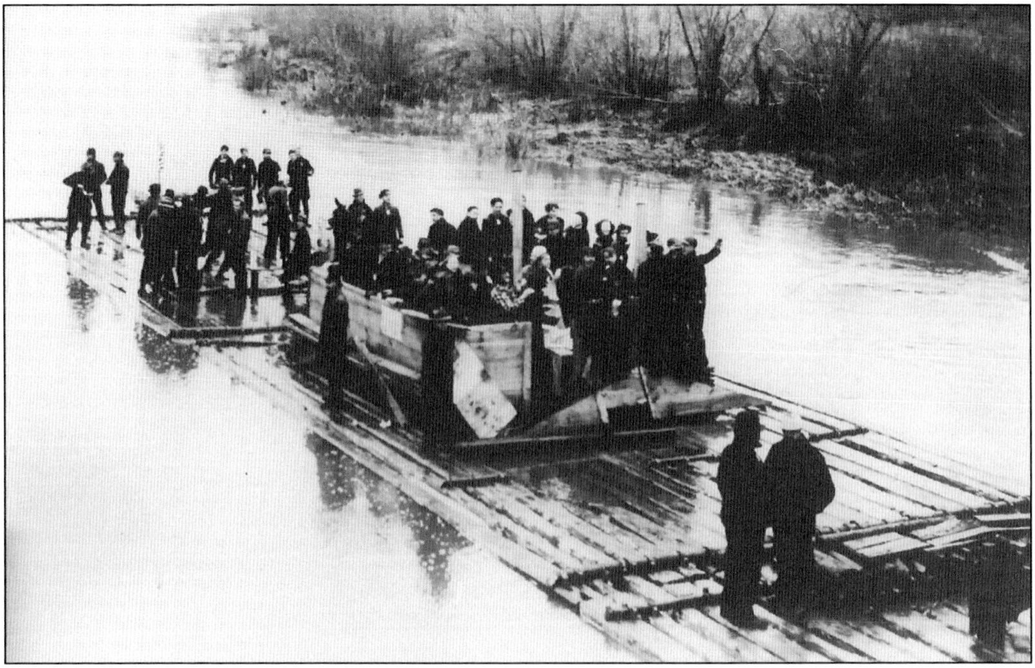

In 1938, a raft was built to honor the rafters, and it embarked on a journey from McGees Mills to Harrisburg. Above, the "last raft" is traveling around a curve at Curry Run. When it reached Muncy, it crashed into a railroad bridge and seven people were killed, including the pilot, Harry "Spot" Conner. (Courtesy Jim Bennett.)

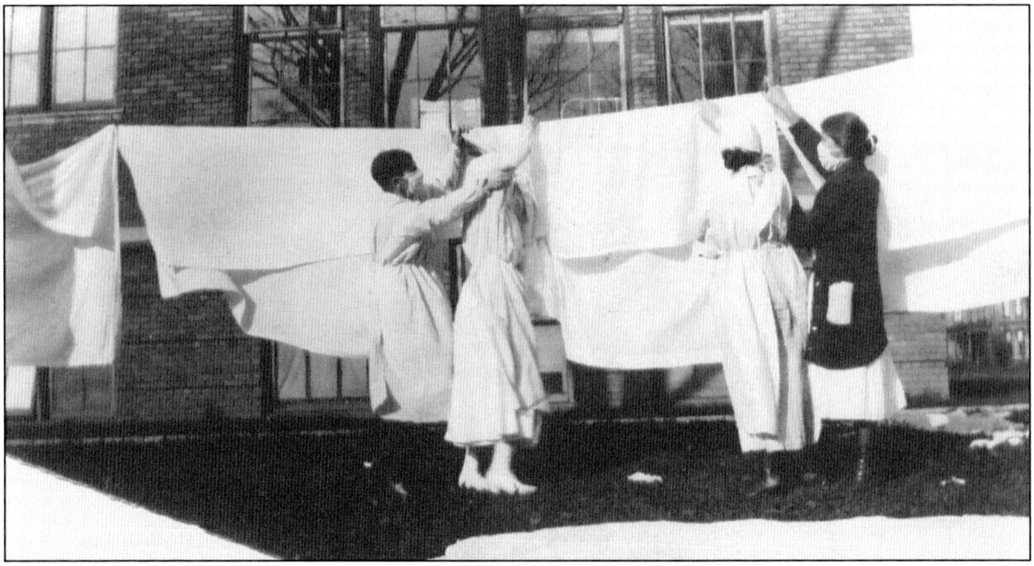

The Spanish Flu swept through the United States in 1918, and at one point, over 1,000 people in Clearfield were ill. Here nurses hang out sheets at the old downtown high school on Front Street in Clearfield, which was used for the overflow of patients from the Clearfield Hospital. Gatherings were limited, and the chairs were removed from the soda fountains so people would not linger there. (Courtesy Clearfield County Historical Society.)

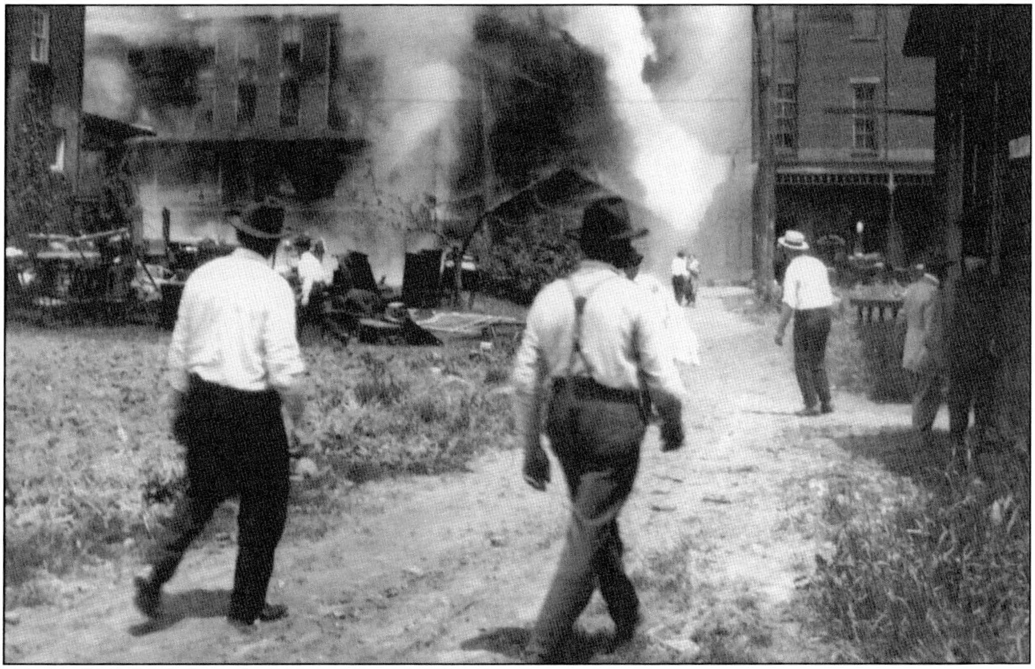

Fire swept through Mahaffey on Sunday, June 27, 1920. The fire, which destroyed the Mahaffey House, started next door in the bakery owned by Edward Nicodemus. It was termed the most disastrous ever to hit the town, wiping out most of the buildings from the bridge to the intersection of Routes 219 and 36. (Courtesy Clearfield County Historical Society.)

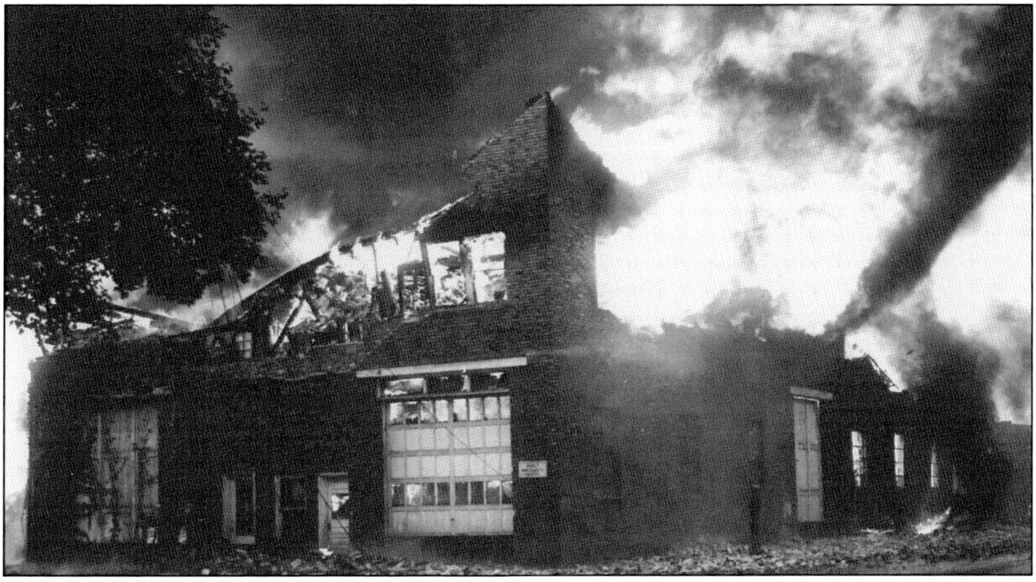

Over $1 million in damage was done by a fire that ripped through the Soult Lumber Company on Williams Street between Merrill and Fulton Streets in Clearfield on September 14, 1959. Equipment and firefighters from seven communities battled the fire for three hours before it was under control. The fire burned poles, shutting off power and telephone service to residents. It was reported that smoke could be seen as far away as DuBois and Philipsburg. (Courtesy Clearfield County Historical Society.)

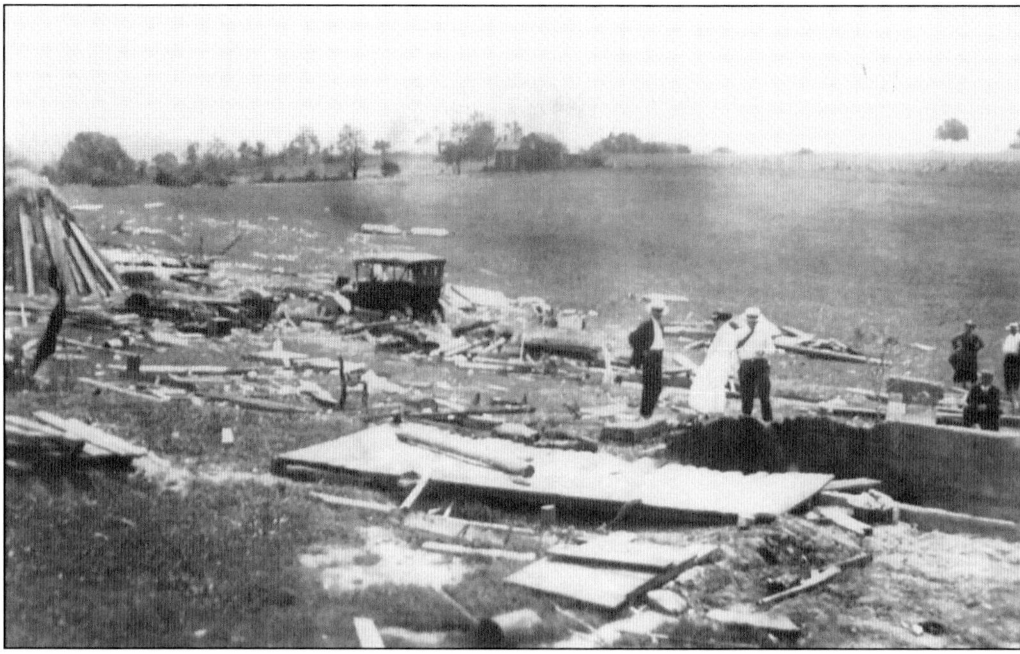

Glen Richey was the target of a tornado on August 22, 1919. It destroyed three homes and damaged five others. Fortunately, there were no injuries. Glen Richey was once a thriving coal town, but like many others in the area, the industry did not last. The social center of the town is now the fire hall. (Courtesy Clearfield County Historical Society.)

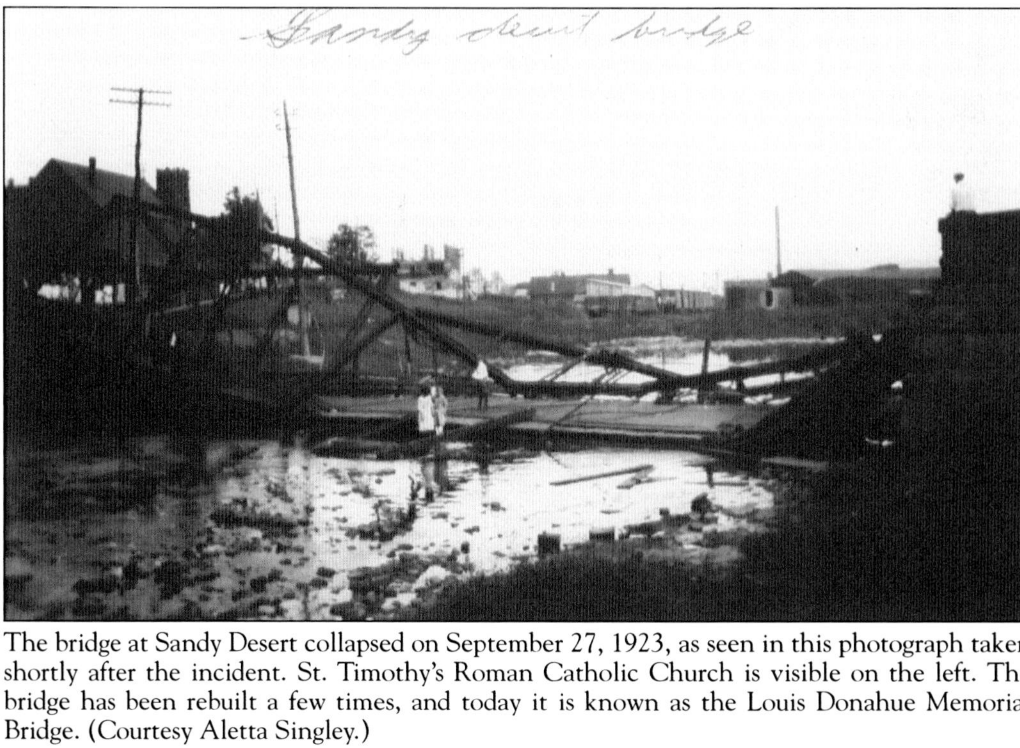

The bridge at Sandy Desert collapsed on September 27, 1923, as seen in this photograph taken shortly after the incident. St. Timothy's Roman Catholic Church is visible on the left. The bridge has been rebuilt a few times, and today it is known as the Louis Donahue Memorial Bridge. (Courtesy Aletta Singley.)

Seven

HOTELS

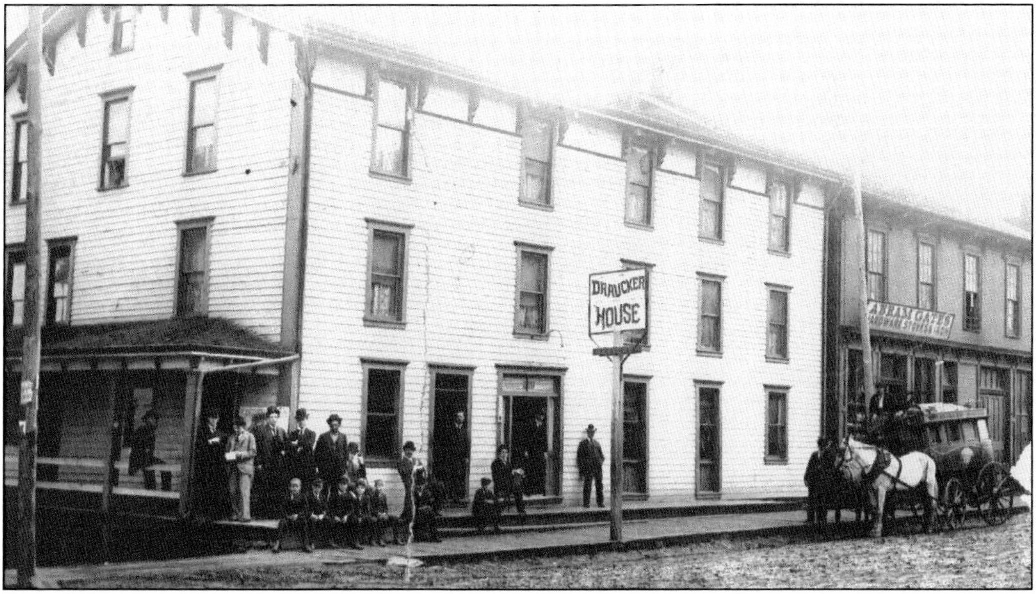

The Draucker House in Curwensville, built around 1820, was located on State Street, just east of Walnut Street. Two stage lines had offices in the hotel, which was operated for over 50 years by three generations of the Draucker family. The New Washington stage line arrived daily at 11:00 a.m. and departed at 1:00 p.m. The building was torn down after being purchased by James L. Smith in 1915. (Courtesy Clearfield County Historical Society.)

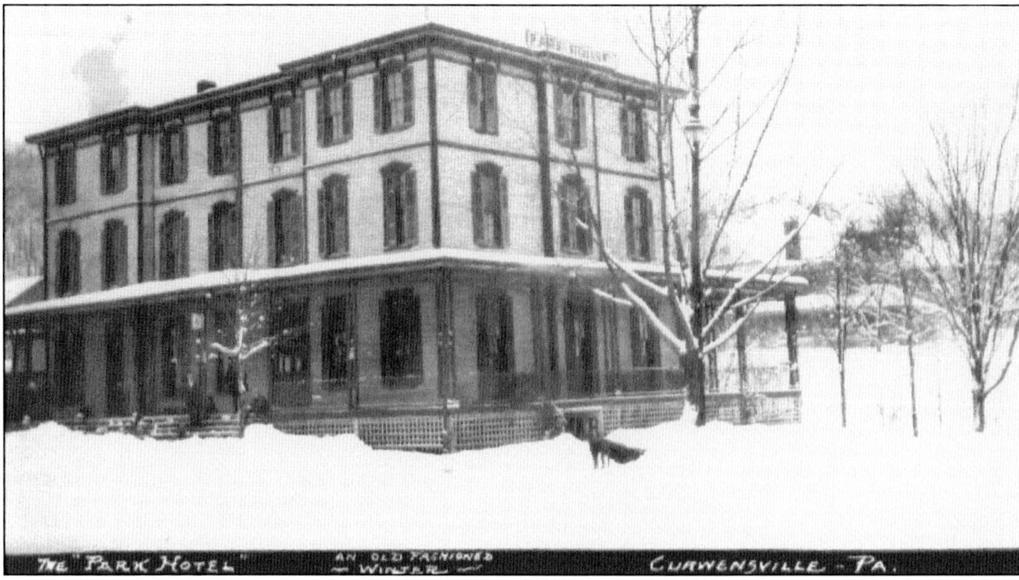

"An old fashioned winter Curwensville PA," reads this postcard from 1910. For over 100 years, the Park Hotel, or Park House, was a landmark located on the corner of State and Filbert Streets. Built in 1881 by a group headed by John Patton, it was torn down in 1989. The hotel had 45 rooms. (Courtesy Curwensville-Pike Township Historical Society.)

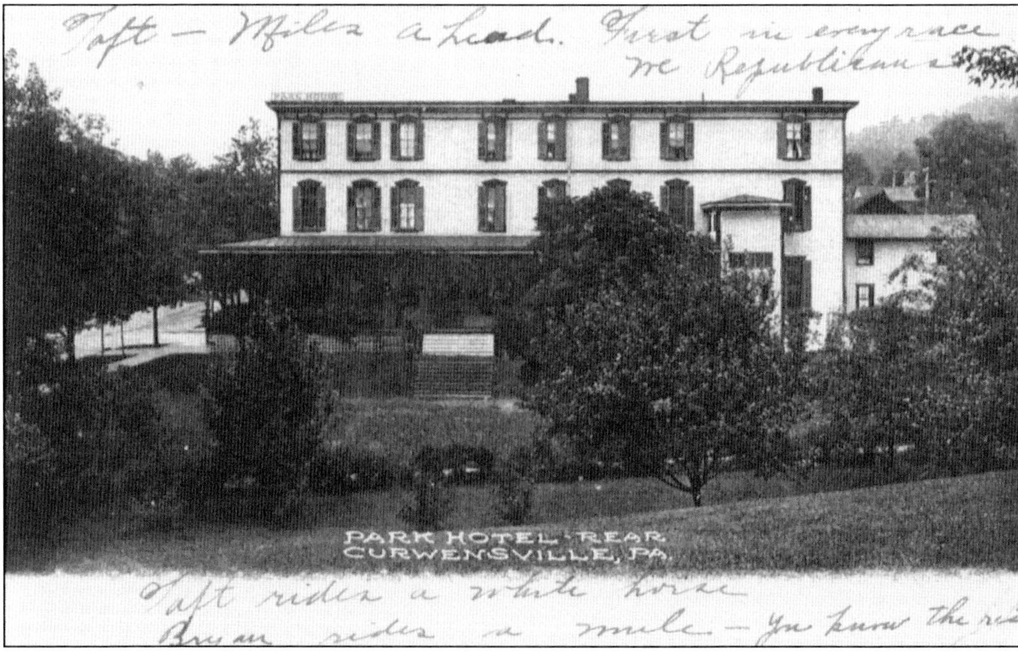

This postcard of the rear of the Park Hotel contains references to the 1908 presidential race between Republican William Howard Taft and Democrat William Jennings Bryan. "Taft rides a white horse. Bryan rides a mule. You know the rest," the sender wrote. Taft defeated Bryan, who had lost two previous presidential bids. (Courtesy Curwensville-Pike Township Historical Society.)

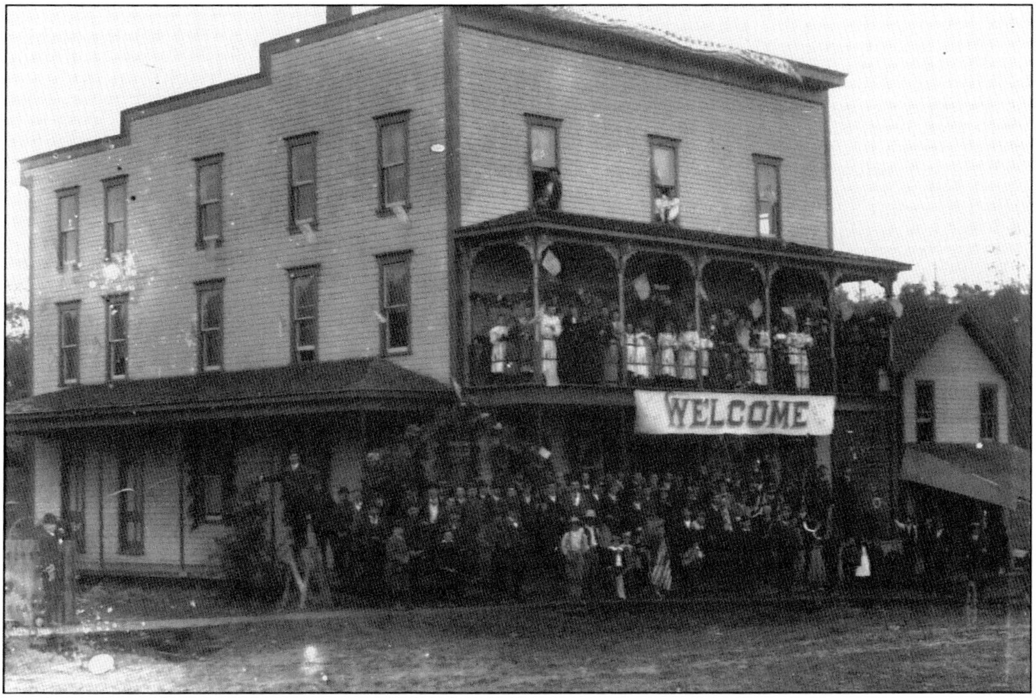

The Central Hotel was built around 1882 by Lewis C. Bloom and currently houses a restaurant and catering business. This Filbert Street establishment was created near the Pennsylvania Railroad station (now Curwensville Feed Store) to give travelers a convenient place to stay. The welcome sign may be referring to the soldiers arriving for one of the Pennsylvania Bucktail reunions. (Courtesy Curwensville-Pike Township Historical Society.)

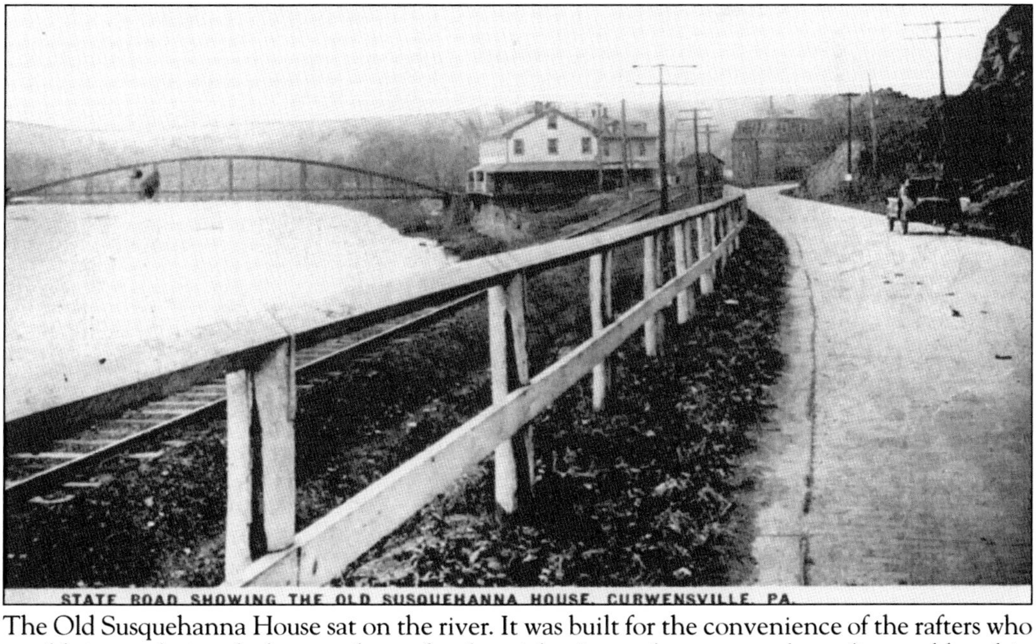

The Old Susquehanna House sat on the river. It was built for the convenience of the rafters who would tie up their rafts here and stay for the night. It was last operated as a licensed hotel in 1903 by John J. McLaughlin. It was torn down in the 1940s. (Courtesy J. Duane Test.)

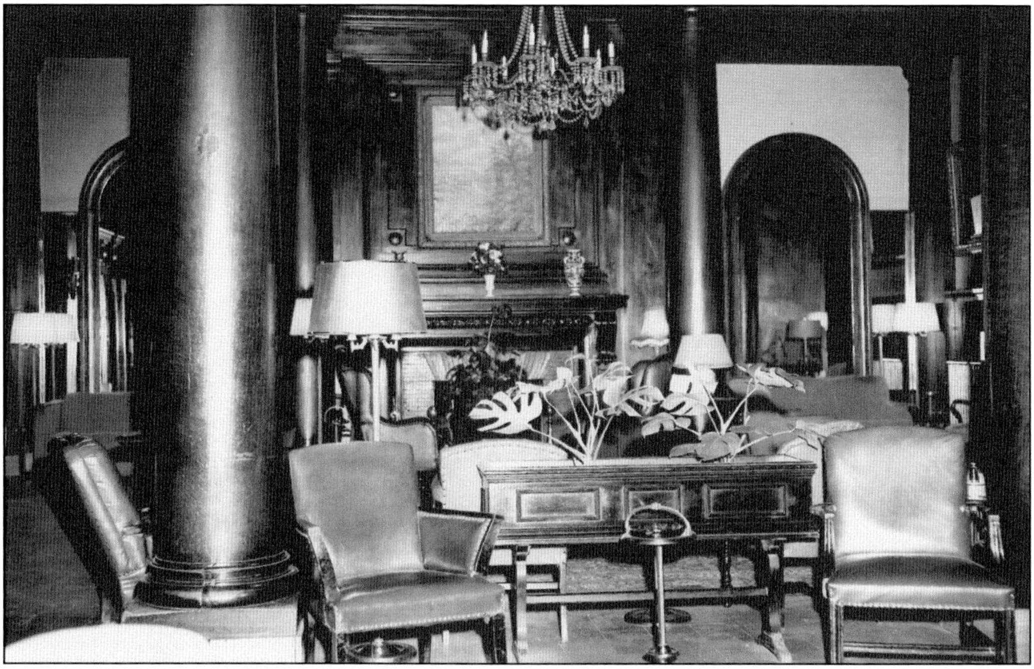

The main lobby of the Dimeling Hotel in Clearfield was an elegant place in the 1950s and featured this chandelier, which originally hung in the Waldorf Astoria Hotel in New York City. The Dimeling was built in 1904 by the Beezer Brothers of Pittsburgh. Today this landmark building is a residence for the elderly. (Courtesy E. S. Shuck Estate.)

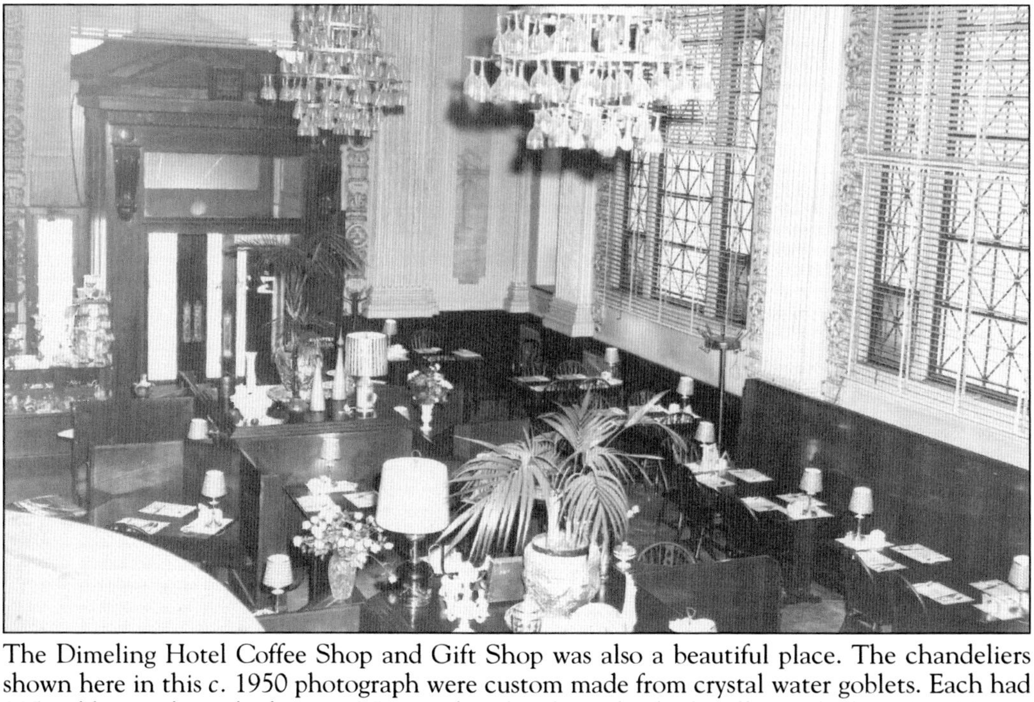

The Dimeling Hotel Coffee Shop and Gift Shop was also a beautiful place. The chandeliers shown here in this *c.* 1950 photograph were custom made from crystal water goblets. Each had 205 goblets and weighed over 175 pounds. The shop also had wall murals depicting Native American life in Clearfield County. (Courtesy E. S. Shuck Estate.)

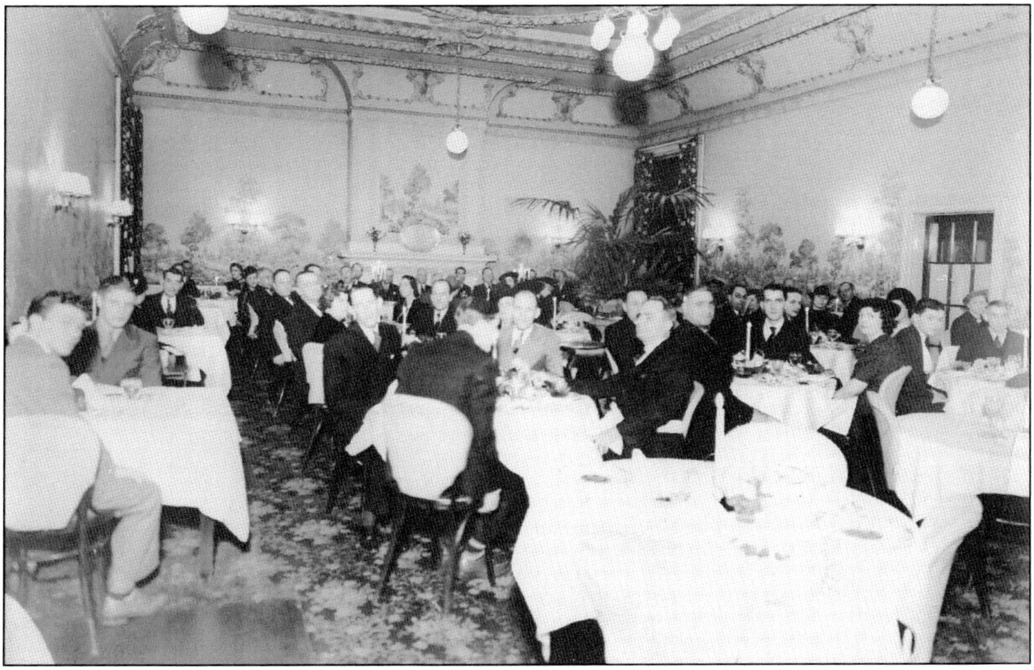

Customers enjoy the food and ambiance in the Dimeling Hotel dining room, which was located on the main floor, in this *c.* 1940 photograph. The owner, E. S. Shuck, did not allow any alcohol to be sold in his hotels. The building also featured a beautiful ballroom that covered an entire floor. Unfortunately, it was lost during the building's conversion into an apartment complex. (Courtesy E. S. Shuck Estate.)

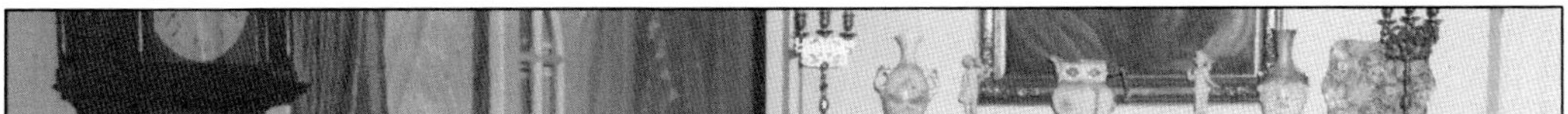

Dimeling owner Shuck relaxes in his apartment at the hotel around 1958. Shuck made a point of making his home in his hotels. He believed either he or his manager should live in the hotel as most problems happened in the evenings. He also owned the Philips Hotel in Philipsburg, the General Pershing Hotel in DuBois, and the Fort Ligonier Hotel. (Courtesy E. S. Shuck Estate.)

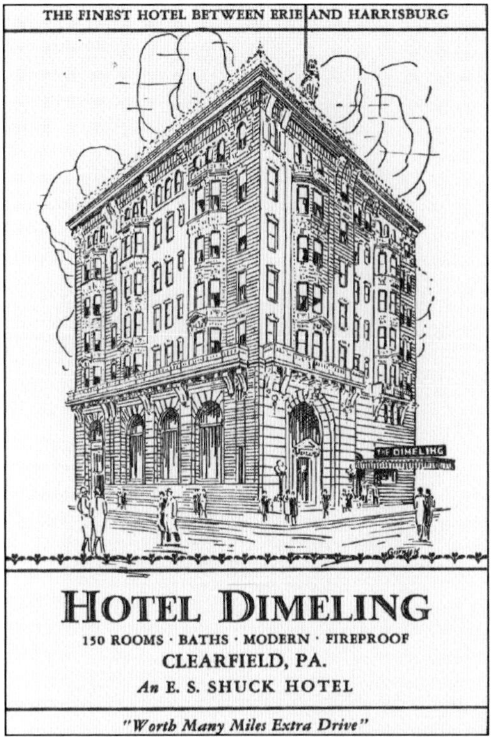

It seems most of the postcards sent from Clearfield featured various views of the Dimeling Hotel. This one from around 1940 describes it as "the finest hotel between Erie and Harrisburg," "modern," having 150 rooms, baths, and most importantly "fireproof." E. S. Shuck owned the hotel from 1926 to 1964. (Courtesy E. S. Shuck Estate.)

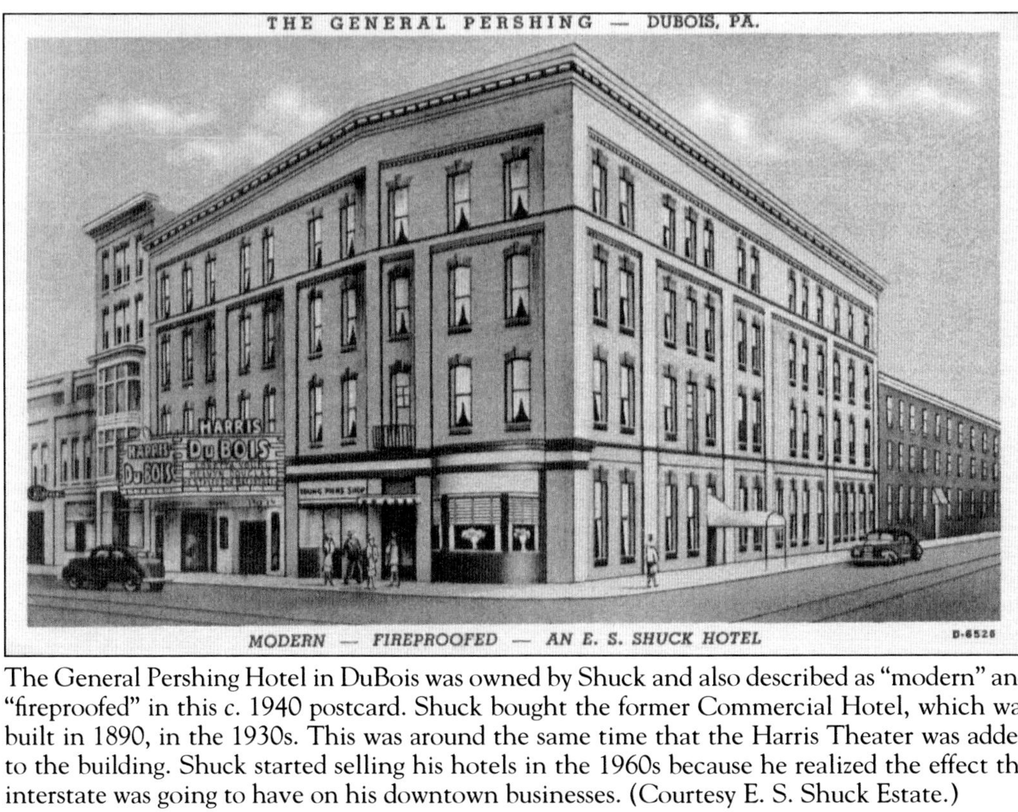

The General Pershing Hotel in DuBois was owned by Shuck and also described as "modern" and "fireproofed" in this *c.* 1940 postcard. Shuck bought the former Commercial Hotel, which was built in 1890, in the 1930s. This was around the same time that the Harris Theater was added to the building. Shuck started selling his hotels in the 1960s because he realized the effect the interstate was going to have on his downtown businesses. (Courtesy E. S. Shuck Estate.)

This rare postcard shows some of last phase of construction of the Dimeling Hotel in 1904. Visible are open windows and sidewalk construction. In the 1990s, a committee was formed to help save this historic structure. This effort led to it being reopened as an elderly housing complex. (Courtesy E. S. Shuck Estate.)

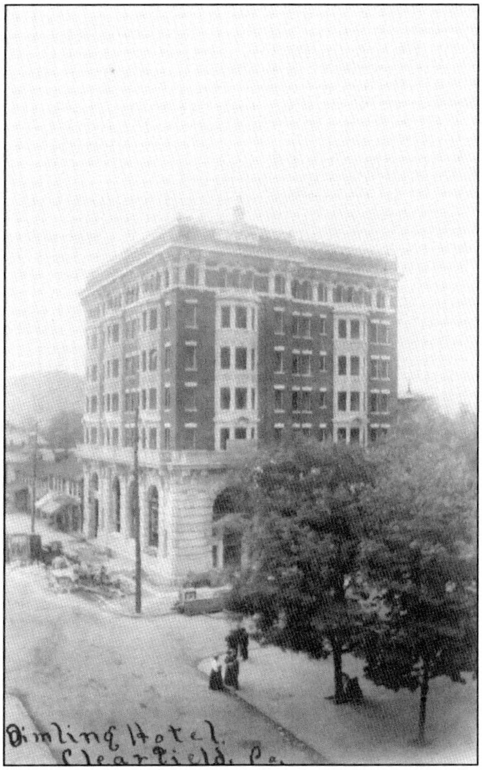

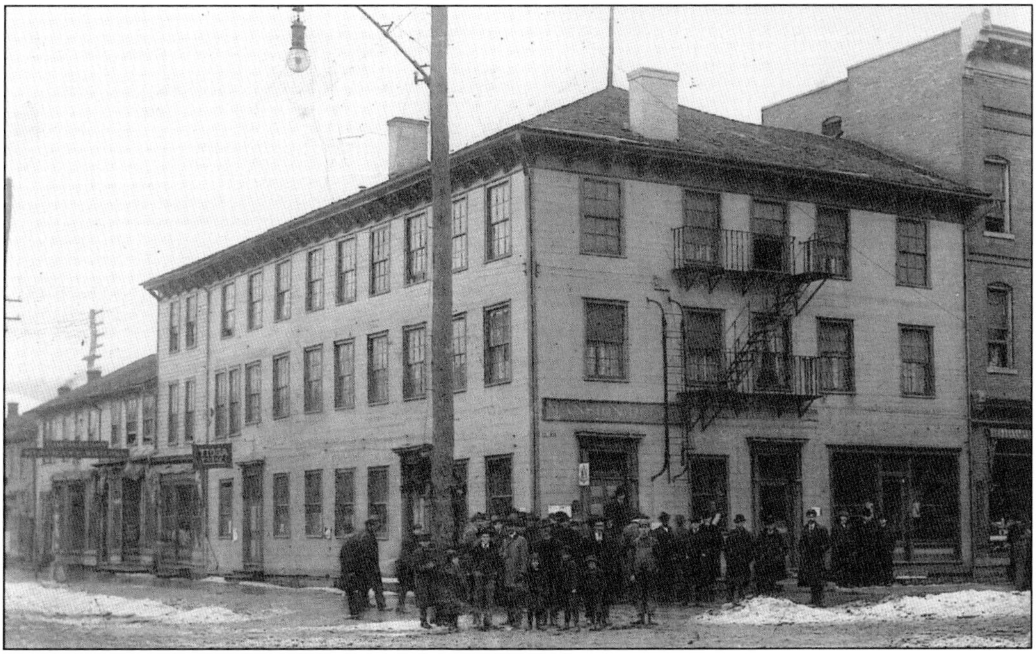

Before the Dimeling Hotel was built, the three-story Mansion House occupied the corner of Second and Market Streets in Clearfield. Prior to the Mansion House construction in 1841, this spot was home to the Collins Hotel, which was owned by Robert Collins and began operating around 1817. (Courtesy Clearfield County Historical Society.)

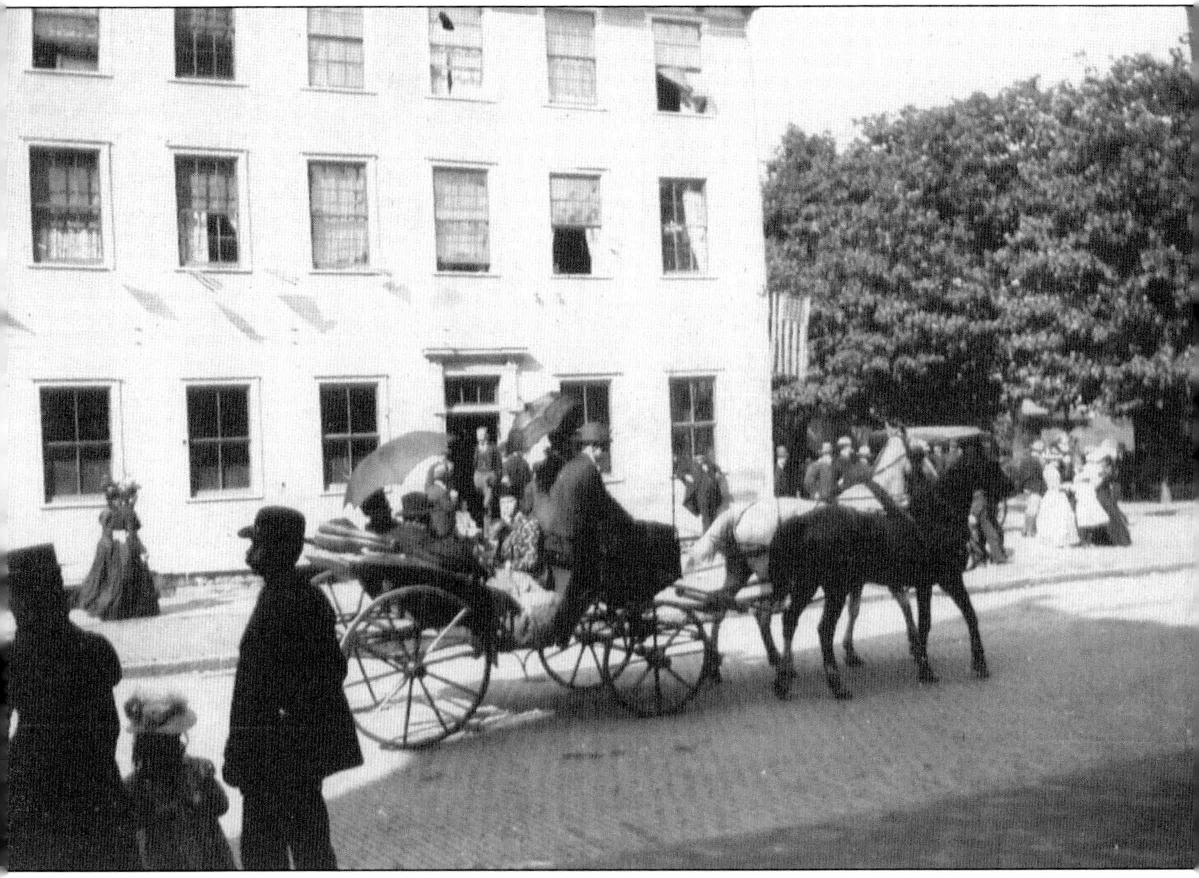

Getting around Clearfield in 1898 involved horses and carriages traveling down brick roads. This carriage, owned by James L. Leavy, passes by the Mansion House, which is on the left. At the far right, the top of the Clearfield County Courthouse is visible. The Mansion House was built by Richard Shaw in 1841. Later it became the property of W. M. Shaw, who sold it to W. C. Cardon, who was the owner in 1876. The three-story building was able to accommodate 80 people. Leavy had a livery stable in town and also was an undertaker and funeral director. Leavy ran a stage line between Clearfield, DuBois, and Curwensville as well. (Courtesy Clearfield County Historical Society.)

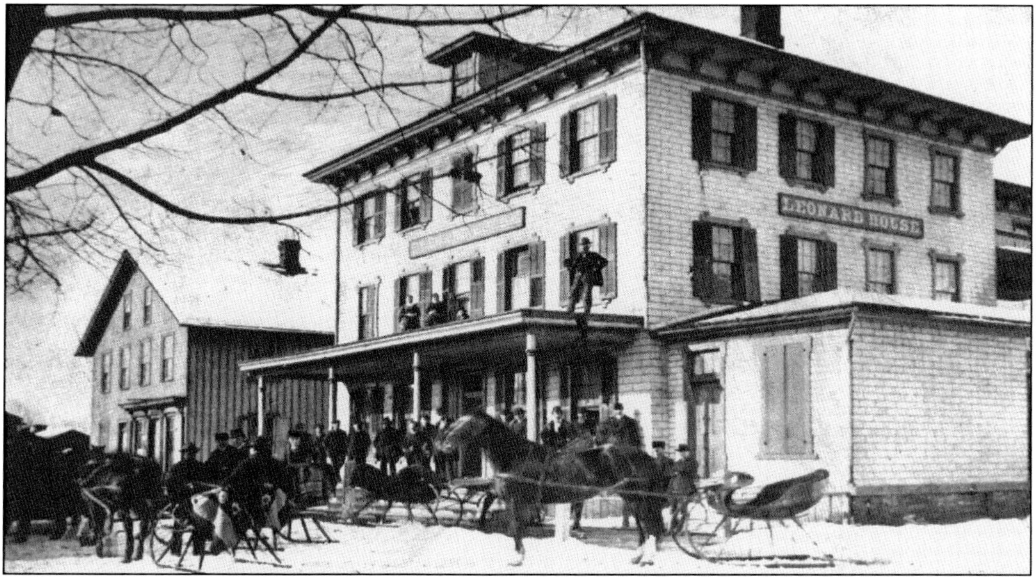

The Leonard House built in 1869 by G. D. Goodfellow was located on the north side of Reed Street between Second and Third Streets, behind the Tyrone and Clearfield Railroad Depot in Clearfield. R. Newton Shaw was the proprietor when this photograph was taken. This hotel was destroyed by fire in the 1930s. (Courtesy Clearfield County Historical Society.)

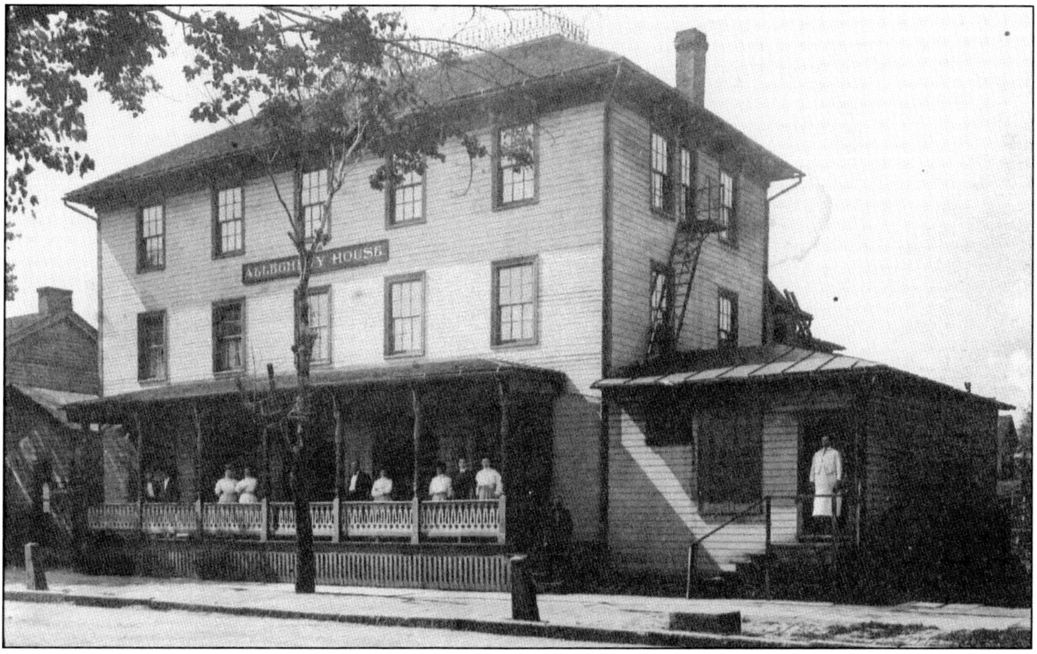

This 1908 postcard features the Allegheny House, which was erected by Caper Leipold in 1868. Located near Fourth Street, it was one of many hotels on Market Street in Clearfield Borough. An advertisement for the business boasted "Rates moderate. Best Accommodations. Steam Heat. Electric Light. Hot and Cold Water." (Courtesy Clearfield County Historical Society.)

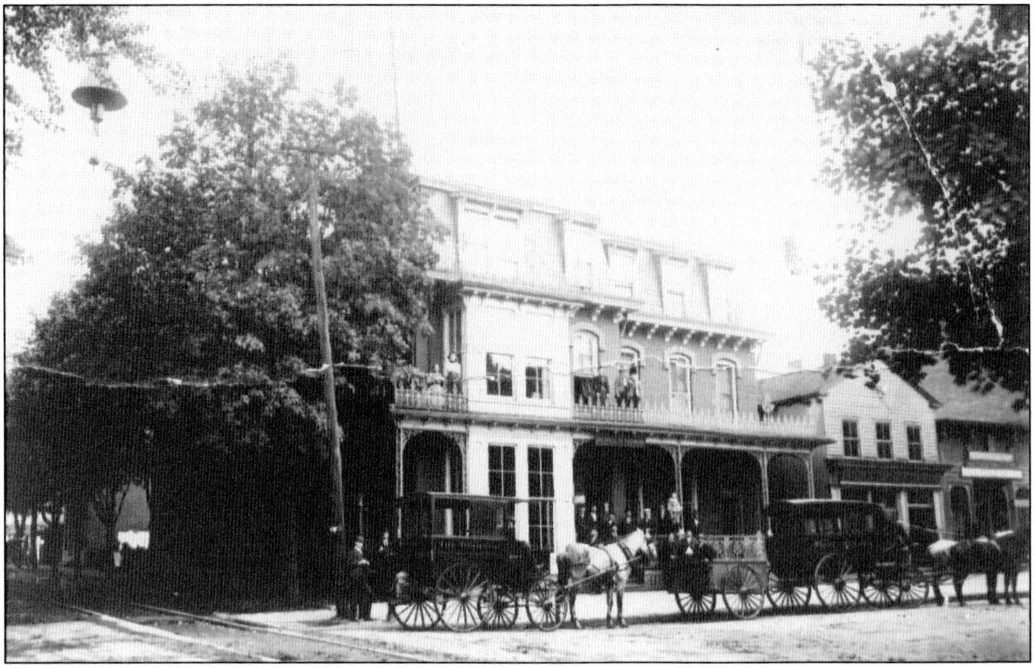

The Hotel Windsor was another popular Market Street hotel. Constructed in 1884 by James Mahaffey, the building still stands at the southwest corner of Third and Market Streets in Clearfield. It has been home to many businesses, including Murphy's and, most recently, a Dollar General store. (Courtesy Clearfield County Historical Society.)

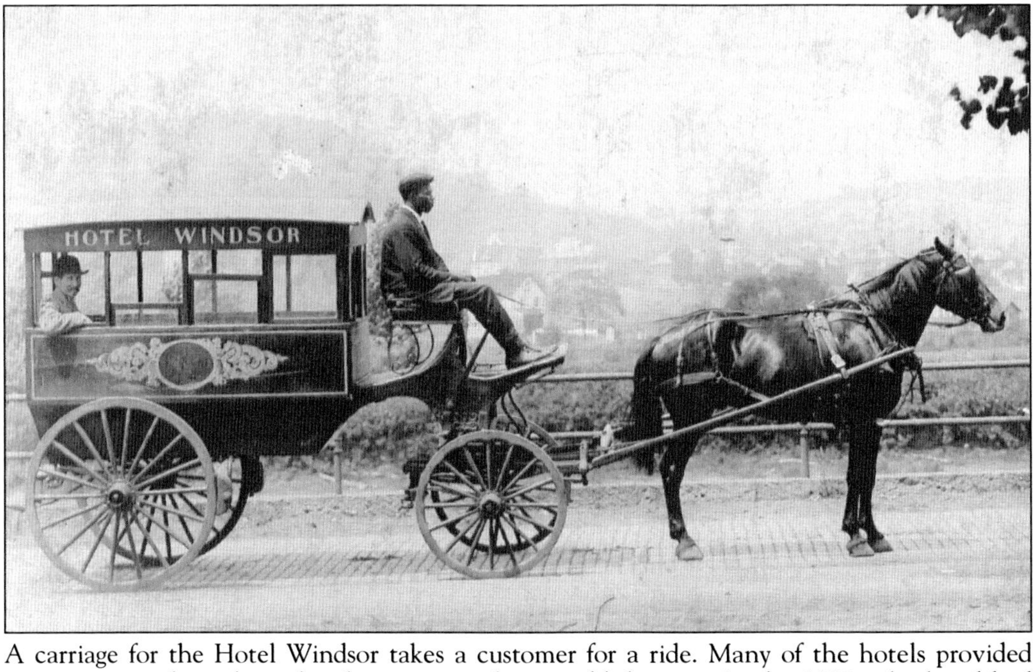

A carriage for the Hotel Windsor takes a customer for a ride. Many of the hotels provided transportation from the railroad stations to their establishments. In the 1880s, the hotel had all the modern improvements of a first-class hotel, including a water supply and steam heat. It could accommodate 150 people. (Courtesy Clearfield County Historical Society.)

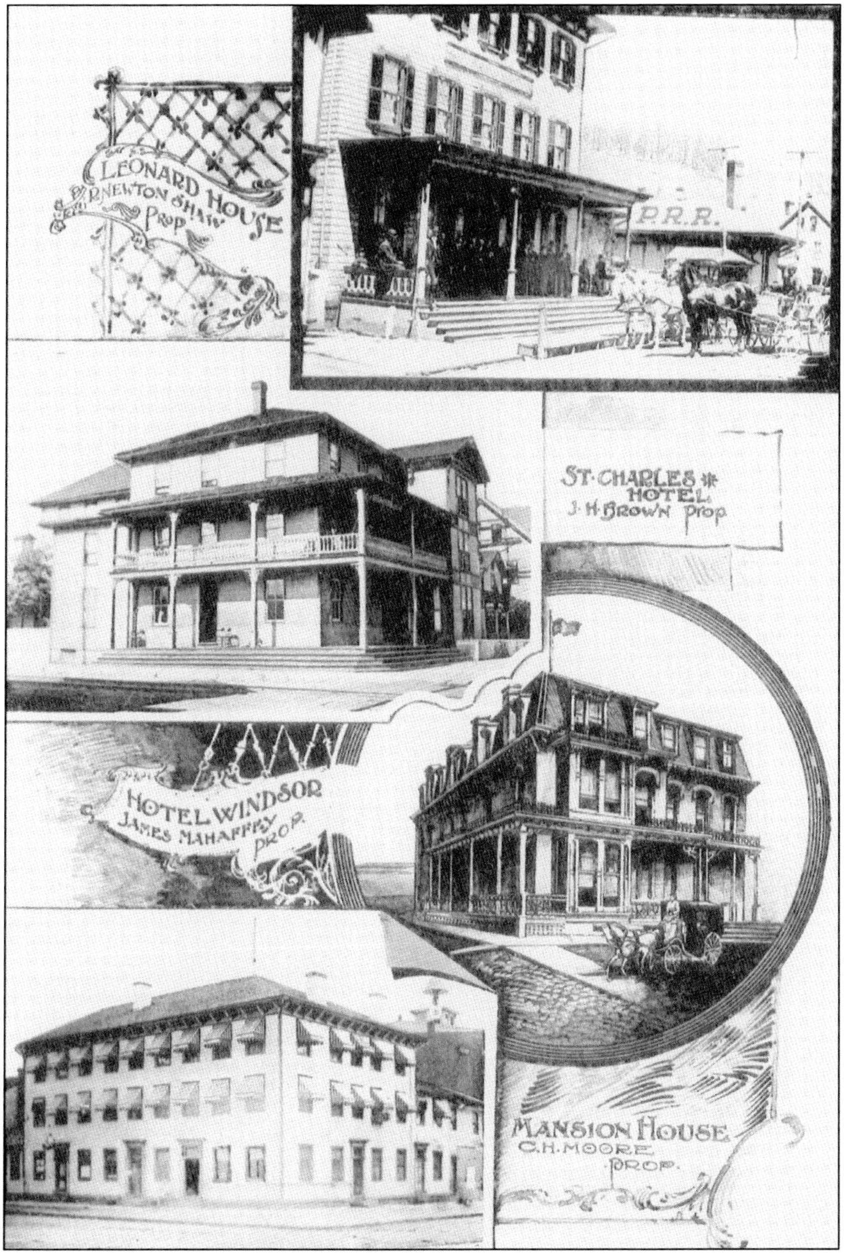

Choosing a place to stay in Clearfield in 1895 could have been a problem. The town had many fine hotels, four of which are featured on this group postcard from 1895: the Leonard House (proprietor R. Newton Shaw) was next to the Pennsylvania Railroad station, which can be seen to the right of the hotel; the St. Charles Hotel (proprietor J. H. Brown), which was built in 1870 and had accommodations for 60 guests; the Hotel Windsor (proprietor James Mahaffey), which was the only brick hotel in Clearfield in the 1880s; and the Mansion House (proprietor C. H. Moore). Of these four hotels, only one is still a business. The St. Charles Hotel building is now a café. The Mansion House and Leonard House buildings no longer exist, but the Hotel Windsor building stills stands on the corner of Third and Market Streets. (Courtesy Clearfield County Historical Society.)

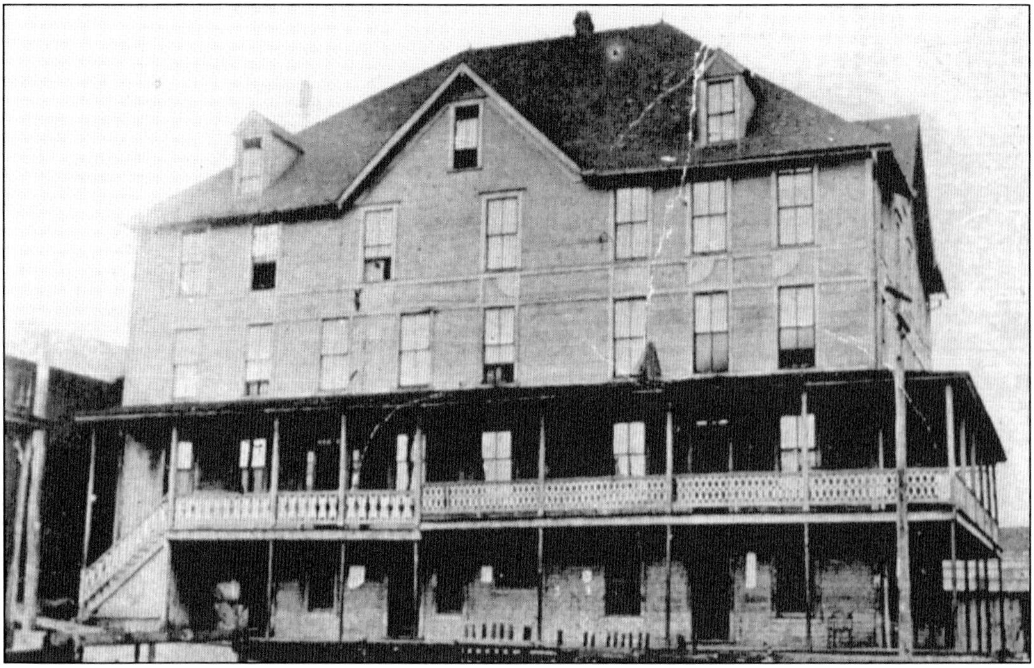

The Mahaffey House, featured on this postcard from 1913, burned on June 27, 1920, during one of the worst fires in Mahaffey history. The fire, which started in a bakery, destroyed most of the structures from the bridge to the intersection of Routes 219 and 36. The possible cause was an electrical problem. The hotel was originally built in the late 1890s. (Courtesy Clearfield County Historical Society.)

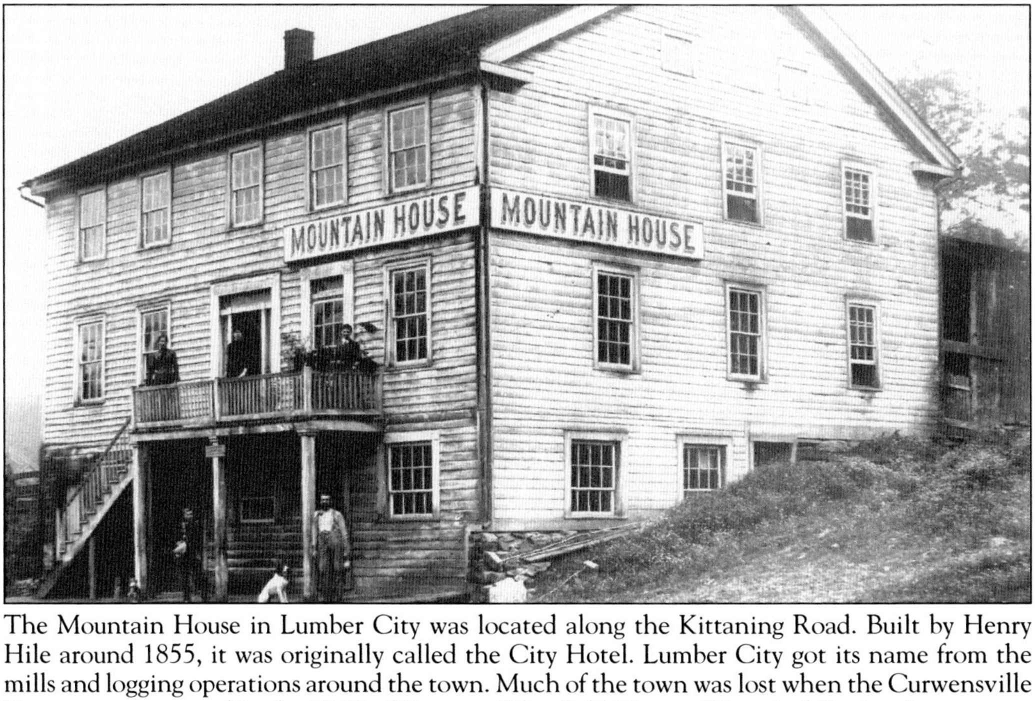

The Mountain House in Lumber City was located along the Kittaning Road. Built by Henry Hile around 1855, it was originally called the City Hotel. Lumber City got its name from the mills and logging operations around the town. Much of the town was lost when the Curwensville Dam was constructed in the 1960s. (Courtesy Clearfield County Historical Society.)

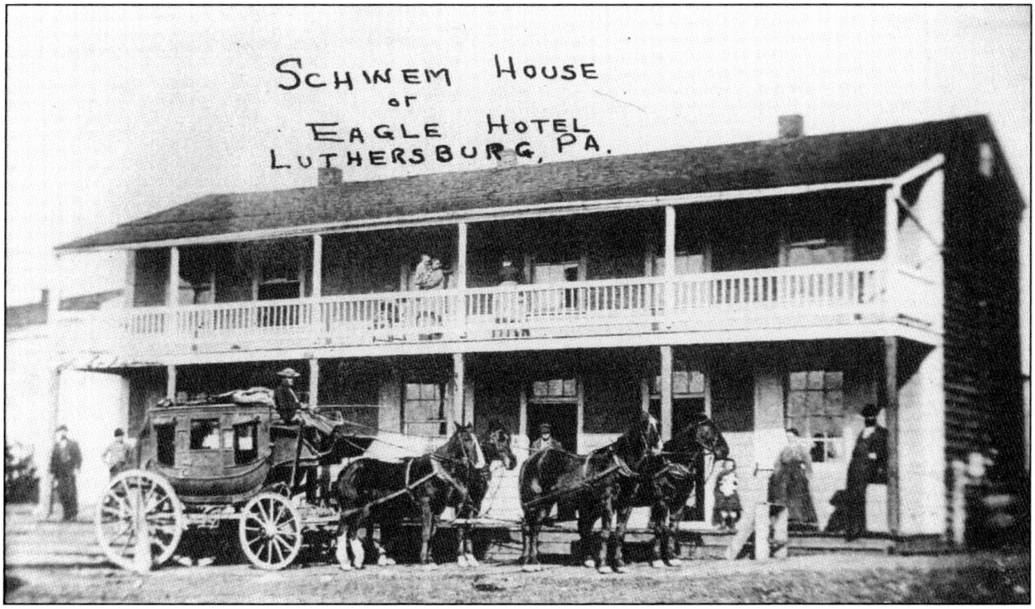

The Schwem or Eagle Hotel was located in Luthersburg. Here a stage makes a stop at the hotel, which was originally known as the Cream Hill Hotel. Seen here are William Schwem, Dr. William A. Means, Annie Schwem Butler, Mrs. William Schwem, Lizzie Weaver, Walter Schwem, and Cooney Long. (Courtesy Clearfield County Historical Society.)

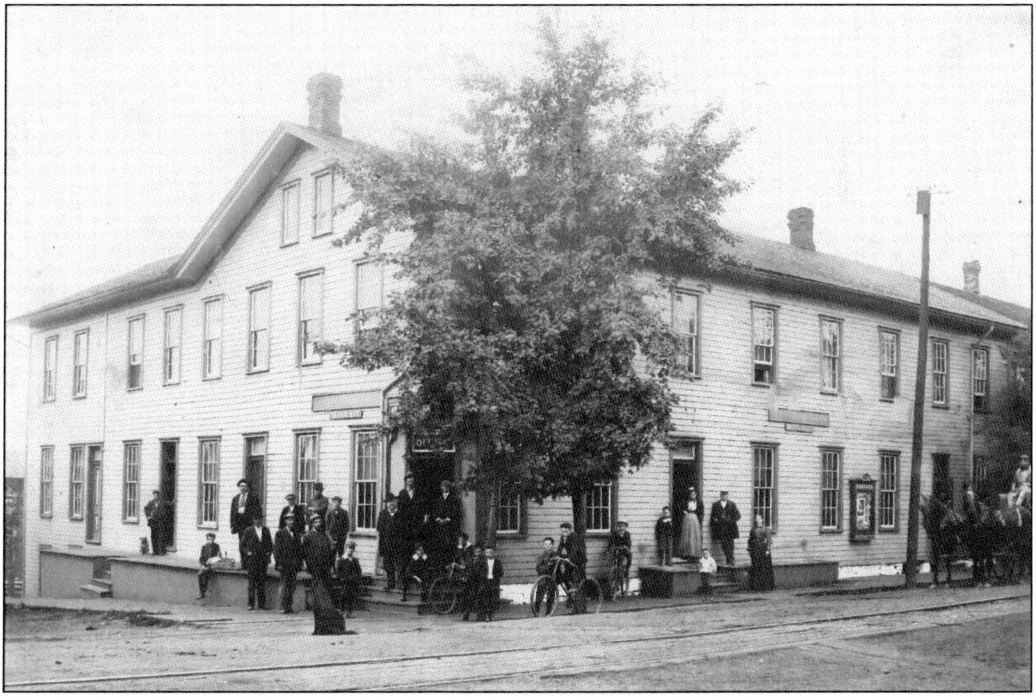

The St. Cloud Hotel on Hannah Street in Houtzdale was near the old train station for the Alley Popper Railroad, which operated from 1893 to 1936. Originally built in 1876, the hotel was refitted when William McKenzie was the proprietor with "heat, bath room, toilet room etc." It burned in 1997. (Courtesy Clearfield County Historical Society.)

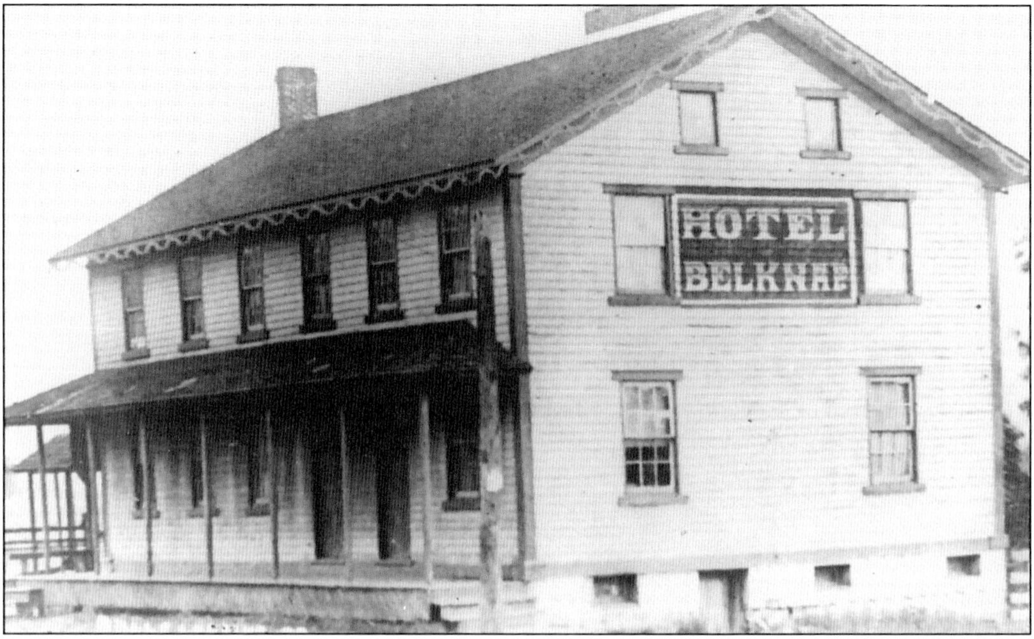

Hotel Belkhar was the place to stay at Bells Landing if one was a rafter in the late 20th century. Bells Landing was originally named Belleville for Greenwood Bell. Later it was changed to Bells Landing because a main landing for the rafters was located here. (Courtesy Jim Bennett.)

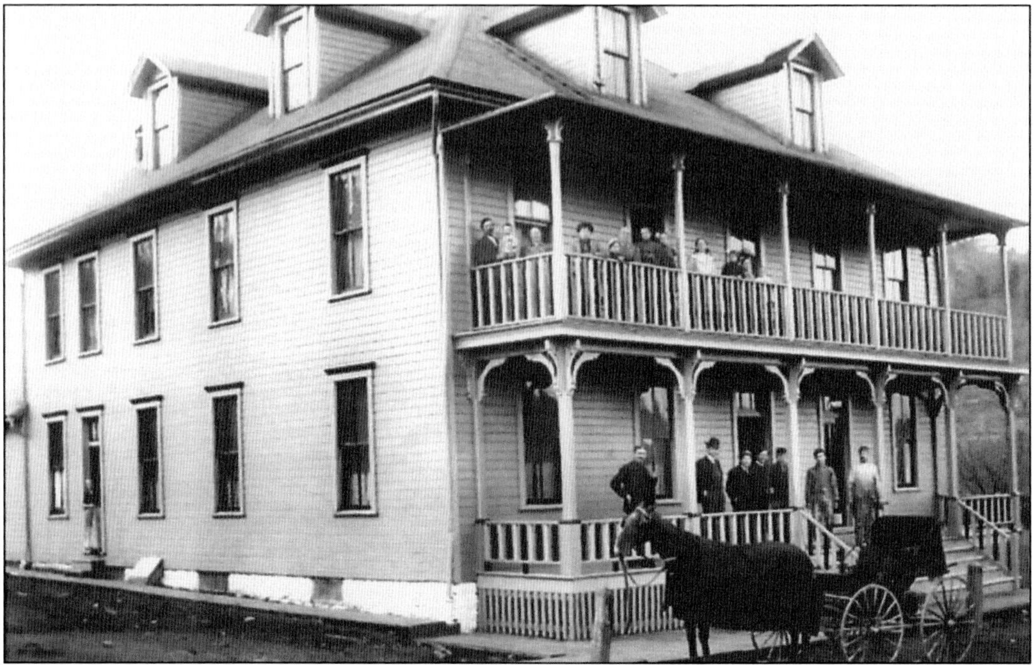

The O'Shanter Hotel was located near the New York Central Railroad station. After the railroad left the area, the hotel was put out of business. It later became a grocery store, run by Karl and Ella Lewis. The building still stands and today is a private residence. O'Shanter is another example of a town that lived and died because of coal in the area. (Courtesy Clearfield County Historical Society.)

Eight

Miscellaneous Postcards

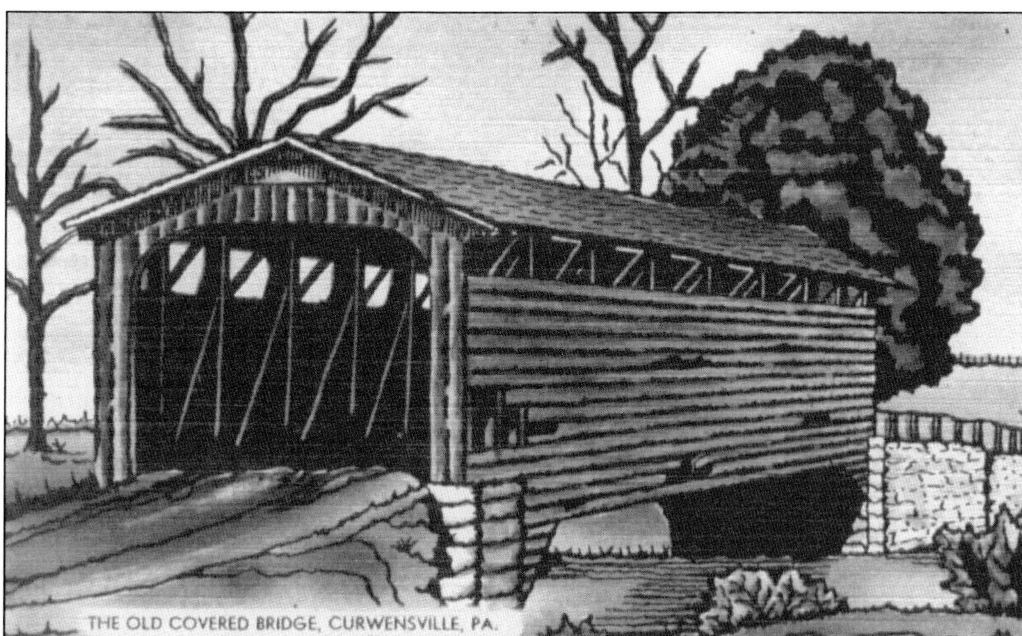

This postcard of the Old Covered Bridge in Curwensville dates back to Curwensville's sesquicentennial in 1949. Information on the back reads, "The Old Covered Bridge, before it was dismantled, was among the oldest of the few remaining bridges of this type in the state of Pennsylvania, and was constructed in the year 1868. Plan to visit Curwensville during the six days appropriate celebration." (Courtesy Dan McDonald.)

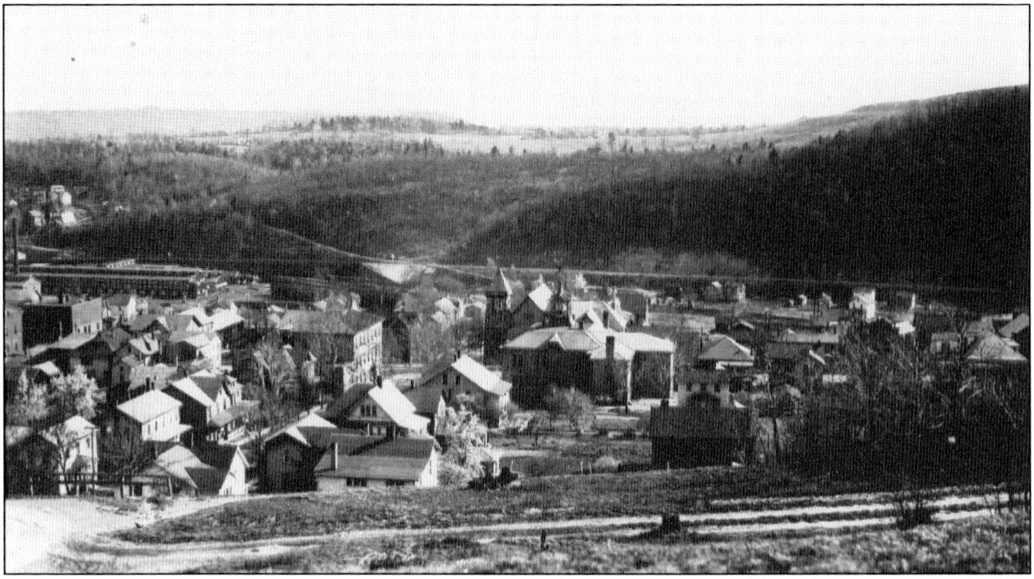

This view from above Curwensville was taken from the hill near Oak Hill Cemetery. The Patton Building, just right of the center, and the Curwensville United Methodist Church, which was located right across State Street, are both visible. (Courtesy Curwensville-Pike Township Historical Society.)

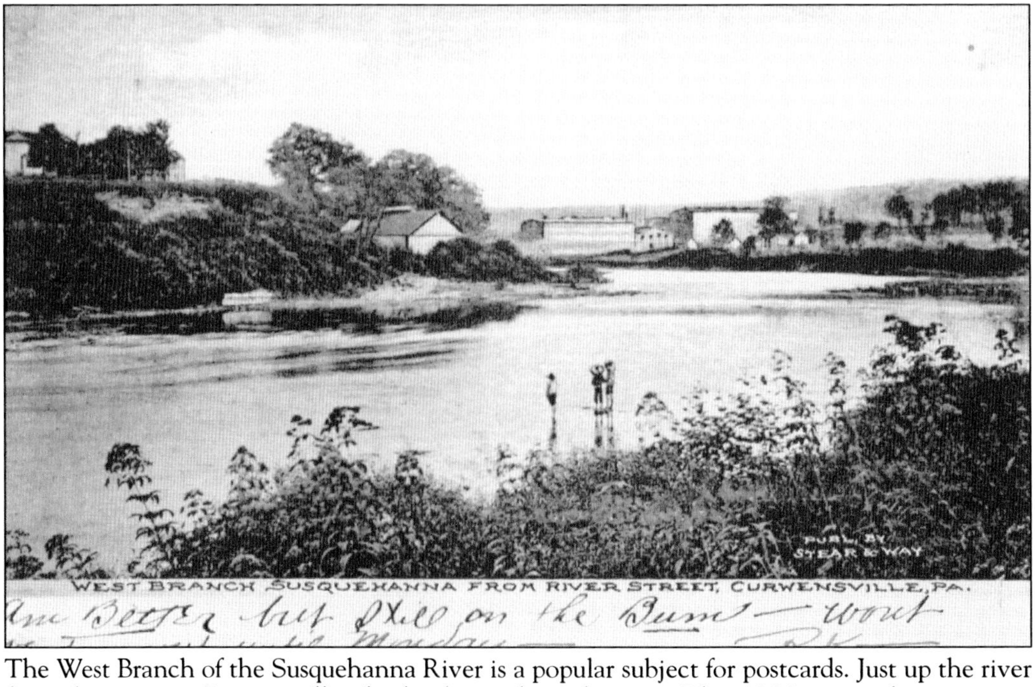

The West Branch of the Susquehanna River is a popular subject for postcards. Just up the river from this spot in Curwensville, the lumberyard can be seen. This 1906 postcard was sent to Punxsutawney by R. K. Way, who was not feeling well according to the notes on the card. (Courtesy Dan McDonald.)

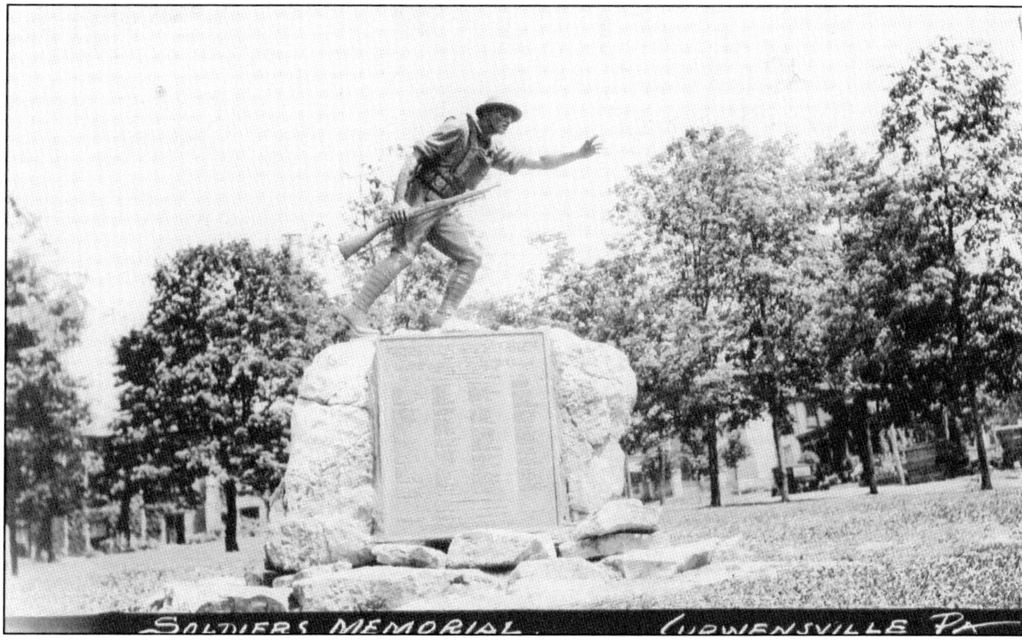

The "Doughboy" monument, or Soldier's Memorial, was dedicated on Flag Day in 1925 to the veterans of all wars. Donated by Col. Edward A. Irvin, this plot was originally intended for a monument for the Pennsylvania Bucktails Company K, which he served with in the Civil War. In 2003, a memorial for the group finally became a reality. This monument stands behind the Doughboy. (Courtesy Curwensville-Pike Township Historical Society.)

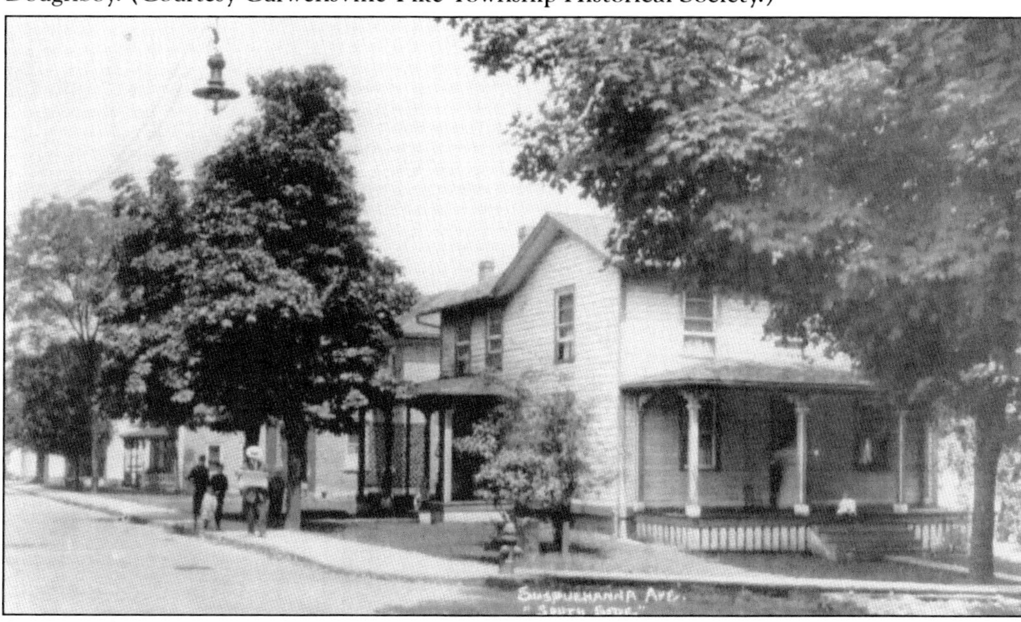

A Susquehanna Avenue home on the south side of Curwensville is featured on this *c.* 1920 postcard. It was built in 1865 by the Schofield family. Currently it belongs to David McNaul and has been in the McNaul family since his grandfather purchased it in 1918. The child on the porch is Jane McNaul, and in the doorway is Jenny McNaul. (Courtesy Curwensville-Pike Township Historical Society.)

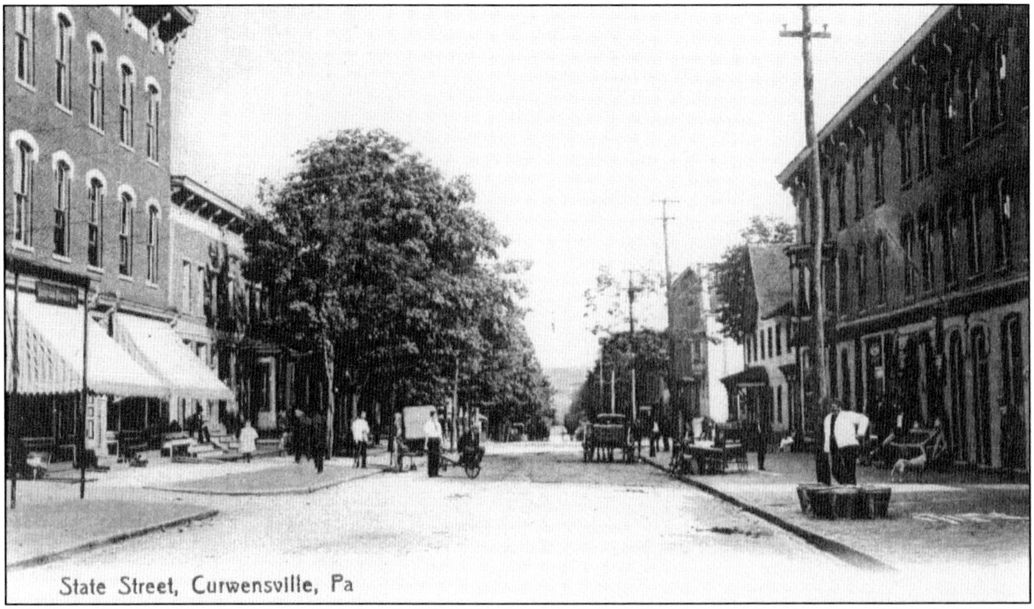

A view of State Street is provided by this c. 1900 postcard. On the left is the block that burned in 1936 and is currently the site of the Curwensville Post Office. On the right is Leib's Drug Store. An advertisement from 1912 reads, "if it's drugs, it's Leib's you want." (Courtesy Curwensville-Pike Township Historical Society.)

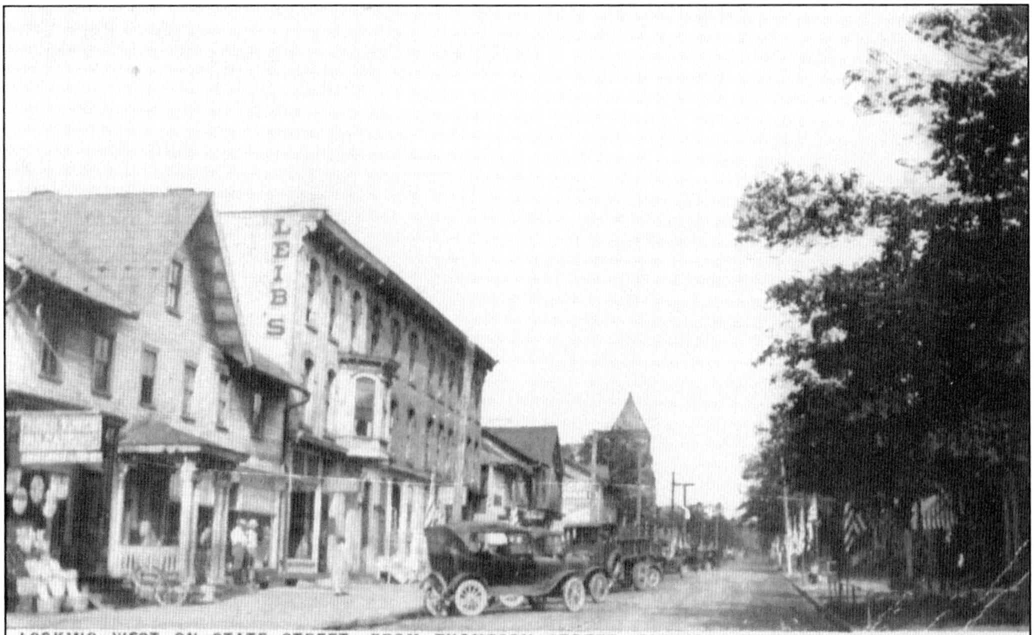

This view of State Street from around 1915 is from the opposite end of the street, looking west toward Thompson Street. On the left are Way's Stationery Store and Leib's Drug Store, and, at the far end of the street, the top of the Curwensville United Methodist Church is visible. (Courtesy Curwensville-Pike Township Historical Society.)

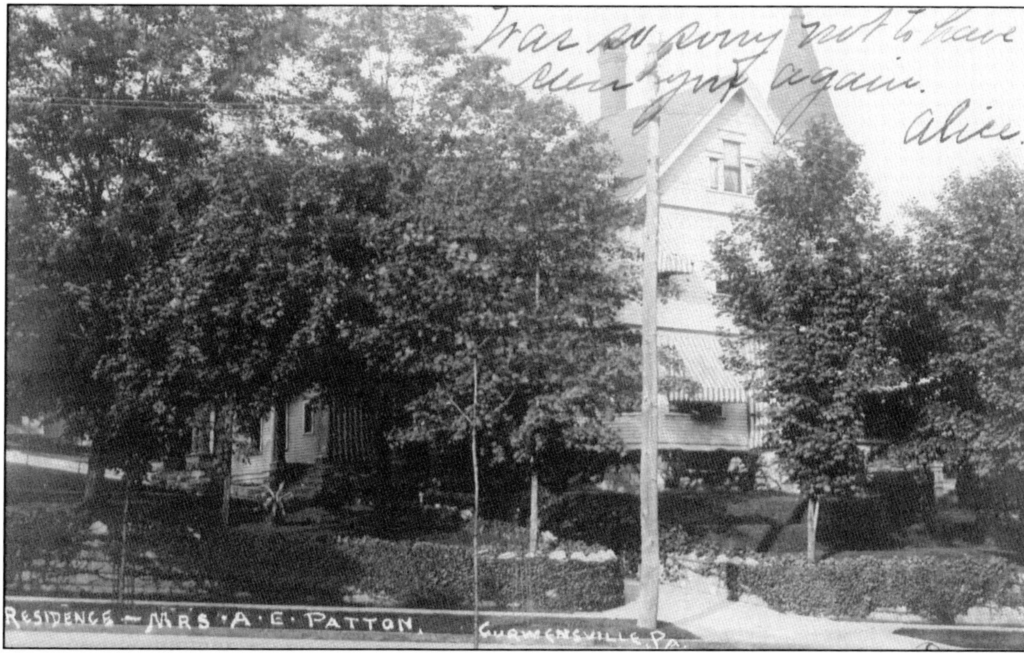

This beautiful home was the residence of Mrs. A. E. Patton, wife of former state senator Alexander E. Patton around 1907. In September 1890, when Pres. Benjamin Harrison visited the area, he stopped to dine with the Pattons here. Unfortunately, the home was lost to fire in 1942. (Courtesy Curwensville-Pike Township Historical Society.)

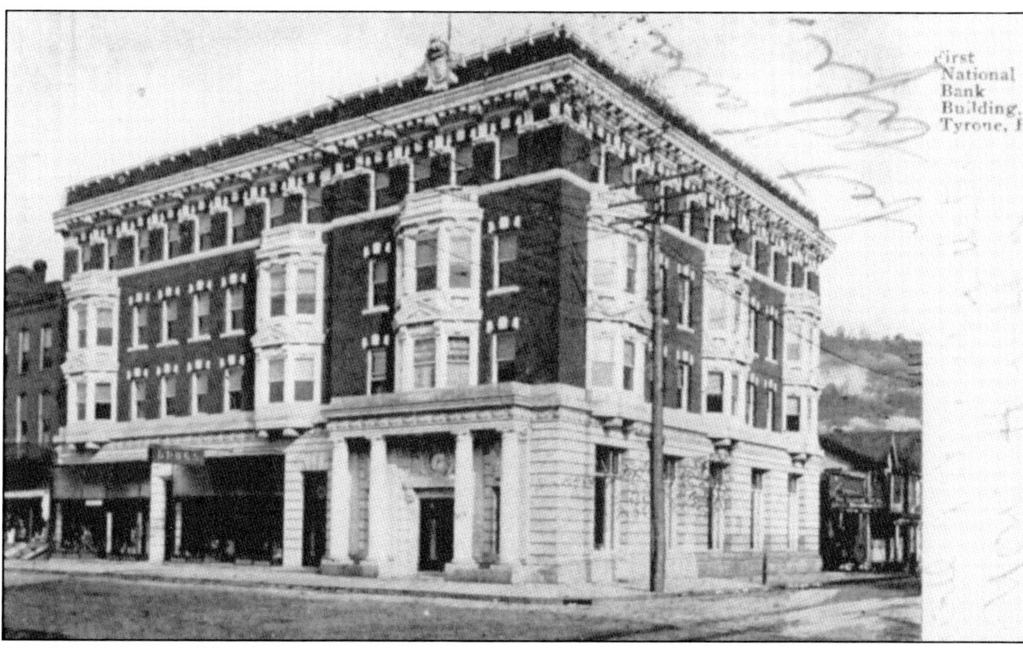

The First National Bank of Tyrone has a familiar look to it for a good reason. It was built by the Beezer brothers, who also built Clearfield's historic Dimeling Hotel. The Dimeling Hotel and the bank were both built around 1904. This postcard is from 1907. This building still stands but has been reduced to one floor, and the outside has been redone. (Courtesy Mark Coudriet.)

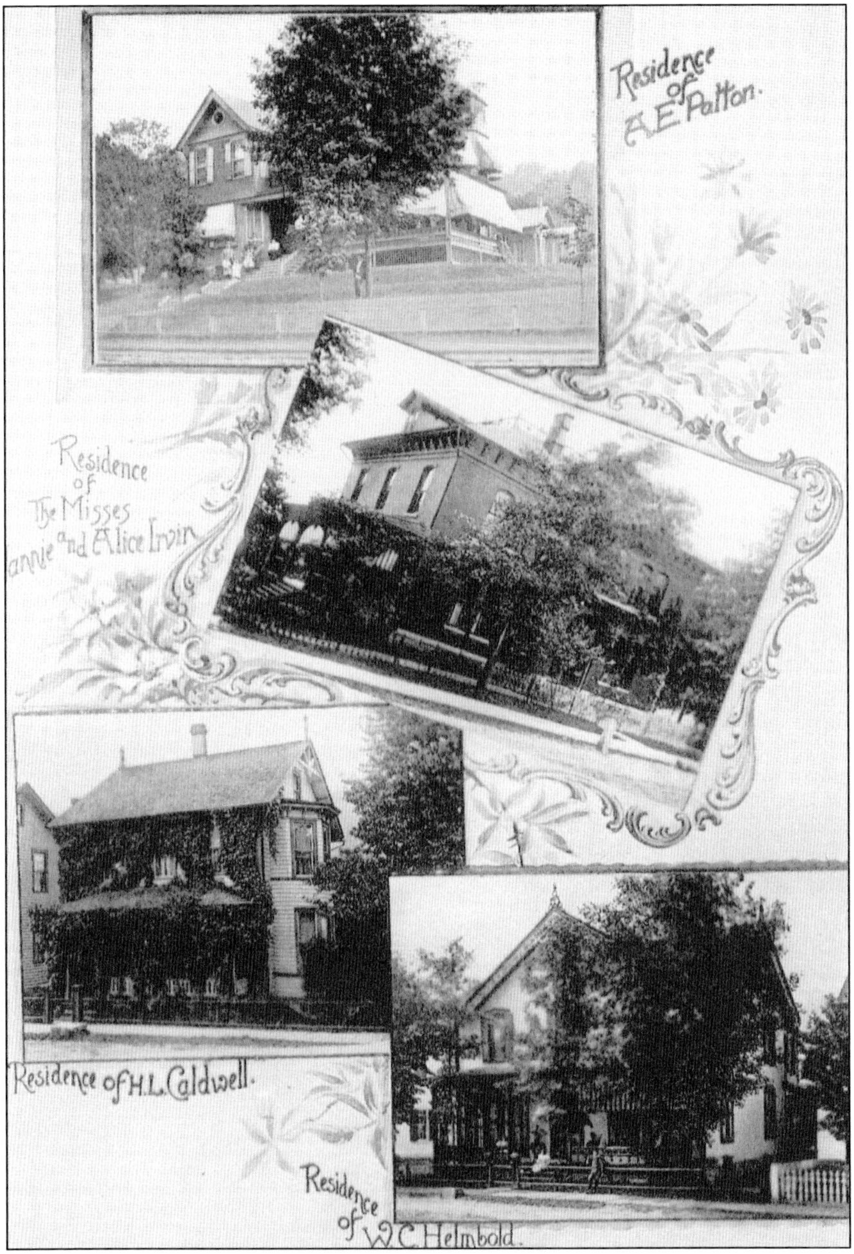

From the *Souvenir of Curwensville* booklet of 1895 comes this postcard featuring some of the magnificent homes of the area. Included are the residences of A. E. Patton, which burned in 1942; Nannie and Alice Irvin, which is now the Strawberry Tree shop; H. L. Caldwell, which is the home of the Curwensville-Pike Township Historical Society; and W. C. Hembold. The man standing on the stairs in the Patton postcard could possibly be A. E. Patton, who died in 1904. The Irvin home was built in 1835 by William and Jane Irvin. Caldwell was a contractor who built A. E. Patton's home, as well as other homes for the Patton family. In the 1870s, Caldwell built his own home on State Street across from the Patton homes. The Caldwell home was donated to the historical society by the family of Mildred Korb Houser after her death. (Courtesy Clearfield County Historical Society.)

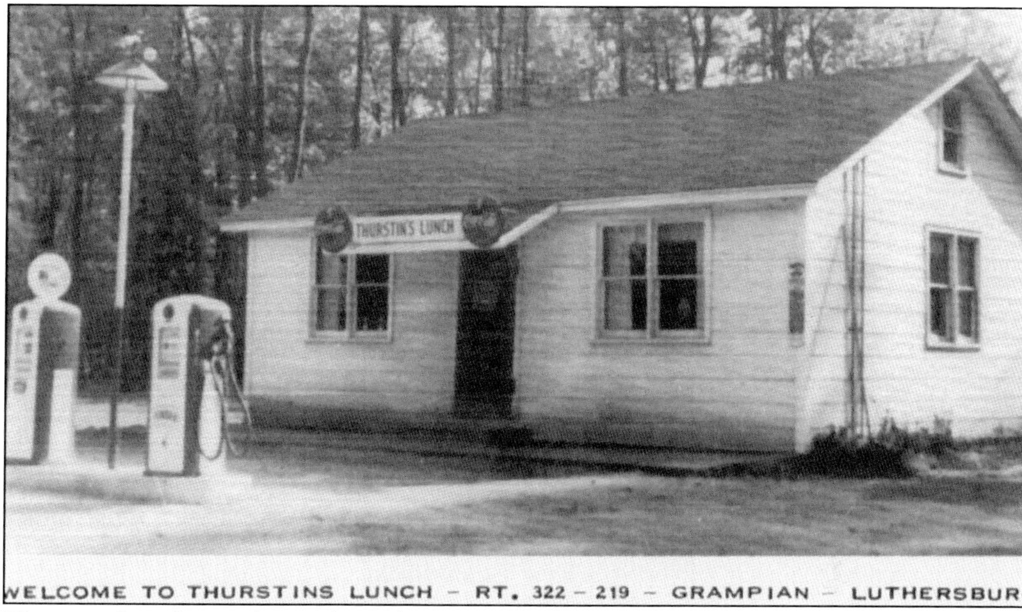

Thurstins Lunch was featured on this postcard from 1956. The dinner and gas station was located on Route 322 and Route 219, between Grampian and Luthersburg. The message on the back reads, "Gone home the old way from Ohio. We had supper here on March 10, 1956." (Courtesy Dan McDonald.)

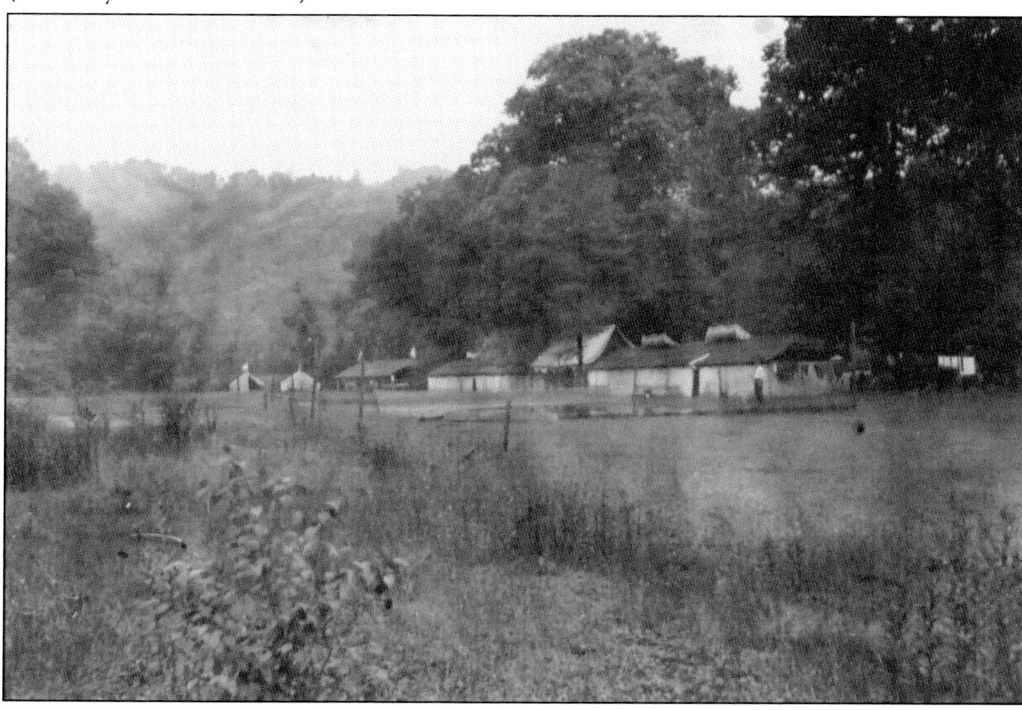

Camp Bonarr was located a few miles from Lumber City on the banks of the Susquehanna. Because of the Curwensville Dam, it is now owned by the state. It was once operated by Sam Watts, but it closed in 1913. This postcard is from a snapshot taken by R. K. Way when he was a visitor at the camp. (Courtesy Clearfield County Historical Society.)

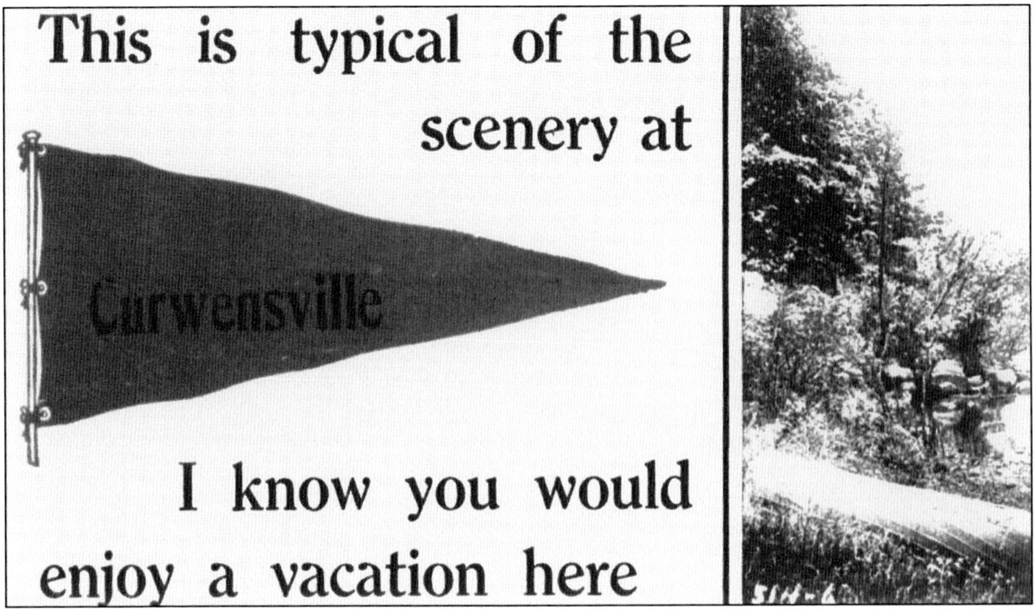

This "typical" Curwensville scene postcard dates from 1912. The photograph on the right appears to show part of the river with a small boat overturned on the shore. It is possible that this was taken at Irvin Park. Postcards of this type were sold in many area stores with only changes made to the town name. (Courtesy Dan McDonald.)

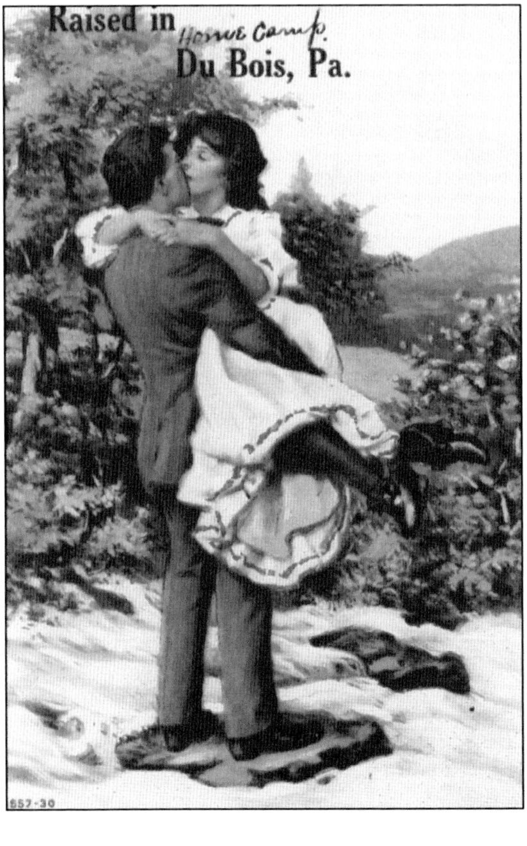

Here is another example of a generic drawing postcard that was printed with the name of whatever local town that the cards would be sold in. The sender of this card was obviously unable to locate one that said "raised in Home Camp," so she adapted this one. (Courtesy Clearfield County Historical Society.)

ADDITIONAL INFORMATION

Julie Rae Rickard is the author of two other successful Arcadia titles, *Clearfield County* from the Images of America series and *Clearfield* from the Postcard History Series. In celebration of Clearfield County's bicentennial, she wrote, produced, and directed the play *Hidden Treasures: A History of Clearfield County*. In addition, she is the author of the spiritual novel *The Destiny of Miro* and the popular short story *The Christmas Stocking*. She is also a freelance writer, reporter, and member of the Clearfield County Historical Society as well as the Curwensville-Pike Township Historical Society. For more information on the author visit thedestinyofmiro.tripod.com or e-mail her at thedestinyofmiro@yahoo.com.

Part of the author's proceeds from this book support the Curwensville-Pike Township Historical Society, P.O. Box 3, Curwensville, Pennsylvania, 16833. Visit its museum, the Korb House, at 836 State Street, Curwensville. For more information about Curwensville, please see the Web site Curwensville.com.

All of the local historical societies can use your support.

The Clearfield County Historical Society is located at 104 East Pine Street, Clearfield, Pennsylvania, 16830. For more information on this society, check out its new Web site at clfdhistory.org or call 814-765-6125.

The DuBois Area Historical Society can be contacted by mail at P.O. Box 401, DuBois, Pennsylvania, 15801 or by telephone at 814-371-9006. Also please visit the society's Web site at home.wrkcs.net/history.

The Coalport Area Coal Museum is located in the Coalport Community Building at 916 Forest Street. It houses over 350 artifacts in 17 displays, featuring the original tools, equipment, texts, scale-model and full-size replicas, and early photographs of our coal-mining heritage. Contact the museum at 814-672-4378 or visit its Web site at business.gsd1.org/CACM.

For more information of Bilger's Rocks, see www.bilgersrocks.com, and for additional information on Clearfield County, go to visitclearfieldcounty.org.

ACROSS AMERICA, PEOPLE ARE DISCOVERING SOMETHING WONDERFUL. *THEIR HERITAGE.*

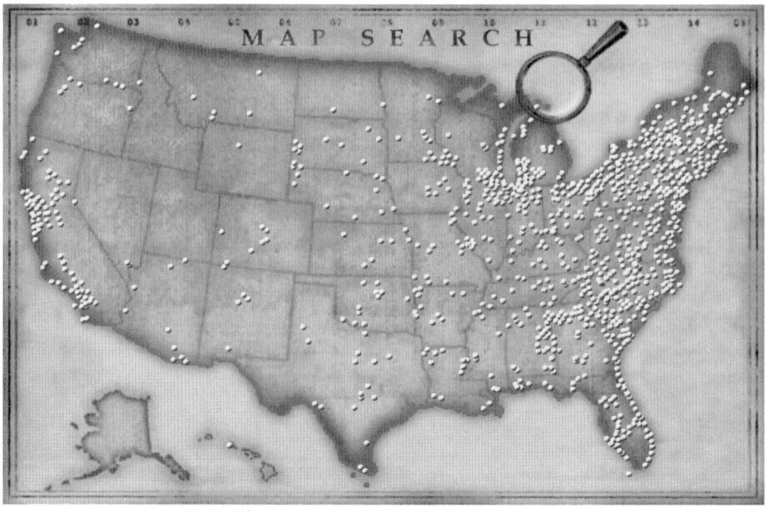